EMPHASIS ART

Self-portraits and portraits of classmates are popular as themes for linoleum prints in upper elementary grades and middle school. It is recommended that the preliminary sketch be made with a blunt-felt-nib pen, black crayon, or small brush and ink that approximates more closely the bold effect of the gouged line.

EMPHASIS ART

A Qualitative Art Program
for Elementary and Middle Schools

FIFTH EDITION

Frank Wachowiak

Robert D. Clements
University of Georgia

HarperCollinsCollegePublishers

To children everywhere who make the teaching of art a never-ending, forever-rewarding adventure, and to their teachers, in both elementary and middle schools, who share in the wonder and discovery. With special thanks to teachers of art around the world and to former students, now teachers and professors of art, who have been so generous in sharing the results of their teaching to help make this book a colorful treasury of child art.

Acquisitions Editor: Christopher Jennison
Developmental Editor: Kathleen Dolan
Project Editor: Olive Collen
Text and Cover Design: Wendy Ann Fredericks
Cover Illustrations: *Front cover:* (upper left) Courtesy of Baiba Kuntz, Glencoe, IL; (lower left) Courtesy of Shirley R. Lucas; (lower right) Reproduced by permission of Jimmy Morris, Athens, GA. *Back cover:* (lower left) Courtesy of David Hodge, Oshkosh, WI; (upper left) David Holzapfel [Gail Genz and Chris Shupin, teachers]; (upper right) Kristin Jade Santobello [Larry Petrash, teacher]
Production Manager/Assistant: Kewal Sharma/Jeffrey Taub
Compositor: York Graphic Services, Inc.
Printer and Binder: R. R. Donnelley & Sons Company
Cover Printer: The Lehigh Press, Inc.

Photos by Frank Wachowiak, Mary Sayer Hammond, David Hodge, Baiba Kuntz, Jimmy O. Morris, W. Robert Nix, the International Child Art Collection, and others are listed on page 295, which is hereby made part of this copyright page.

EMPHASIS ART, Fifth Edition
Copyright © 1993 by HarperCollins College Publishers

Library of Congress Cataloging-in-Publication Data

Wachowiak, Frank.
    Emphasis art: a qualitative art program for elementary and middle schools / Frank Wachowiak, Robert D. Clements.—5th ed.
        p.   cm.
    ISBN 0-06-500603-8
    1. Art—Study and teaching (Elementary)   2. Art—Study and teaching (Secondary)   I. Clements, Robert D.   II. Title.
N350.W26 1993
372.5′044—dc20   92-26534
                                                                    CIP

95   9 8 7 6 5

Contents

Preface

This fifth edition of *Emphasis Art* is based upon Frank Wachowiak's teaching of art to children, beginning with his first elementary-school art classes in rural Minnesota and continuing for the next 50 years. His creative encounters with children enriched and colored his life, and he found in the happy, charged environment of children's searching, discovering, and creating that it was easy to stay young at heart. Although Frank's health nowadays prevents his involvement in this new edition, his inspiring words, the beautiful examples of children's art, and his clear technical directions continue in this new edition. His belief in the intrinsic worth of the art-studio experience is still central. The emphasis is on art—art as an adventure; a flowering; a celebration; and a discipline with its own singular demands, unique core of learnings, and incomparable rewards.

Allowing children to discover how their innate desire to react and respond verbally to their own artwork and to that of others can enrich their studio art experience. At every stage of human development, a response to art is an exploration of the self and of human nature! Art educators have identified art criticism, art history, and aesthetics as the formal disciplines that can best aid students in this exploration. These three areas, along with studio production, comprise the elements of discipline-based art education (DBAE). This philosophy has evolved in recent years to supplant art appreciation and become an important framework for a rigorous and challenging study of art at all age levels. New material in this edition will focus on how DBAE can be incorporated at each developmental stage. Including the three disciplines will meet the needs of teachers in the increasing number of school systems, colleges, universities, and states (through state education departments policies) which mandate that art education be treated in the four areas of art criticism, art history, aesthetics, and art production.

While the last edition had, in the body and in its appendixes, separate sections of related material dealing with children's development, a sequential curriculum, and an art program over the years, these three sections have now been organized into five chapters (Chapters 3 to 7). This material on sequential development is discussed not only in terms of art production but also in terms of art criticism, art history, and aesthetics.

In the 1990s, an important aspect of education receiving much attention is multicultural education. This text has always been pioneering in one important phase of multicultural art education, showing children's art from around the world. Now a section on other ways in which art can promote multicultural education, mainly through art criticism, has been added in Chapter 1 and throughout Part III.

The chapter on art for children with special needs has been enlarged to reflect new terminology, new approaches, and new attitudes, which I have become familiar with through my association as a Fellow of the Georgia University Affiliated Program for Persons with Developmental Disabilities. Because of federal legislation mandating the placing of children in the least restrictive, most normalizing environment, teaching children with significant mental and physical challenges is increasingly becoming the responsibility of every teacher. Teaching the artistically talented or gifted child has now been developed as a separate chapter.

New material has been added in Part II, "Teachers and Teaching," on teaching strategies, to make it serve the needs of beginning teachers who may have questions regarding management and discipline in the art classroom. In this section, a new chapter has been added on writing lesson plans using instructional objectives. For the past two score years, school systems have increasingly demanded clearly spelled out instructional objectives, competency-based education (CBE), and accountability. To be sure, no teachers have ever been more accountable than those who teach art, for every display of student art shows immediately to any and all perceptive viewers the students' demonstrable skills. This chapter now demonstrates how instructional objectives can serve not just as a way to meet the planning requirement of the school's central administration, but also as the teacher's central vehicle for evaluation. In addition, this chapter provides an example of one format by which lesson plans can meet many kinds of educational goals.

Other changes in this edition include the addition of new illustrations. Examples of postmodern art are included. Recommendations for activities in computer art, video, and architecture have been added. A new section added to Appendix A, "Art Materials," deals with hazardous art materials.

The response of educators at all levels to the fourth edition of *Emphasis Art* has been gratifyingly positive. The book's clarity, structure, and wealth of colorful illustrations have found enthusiastic endorsement. The art teaching strategies, motivations, techniques, and evaluative procedures described are based on actual experiences and observations of outstanding elementary- and middle-school art practices both in this country and abroad. This revised edition again concerns itself with the adventures, joys, responsibilities, problems, and rewards of teaching art to children; with the strategic, guiding role of the teacher; with projects based on perennial, universal art principles; and with the ongoing evaluation of lesson objectives in design and composition, art history, art criticism, and aesthetics.

Emphasis Art is designed first and foremost for elementary- and middle-school teachers of art who want to augment and enrich their art programs. It is also proposed as a text for the college or university student in search of high-caliber elementary- and middle-school art practices. It offers a lucid description of a proven, dynamic program for those veteran teachers who seek continuing challenges, new techniques, and classroom-tested art projects for their instructional repertoire.

I wish to acknowledge the assistance and contributions of the following individuals who have contributed. Those who coauthored earlier editions: Theodore K. Ramsay, professor of art, University of Michigan, Ann Arbor, coauthor of the first and second editions of *Emphasis Art;* and David Hodge, professor of art, University of Wisconsin, Oshkosh, coauthor of the now out of print *Art in Depth.* Those who taught with Frank Wachowiak in his University of Georgia children's art classes include the following people: Mary Hammond, professor of art, George Mason University, Virginia; Jimmy O. Morris, fine arts coordinator, Athens, Georgia; Patrick Taylor, professor of art, Kennesaw College, Kennesaw, Georgia; Allison Free and Julianne Hutto, Athens, Georgia. Colleagues at the Art Department at the University of Georgia have helped: W. Robert Nix, Claire B. Clements, Carole Henry, Andra Johnson, Heta Kauppinen, and Diane Barret. The beauty of this book has also been made possible through the contributions of art teachers from around the nation and world: Chen huei-Tung, Tainan, Taiwan; Jean Grant, coordinator, arts and humanities, Department of Defense Dependents' Schools (DODDS), Atlantic Region; Eric Ma Presado, Manila, Philippines; James McGrath, coordinator, arts and humanities, DODDS, Pacific Region; George Mitchell, Atlanta; Federico Moroni, Santarcangelo, Italy; Michihisa Kosugi, Saga, Japan; Baiba Kuntz, Winnetka, Illinois; Shirley Lucas, Oshkosh, Wisconsin; Alice Ballard Munn, Anchorage, Alaska; Norihisa Nakase, art education liaison, Tokyo, Japan; Michael F. O'Brien, American High School, Seoul, Korea; Ted Oliver, Blairsville, Georgia; Linda Riddle, Heidelberg, West Germany; Carolyn Shapiro, Brookline, Massachusetts; Mary E. Swanson, Nashua, New Hampshire; and Diane Turner, Laurens, South Carolina, and Barry Moore, Normal, Illinois. Also Faye Brassie, Emily Harris, David Hawell, Mary Lazzari, and Lawrence Stueck, all from Athens, Georgia. I also want to thank the following persons for giving permission to use published material: Masachi Shimono, editor, Nihon Bunkyo Suppan, Osaka, Japan; and Professor Osamu Muro, executive director, *Art Education Magazine,* Tokyo, Japan.

I would also like to thank the following reviewers for their comments and suggestions during the revision process: Victoria J. Fergus, West Virginia University; Roxanna S. Albury, Lander College; Chuck Peterson, St. Norbert College; Mary S. Hammond, George Mason University; Willet Ryder, York College; Amelia C. Watson, Cleveland State University; Rebecca Bailey, Meredith College; Marion F. Jefferson, University of Miami; Cheryl A. Grossman, University of Missouri–Kansas City; and Tina Weil, National–Louis University.

To the members of the editorial and production staff at HarperCollins, my grateful acknowledgment for their contributions, especially those of Christopher Jennison, executive editor, Kathleen Dolan, developmental editor, and Olive Collen, production editor.

Robert D. Clements

Previous page: A 12-year-old's gloriously painted pattern of red figures with white faces, Jamaica.

CHAPTER 1

The Role of Art in Society and in the Schools

Art in Society

On the one hand, art is an international language; it is universally accessible even to those who have little knowledge of how it was used in a culture. Through its organization and content, it communicates some of its meaning without words. Yet on the other hand, it is relative to the culture, to the time and place of its creation. For the members of any cultural group, art provides a mirror and helps them to have a unique sense of cultural identity. Art is one of the main ways for transmitting, maintaining, and analyzing culture. It is a way for people to find out about a culture. Culture is not just a people's artistic, musical, food, holiday, and historical heritage. It is also the shared values, attitudes, belief systems, and cognitive styles that affect a group of people's behavior and serve to direct them in their lives and to give their lives meaning. Study of the arts and humanities enriches daily life, helps maintain civility, and develops a sense of community.

The arts are important to a nation's people and to their culture. More Americans go to museums than to sporting events. Over a million Americans from all communities and cultures call themselves artists. All communities and all cultures make art because art makes events special. When art is made to celebrate ordinary experiences, these experiences take on a special quality. By making events and things stand out from the commonplace, art transforms and reorganizes our conceptions of the world.

Multicultural Pluralism

America is becoming increasingly multicultural. More and more, both our nation in general and the specific arts in our nation are addressing the importance of multiculturalism. For example, one of the major focuses of postmodern art, the term applied to much of our contemporary art, is the relationship of art in a particular culture to social and political issues. This new interest of contemporary art in things sociopolitical is a radical departure from earlier movements, such as abstract expressionism, which avoided sociopolitical involvement. As anyone knows who has visited a museum of modern art recently or seen artworks such as Nancy Spero's and Leon Golub's works about brutality, Judy Chicago's and Mary Kelly's pieces about women and motherhood, or Nam June Paik and Joseph Beuys's video about whales, art has become an agent for social change.

Not only have postmodern artists become agents for change, but museums as well are beginning to move in a new direction. As one of society's major institutions dealing with the transmission of culture, the museum in America plays a major role in determining what is considered art. Museums have now begun to mount such exhibitions as Hispanic-American artists, women artists, and Harlem's African-American artists. But multicultural progress is slow. Ninety percent of museum exhibitions in the past decade had a Euro-American focus, and cultural institutions are increasingly being challenged to take into account the values, attitudes, and beliefs of minority cultures.

Just as today's artists, museums, and society in general make efforts to create a just society serving all its citizens, teachers in the schools are striving to give equitable treatment to the cultural contributions of their students' ethnic groups. As the student populations of American schools become more multicultural, it is essential that teachers of art design curricula that promote the appreciation of diverse cultures' art heritages. In designing a curriculum, we must ask: Whose culture is being taught? In addition, we must ask if the culture is one in which contributions are made both by men and by women. Female artists have generally been ignored by the museums and by the art establishment.

Art curricula should recognize the students' diversity of class, race, and gender. Art is a natural area in which to combat ethnocentrism and monoculturalism, where European culture is seen as *the* central culture. Newer art programs emphasize the idea that culture is specific. The goal is not to add "multicultural" ingredients as new elements to education but instead to make education truly multicultural. Teachers need to be open to and nonjudgmental about diverse cultural experiences. They should use their students' preferred styles of learning to make the art curriculum more relevant to the disenfranchised groups that have suffered prejudice. Artistic experiences that are encountered in daily life should guide the development of the curriculum.

Teachers do not set out purposefully to culturally suppress a particular group; rather they do so unintentionally. But the effect is similar in both cases. Taking education out of the hands of a particular ethnic group and imposing the dominant society's values leads to feelings of alienation and frustration. There are two ways to move beyond the approach of suppression, in which nothing in the minority culture is considered worth preserving, toward multiculturalism. In the first, assimilation, the cultural heritage of the minority group becomes part of the majority culture. The second way involves a kind of cultural pluralism: the minority group retains its cultural traditions at the same time that it adopts practices necessary for the smooth functioning of society as a whole.

Past practices have led to inequities, omissions, and stereotyping. What content should be covered in school? There is a debate between elitists and populists concerning how much effort should be devoted to studying the classic masterpieces and how much devoted to studying folk art, popular arts, and commercial art. Elitists say that the great art masterpieces should be studied because they concern universal themes and have stood the test of time in meeting peoples' needs. Others say that informal art forms, such as folk art and video, are more relevant and lend themselves to increased interpretive possibilities. New methods in the teaching of art history emphasize the interconnectedness of political, social, and economic issues.

Top: *Though art communicates some of its meaning across eras and cultures, its creation is relative to its culture. It helps to create a sense of cultural community and identity.* Dropped Bowl with Scattered Slices and Peels, *1989, Claes Oldenburg and Coosje van Bruggen, Art in Public Places Program, Miami, Florida.* **Middle:** *Native American kachina.* **Bottom:** *Mola (reverse appliqué) by San Blas Indians.*

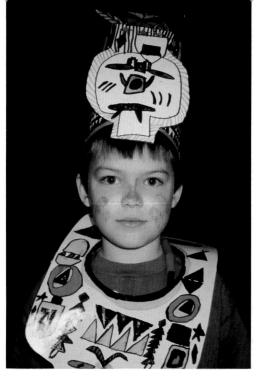

An appreciation of Native American culture is brought to these second-grade children through examining the myths and art of the northwest and southwest Native American cultures. Each second-grade class selected its own power animal. **Top, left:** Wolf kachina with exciting patterns. **Bottom, left:** Blue bird kachina based on southwest Native American stories. **Top, middle:** Boy with symbolic collar and headpiece. **Top, right:** Black and white striped doll based on Hopi clown kachina. **Bottom, right:** A girl in white costume enacts the northwest Native American myth of how the loon lost her voice.

Examples of some multicultural approaches for your classroom are: Why do the people in our community do art, as different from in other lands? How do people in our community and elsewhere make art to mark life transitions and other social purposes? In our area, how does art bring about a sense of community? How are the customs of our culture shown in the art of our community? What knowledge and skills are necessary to produce art in our particular community and in other countries?

Begin with the students' own beliefs and values and community to draw on what is familiar to them. Appreciation should not be disseminated in a top-down manner. Strive to make the classroom a more democratic place by incorporating the neglected peer group's subculture. Form students into small groups from different cultural backgrounds and have them explain and defend why they like the art that they do.

In the artworks discussed in class, show a willingness to address issues of racism, sexism, and inequity, and to discuss the struggle for power. For example, you might ask, "Do the people shown have control over their own lives, or are they controlled by others? How does the artist convey this?" Studio activities can promote culture pluralism. However, just making a kachina doll will not necessarily result in multicultural understanding. Sociopolitical issues should be addressed whenever possible.

Most obviously, you can promote multicultural understanding through your choices of material to study. You need to decide how close or remote the cultural connection should be. For example, are the needs of Hispanic-American youths more directly met by a study of Pre-Columbian culture or by the study of contemporary Hispanic-American culture? In showing the materials from diverse cultures to the class, it is necessary but not sufficient to cite the artist's ethnic origin. Also discuss how the artist's ethnicity might have affected his or her art.

Natural sources for materials are the school library and the social studies curriculum. (For example, one current social studies text contains 600 reproductions of artworks.) Multicultural education can be reinforced by visits to art museums and by use of audiovisual materials, such as slides and videotapes. Materials from diverse cultures

---

Communities use the arts to celebrate their historic heritage and myths. Elementary-school children from Tainan, Taiwan, have depicted their culture's traditional festivals and pageants. **Top and bottom:** *The Dragon Dance.* **Middle:** *The River Festival.*

School Arts Magazine, January 1991, Courtesy of Davis Publications, Wooster, Massachusetts.

Artist Eddie Edwards and students at Martin Luther King Elementary School, San Diego, created this mural about Reverend King's dream, "We shall overcome." It is described in Kay Wagner's article "A Mural Worth a Million Words."

can be included in the still life and model arrangements you and your students put together. For example, these might include Indian and African tie-dyed cloths and shirts, umbrellas from Far Eastern countries, travel posters, and models dressed in ethnic costumes. Another way to promote multicultural education is through art exchanges between schools in other countries. The art program you provide your students can help them to feel pride in and connectedness to themselves and their own cultural backgrounds, to other people, and to other cultures.

Art in the School

What kind of curriculum should America's nearly fifty million schoolchildren be taught? Where does art fit in? Americans do believe in arts education. One national survey found that almost all feel it is important for children to be exposed to the arts. A large survey of U.S. schools by John Goodlad found that parents do not want and never have wanted a "back to basics" curriculum. Instead they want a curriculum based on four areas: academic, vocational, social-civic-cultural, and personal.

In the social-civic-cultural area, the art goal, as described in the above material on multiculturalism, is to apply basic concepts in the fine arts and humanities to the appreciation of the aesthetic contribu-

tions of other cultures. Under the personal area, which also includes the arts, a goal is to expand one's ability to use leisure time effectively. Students surveyed consistently rated the arts as more interesting and enjoyable than academic subjects. However, about arts classes, Goodlad (1984) wrote:

> I am disappointed with the degree to which the arts classes appear to be dominated by the ambience of English, mathematics and other academic subjects. Arts classes, too, appear to be governed by characteristics which are best described as "school"—following the rules, finding the one right answer, practicing the lower cognitive processes. [The arts] did not convey the picture of individual expression and artistic creativity toward which one is led by the rhetoric of forward-looking practice in the field.

The qualitative approach to art teaching brings with it an attitude of rigor and of the need for artistic creativity. Art requires a high level of abstract reasoning. The new curriculum in art criticism and aesthetics requires analysis and interpretation and is another way to include higher-order cognitive processes in art. Through the study of art, we become able to judge our efforts by the highest standards. America needs citizens who can think for themselves, communicate effectively, and appreciate our nation's ethnic diversity. Art education is needed to develop better educated human beings, citizens who will value and evolve a worthy life. In the art classroom, all of the rationales for education can be addressed: academic excellence, cognitive development, social adaptation, social change, and personal growth. The goal of education is to help students to develop both their intellectual capabilities and their capacity to express their thoughts and feelings. These come together in art, and this coming together, in large part, accounts for the power of art.

In art classes, enriched and stimulated by a teacher's varied and challenging motivations, children learn to see more, sense more, and recall more. They become more aware of their changing and expanding environment. They realize that making art is not something special done by special people. Everyone can put one's imprint on a piece of art. The aesthetic state can be likened to that of the human infant: nonspecialized, nondirectional, inquisitive, imaginative, open, and creative. The teacher of art in the elementary school can begin very early to talk to the young child about the exciting wonders and uses of design and color. Children readily understand the ideas of using dark and light values or dull and bright colors for contrast, of creating big and little shapes for variety, of repeating a shape or color to achieve pattern, and of drawing things large to fill the composition. Children

Courtesy of David Hodge, Oshkosh, Wisconsin.

The child's knowledge of science, nature, and art come together as the child represents the natural world, which can be as near as the schoolyard. Teachers should take advantage of the immediate environment—the school playground, *the cafeteria kitchen, the band room with musical instruments—as a visual motivational resource. Here the children are employing 18- × 24-inch sections of hardboard as sketching pads for drawing.*

who express their ideas, responses, and reactions with honesty, sensitivity, and perceptiveness in a framework of compositional principles and design create art. For the majority of students, this sense of design and art structure must grow from the many planned art-life experiences and happenings provided by the resourceful teacher.

A Qualitative Approach to Teaching Art

All persons can engage in art-making behavior. However, some people think that anything a child draws, paints, or constructs is art. It may be called art, but the question remains as to whether it is a work of good or bad art. It may indeed be a child's visual statement, but it is not necessarily a quality work of art. To have art quality, it must, as much as possible, be expressed in the language, structure, and form of art.

Very often what some observers call "art" in a child's drawing is not art at all, but simply a visual report that relates to factual writing. Art, on the other hand, is more akin to poetry, which, like all fine art, comes to life when it distills the essence of an experience in highly expressive and discriminative choices. This is how the qualitative method of teaching art differs from other methods. In poetry one discovers that the quality of the verse often depends on the choice use of an expressive word, phrase, or couplet and on effective alliteration, meter, rhythm, and sometimes rhyme. Likewise, in the most evocative, colorful art creations of children, one sees how artworks that employ art principles result in a unity and a rich design that distinguishes them from ordinary, relatively impoverished, expressions.

Where qualitative teaching differs from other methods is that it requires the teacher to go beyond initial stimulation. In general, all art methods emphasize the teacher's responsibility for keeping students engaged in worthwhile experiences so they may have something meaningful to express, draw, paint, print, model, or construct. Often they help the children recall a past event or provide new visual enrichments through a field trip, a model brought to class, dramatization,

Athens Academy, Georgia.

Above: *Animals, their differences and habits, are shown in this mural made by third-grade children who pasted small yarn scraps to a hard backing.* **Below:** *Second-grade children learned about poisonous and nonpoisonous snakes through creating this stitchery mural.*

Oconee Elementary School, Georgia. Courtesy of Mary Ruth Moore.

Grade 2, Athens, Georgia. Courtesy of Mary Sayer Hammond, Fairfax, Virginia.

A qualitative artwork, such as this "pet in a garden" oil pastel, takes time to create. On 12- × 18-inch violet-colored construction paper, it took three 50-minute class periods. The preliminary drawing was made in school chalk, then reinforced with a large-sized, black felt-nib pen. Color was then applied up to, but not covering, the black lines. Instructional objectives for color were to use color imaginatively and to repeat colors for unity. The animal (pet) was drawn first and the garden environment added afterward. See the child at work on this painting in the circle illustration at the right.

film, dance, musical recording, story, or poem. But for qualitative teaching in art, this initial stimulation is not enough. The teacher must also guide the students as they express their responses from preliminary drawing through to the finished product.

Every time children create a work of art—painting, collage, print, sculpture—they should be encouraged to evaluate their efforts in terms of the lesson's instructional objectives, beginning with the initial sketch. If nothing is said about design, structure, composition, line, value, color, contrast, pattern, and other aspects of the artwork, it is presumptuous to assume that students will develop in aesthetic awareness and artistic potential.

Students who persevere when they make art create more fulfilling, rewarding, and exciting art when they are guided to become more fully aware of their environment. If their contact with the world, the people in it, and nature is superficial and if their identification with and their response to visual stimuli are minimal, they are apt to be content with a hasty, casual, lazy, noncommittal, shorthand statement of an event. Stereotyped interpretations such as stick figures, lollipop trees, box houses, and two curved lines for a bird are seldom based on children's richly observed experiences in distinguishing identifying characteristics and noting differences in things. Without the teacher's help, the average child's art production, limited by abbreviated time schedules, tends to be cursory and sterile.

Teachers who see examples of children's art like those in this text often inquire how long it takes the children to complete projects of the quality illustrated. They no doubt sense that the artworks enriching this text are not the result of a single 45-minute art lesson. In most instances the motivation and the preliminary drawing alone take one period. A completed project may take three to four art periods, depending on the age of the child or the grade level. When art is scheduled only once a week, some classroom teachers of art are concerned that, should a project extend over a period of several weeks, they could not hold the children's interest. A way to deal with time constraints and still produce qualitative art is limiting the size of the paper—for example, using 9- ×12-inch surfaces instead of 12 × 18 inches for detailed compositions and 12- ×18-inch paper instead of 18 × 24 inches for expressively free tempera paintings.

Qualitative art experiences should have a regularly scheduled and undisputed place in the curriculum of elementary and middle schools. When art is not allotted sufficient time in the school week, when it plays a role subordinate to every other subject in the classroom, and when it consists mainly of peripheral activities and stereotyped holiday decorations, it is unrealistic to expect it to perform a vital role in children's creative growth.

Imaginative underwater themes intrigued the Japanese children who painted these rich interpretations of oceanic exploration and adventure. When youngsters are capable of producing such rich visual statements, why allow them to settle for stereotyped, minimal results?

When art is taught purposefully and qualitatively and the instructional objectives to be mastered are made clear, beautiful work results. **Top, left:** *A Cape Town, South Africa, farm scene has clear areas of glowing color. Age 7.* **Above:** *A St. Petersburg, Russia, scene of children playing in the snow uses the figures of many children to fill the page, age 6.* **Left:** *A market scene from Turkey shows depth through vertical placement. Colors are delightfully carried throughout the scene. Age 11.*

Instructors faced with today's overloaded classes and limited time schedules often do well just to keep the students under control. Teachers can maintain an effective, positive, and productive atmosphere in their classes when they can alert the students to an awareness of the project's instructional objectives and the satisfaction to be achieved in a purposeful art endeavor. Art taught effectively, purposefully, and qualitatively has a body of knowledge and skills to be mastered. It has unquestionable merit as a unique avenue to mental, social, and individual growth. Artistic creativity should be recognized, lauded, and embraced as a living and learning experience in its own right. Indeed, if taught imaginatively and qualitatively, so that every art lesson augments and enhances the students' skills in basic learnings and in perceiving, reading, analyzing, and building a vocabulary, then art is education.

CHAPTER 2

Fundamentals of Art: A Review

A high-quality methods course, whether directed to the classroom teacher or the teacher of art, should provide students with aesthetically significant, in-depth art experiences. Art concepts based on recurring compositional principles employed in the visual arts, both past and present, should be central features of college or university-level art education programs. The studio content should be characterized by a deliberate and continuing emphasis on sensitive and expressive drawing experiences. Preliminary sketches or drawings, evaluated in an art context, should be the rule in the majority of studio projects. Beyond college and art course training, teachers of art in our elementary and middle schools can grow creatively and professionally if they continue to read articles on painting, sculpture, printmaking, architecture, and crafts. There they will discover recurring references to the basic elements of art—line, shape, color, value, form, space, texture, and pattern—as well as discussions of art's fundamental principles—balance, rhythm-repetition, variety, emphasis, domination-subordination, radiation, and unity. Art creation is a continually challenging adventure, providing few shortcuts to successful composition. Yet there are some constant elements that teachers can always turn to and use with confidence in instructing the children in their art classes.

Line

Line in art is a human invention, a unique method of perceiving and documenting the visible world. Therefore, a primary concern of teachers of art should be an understanding and implementation of the linear image. The line drawing is the basic structural foundation of all graphic composition and pictorial design. Expressive, sensitively drawn lines vary in weight, width, and emphasis. They may be delicate, bold, static, flowing, rhythmic, ponderous, hesitant, violent, or

dynamic. They are achieved through freedom and spontaneity or through thoughtful and deliberate action. They may converge, radiate, run parallel, meander, twist, skip, and crisscross to create confusion, flow, rhythm, order, or chaos.

An object or image is usually more visually exciting when delineated in a variety of expressive lines. Lines sensitively drawn can create and define shapes, values, and paths of motion. Teachers and students should turn to nature and select objects for limitless sources of line variety: frost, roots, spider webs, water ripples, lightning, veins in leaves, feathers, seashells and coral, grain in wood, cracks in ice and dried mud, insect wings, bridges, road maps, shopping carts, bird cages, wicker furniture, and tree bark and branches. Children should be provided with many opportunities to study and express their ideas in line and pattern in their myriad forms.

Shape

A study of pictorial design, of composition in painting, prints, and posters, eventually centers on the *shape* of things. The shapes created by lines merging, touching, and intersecting one another take many forms. They may be square, rectangular, round, elliptical, oval, triangular, or amorphous. They may emerge as nonobjective, figurative, or free-form. Shapes can also be created by ink or color washes, charcoal smudges, paint pourings, object printing, and paper cutouts. The achievement of varied, expressive shapes in a developing composition provides students with one of art's most stimulating challenges and rewards.

Nature is by far the richest source of inspiration for the study of variety in shapes. Natural forms and configurations such as those found in tree branches, leaves, seashells, eggs, nuts, petals, berries,

Lines depict a variety of types of fish, and the lines of the seaweed create interlocking shapes of various sizes which tie the design together.

and feathers are usually much more varied and subtle than those based on precise formulas. Perhaps that is why artists turn to aging, dilapidated buildings for their drawing inspiration instead of the coldly geometric shapes of much contemporary architecture. There is far too much reliance on formulas and rules of perspective in the rendition of tabletops, doors, windows, fences, roofs, and sidewalks. Teachers should encourage students to use artistic license to give vitality to static imagery through meaningful distortion, omission, exaggeration, and free-form interpretation.

The shapes of objects or figures in a composition such as trees, houses, people, animals, furniture, and vehicles are generally called "positive shapes." The empty area around them is referred to as "negative space," even though this space may include ground, water, and sky. In most instances, when the positive shapes are varied in size and shape, the negative spaces or shapes are consequently just as varied and as interesting, thereby enhancing the composition.

Value

Value, especially the contrast produced by juxtaposing a variety of values, plays a very important role in pictorial design. *Value*, simply stated, refers to the light and dark elements in a composition. Every shade (dark value) and tint (light value) of every color or hue has a place on the value scale. An attractive disposition of values in a picture is even more important than color. Values when repeated create movement in a painting, leading the viewer from one part of the composition to another. Value analyses of master paintings and prints can help students understand and appreciate the principles employed in achieving successful light and dark orchestration. Compositions with sharply contrasting values are generally more dramatic and dynamic in their visual impact.

When famous American artist Georgia O'Keeffe was studying to be an art teacher, her professor at Teacher's College of Columbia University, Arthur Wesley Dow, emphasized in both his lectures and his writings the importance of value. Many people acknowledge that the value patterns seen in O'Keeffe's paintings are one of their strongest features.

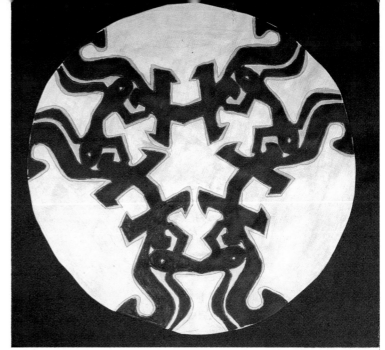

Courtesy of Fay Brassie, Athens, Georgia.

From a linear design of a middle-school student's initials, an attractive design of trilateral symmetry develops.

Color

Can you imagine a world without color? How dull it would be. *Color* has three properties or components: *hue*, the name of the color, *value*, the lightness or darkness of the color, and *intensity* (saturation), the brightness or dullness of the color. Unfortunately, its most amazing property is often ignored. Color has magic!

Color in painting is a continuing challenge to art students, teachers of art, and, often, artists. It is not uncommon to observe students performing with confidence and success when they draw or compose in line or in black and white values only; yet they are completely at a loss when they tackle color. Fortunately, successful strategies in color usage exist: to employ intense colors sparingly, to limit the total number of colors or to use related colors, to neutralize certain colors, and to create value patterns.

Limitation definitely plays an important role in the mastery of color orchestration. Sometimes students may be advised to limit their palettes to black, white, and one color in all of its various tints and shades, a system which is very effective. Another suggestion is to use

The curvilinear shapes of fish and crescents were paired up in the spiraling, radiating design of this upper-elementary-grade class mural.

The arrangement of values is often more important than the arrangement of hues. Notice the repetition of light and dark shapes and how they fill the composition of this acrylic polymer painting. Professor David Hodge, Seated

Figure: Margaret Mary, 1964 (48 × 48 inches), Art Department, University of Wisconsin, Oshkosh. Professor Hodge is the coauthor of Art in Depth, a Qualitative Program of Art for the Adolescent.

Reproduced by permission of Jimmy Morris, Athens, Georgia.

For this story illustration of messenger boys in the snow, a Japanese upper-elementary-grade student used only very dark and very light values to create a bold pattern.

Courtesy of Shirley Lucas, Oshkosh, Wisconsin.

One color dominates each of these paintings and provides unity. Notice the mixtures of blue and violet and blue and green in the top painting and the mixed yellow-brown color in the yellow painting. Small areas of other colors provide brilliant contrast. The theme "if I ran the circus" was the motivational catalyst that prompted these two action-filled tempera paintings by fourth-grade children.

analogous or related colors, those adjacent to one another on the color wheel, for example, blue, blue-green, green, and yellow-green. Two or three colors are usually enough, five colors are too many. One color should dominate and set the tone for the whole color scheme.

To avoid pitfalls of clashing color or strident chromatic relationships, students should be counseled to minimize the intensity of colors in a composition. This process, sometimes referred to as "neutralization" or "dulling" of a color, involves mixing or combining a color with its complementary hue, which can be found opposite to it on the color wheel. Examples of complementary colors are red and green, and blue and orange. Find the opposites in each; as Vincent Van Gogh wrote to his brother Theo, "While painting, I perceived for the first time how much light there was in darkness." Many colors now available in crayon, oil pastel, and tempera are already neutralized, for example, sienna, brown, umber, ochre, and chrome green.

A fraction of bright, intense color will hold its own against a more generous employment of neutralized colors. Surrounded by duller colors, brighter colors in the middle of the picture give it a sense of glowing light. Colors can be repeated to create movement and unity, but it is recommended that the size and shape of the repeated color be varied for effectiveness. Dark, cool colors generally recede; bright, warm colors usually advance. Complementary colors such as red and green in their fullest intensities create vibrant contrasts when juxtaposed. Black, grey, and white can be combined with

any color scheme without creating harmonic conflicts. Often, as in the case of black outlining, the dark linear accent gives a contrasting sharpness and sparkle to the composition. The character, identity, and impact of a color depend a great deal on the colors adjacent to or surrounding it. For example, a green shape on a turquoise background may be relatively unnoticed, but intense orange against an intense blue (a complementary relationship) will vibrate and arrest the eye.

Ironically, to make colors beautiful, we must consider first not hue but value, for it is the main pattern of values or shade which give a

A sixth-grade child's quadrilateral design is derived from a beetle. Subtle red variations and accents of blue and yellow surround the reddest red which glows from the center.

picture its overall effect and strength. It is more important to vary the shades than to vary the hues. Contrasts of light colors and dark colors will make a picture bold.

The painters of the postimpressionist era, including Franz Marc, Marc Chagall, and Odilon Redon, and contemporary colorists such as Karel Appel, Helen Frankenthaler, Richard Anuskiewicz, and Victor Vasarely, have provided the art world with eye-opening creations in color, resulting in surprises such as blue horses and multihued people. Teachers and students should turn, too, for inspiration in color usage to the luminous stained-glass windows of Gothic cathedrals, the jewel-like miniatures of India and Persia, the shimmering mosaics of Byzantium, and the fascinating ukiyo-e color woodcuts of Japan.

Space

Space is an element in pictorial composition and in abstract design that often confuses the student. In two-dimensional art expression *space* is sometimes designated as the negative area between positive objects. This kind of space is often referred to as "decorative" or "surface" space. Another category of space to be considered is space-

Space is shown by overlapping and diminishing sizes of the heads. This gives an effect of hundreds of dancers in the community folk dance celebration. The painting is by an 11-year-old from Kastamonu, Turkey.

in-depth. Common pictorial devices for achieving the illusion of space-in-depth on a two-dimensional plane, as in a painting, are

- Diminishing sizes of objects as they recede in distance
- Drawing sharp, clear details in the foreground and blurred, indistinct elements in the background
- Overlapping shapes or forms
- Drawing objects farther away from the observer higher on the picture plane
- Using bright, intense colors in the foreground and dulled colors in the background
- Employing perspective-creating techniques such as converging lines and horizon levels

Reproduced by permission of Jimmy Morris, Athens, Georgia.

Space is created by diminishing tree sizes, progressively lightened in the distance. The Japanese primary-grade child has drawn the figures front view while the wagon is drawn top view. This charming way of representation is called a mixed-plan-and-elevation view.

Courtesy of Mary Sayer Hammond, Fairfax, Virginia.

Imaginative patterns of circles, checkerboards, stripes, and diamonds grace this upper-elementary child's oil pastel on pink paper. It was drawn with white chalk and inspired by a stuffed bird and photos of birds.

As students move into middle school, they discover other means of creating space through shading and foreshortening. Some of this expertise in space handling comes intuitively, but most children must be guided in mastering the intricacies of perspective and space-in-depth. Rules of perspective should not be imposed on children unless they indicate a need for them. One cannot guarantee the success of a composition by simply applying the canons of perspective.

Texture and Pattern

Texture and pattern are usually considered as adorning elements or secondary elements which add richness and variety. However, they can also become the main feature of a design, as, for instance, in the design of floor tiles or in the repetitions of windows and columns in a work of architecture. Some names for textures are rough, smooth, actual, implied, bumpy, and jagged. Artists such as Rembrandt, Rubens, and Velasquez were virtuosos in painting the textures of hair, silk, velvet, and fur.

Some types of patterns are regular, irregular, stripes (bands), zigzag (chevron), scallop (fish scale), plaid (crossband), notched (cren-

Courtesy of David Hodge, Oshkosh, Wisconsin.

Clay is the supreme material for creating textures. Buttons, wire mesh, bottle caps, and kitchen tools can be helpful.

Courtesy of Baiba Kuntz, Glencoe, Illinois.

Teachers can help students to see the series of patterns and shapes in nature's leaves and seeds. These exquisite sunflower oil pastels on black paper have compositions which fill the page. The leaves, arranged alternately on the stem, run off the edges of the picture to create dramatic black background shapes. The leaf veins are carefully drawn. In the middle picture a flower is drawn *side view; in the right picture, leaves are drawn side view. The petals are colored in variations of yellow, the leaves in variations of green. It would be wonderful if children everywhere could have the experience of studying with an art teacher who brings out the best in them, as was the case with these students.*

ellated, and checkerboard (counterchange). Patterns can be created by setting up a series of parallel lines or lines which crisscross, often at right angles. These lines can be straight, curved, wavy, or jagged.

Patterns in nature usually have a mathematical basis. For example, the arrangement of seeds in the head of a sunflower and the bumps on a pineapple are two of the many natural occurrences of the mathematical series called a *Fibonacci series*. Such seemingly random patterns as those formed by the branches of a tree or the indentations on a coastline are in fact governed by the same geometric phenomenon, *fractal geometry*.

Both pattern and texture can be created by the repetition of individual elements, for example, lines to make grass or circles to make apples on a tree. Patterns are usually made up of the repetition of one or more clearly discernible shapes. In textures, on the other hand, individual elements are merged together into the whole and are difficult to distinguish. It is sometimes hard to make a clear distinction between pattern and texture. For example, apples on a tree seen from a distance would create a texture; apples on a tree seen from up close

would create a pattern. Microscopes and telescopes can further determine whether something is seen as a texture, a pattern, or a shape.

Both pattern and texture can be used overall. On the other hand, they may take on even more importance when they are used judiciously and separated by empty, plain areas of a solid, unvaried color. When a texture changes in a progressive way, for instance, from distinct in front to blended together in the distance, it is called a *textural gradient*. This phenomenon can be seen in views of the ocean's waves, clouds, and fields of trees and crops.

Balance and Symmetry

Line, shape, value, color, space, texture, and pattern are the *elements* of design. Balance, symmetry, and variety are the *principles* of design. An important avenue to effective picture making is the sensitive exploitation of balance or symmetry. Both teachers and students should be familiar with the two types of compositional balance: symmetrical

or formal balance and asymmetrical or informal balance. Formal balance has gone in and out of favor as styles have changed. However, in general, a symmetrical arrangement in which objects or figures on the right balance similarly weighted components on the left makes a more rigid, static composition.

A common misconception about art composition is that emphasis can be achieved by drawing something very large and placing it in the center of the picture. Size and placement in the composition by themselves do not ensure domination. The object to be noticed must exhibit other attributes as well; contrasting value, color, and detail will usually attract the viewer's attention. While there are no hard-and-fast rules, often a pictorial creation is much more interesting and attractive when the principal subject is not placed exactly in the center of the composition.

Variety, Emphasis, and Domination-Subordination

Variety in composition and design has always played a significant role. Analyses of past and present art masterpieces reveal the artists' reliance on, and constant use of, a variety of shapes and forms in their compositions. Seldom does one discover two shapes that are alike. Look at a score of multifigure paintings by recognized artists throughout the centuries and you will discover endless variety: No two heads are on the same level, no two figures are in the same position, and no two figures stand on the same levels in the foreground.

In nature, examples of variety are evident in the wings of a butterfly, the stripes on a zebra, the spots on a leopard, the feathers on a bird, the scales on a fish, the web of a spider, the cracks in an ice flow, or the frost on a windowpane. No two are alike. Although humans are nature's children, unlike the embodiments and creations of

Top: *No two cabin cruisers are alike in the riotous variety of this primary-grade child's wonderful marker pen harbor scene. How delightful are the beach house architecture, the intensely colored empty spaces, and the wind-swept trees and hairstyles.* **Middle:** *In nature, few examples of patterns are as striking as the leopard's spots. The third grader has camouflaged the leopard in an equally exciting pattern of a triangular grass motif in a multicolor checkerboard environment.* **Bottom:** *In the fifth grader's Antarctica scene, the largest penguin is four times as large as the distant penguin. This creates an effect of space, as does their all being at different levels.*

Middle: Courtesy of Mary Sayer Hammond, Fairfax, Virginia.

Courtesy of Mary Sayer Hammond, Fairfax, Virginia. Middle picture reproduced by permission of Jimmy Morris, Athens, Georgia.

the natural world, they must learn to employ variety in their graphic imagery. Variety as a vital element in pictorial design can be employed in every aspect—line, shape, value, color, pattern, texture—to give excitement and interest to a work of art, but it must be counterbalanced by a repetition of those art elements if the desired unity is to be achieved. Related to variety are the concepts of *emphasis* (that one object or motif should stand out above others) and *domination-subordination* (that equality is to be avoided in favor of one object or motif being major). The most successful compositions employ both major and minor areas of emphasis. Variety in the compositional placement of objects can be achieved by having objects:

Change in size and shape
Begin on different planes
Terminate at different heights
Touch the edges of the picture plane at different points, creating lines into the
     composition
Strategically overlap one another to create even more varied shapes and nega-
     tive spaces

The Basic Elements and Principles as a Foundation

The basic elements and principles can provide a practical design foundation on which to build a qualitative art program over the years. Art knowledge is acquired as these concepts are revisited time and again in the context of different assignments. In most instances and in most classrooms, students' knowledge and application of composition and design principles, as exemplified in art masterpieces and in the art around them, enhanced by a growing appreciation of design in nature, will prove both successful and personally rewarding. The development of ability in making and thinking about art requires a continuing exposure, at various developmental levels, to certain core concepts such as the basic elements and principles of composition and design.

Overlapping, forms touching the edges at different points, and imaginative use of color were emphasized in these primary-grade oil pastels of multicolored cats.

The Shapes of Time: Iowa City, 1964 (mixed-media collage, 18 × 24 inches), Ted Ramsay, Professor of Art, University of Michigan, Ann Arbor. Collection of the author.

By using the art elements and principles over the years, artists achieve mastery in their use. Notice here the shapes, their varied sizes, values, hues, and textures, as they strike the edges of the collage. What occurs at the edges of a picture gives a composition strength.

CHAPTER 3

Considerations Regarding a Sequential Art Curriculum Based Upon Children's Development

Children from the first through the eighth grades respond and grow in a program in which art fundamentals and techniques are not left to chance but are taught sequentially, purposefully, and imaginatively. This chapter provides a background for considering child development in art. The subsequent four chapters give specific recommendations.

Children's Similarities

Children everywhere have much in common. They react in similar ways to their environment. They laugh and cry, play, act, sing, and dance. They delight in seeing and manipulating bright, colorful objects, games, machines, and vehicles. They respond to sympathetic, supportive voices and to loving, nurturing hands.

Likewise, children the world over draw in very much the same manner during the early developmental stages. Long before we learn how to respond to the world cognitively, we respond to it aesthetically: through touch, taste, smell, feel, and sound. Preschoolers begin with random, haphazard marks and then move on to explore some of the twenty kinds of scribbles which have been classified (Kellogg, 1970). These include:

Patterns of marking in strokes
Patterns of dots
Vertical, horizontal, diagonal, circular, curved, and waving lines
Placement of patterns on the page, such as overall, quarter page, centered, in
    halves, along a diagonal axis, and following the shape of a two-cornered
    arch, a one-corner fan, or a two-corner pyramidal form

Rather than thinking of these as "scribbles," a term which has negative connotations to some people, one can think of them as presentations, in contrast to children's later *re*-presentations.

Gradually acquiring more control and the desire for representation, children move on to simple, geometric, schematic symbols. They confidently and proudly give to their drawings names and titles which might change from one minute to the next. They then progress to tadpolelike forms and semirealistic interpretations. Contrasted to later

Moving beyond the scribbling stage, the young child begins to use geometric shapes to make representations. Butterflies in the Garden *shows a wonderful intuitive use of color in the multihued flower petals and cheerful use of background washes. White crayon lines are especially effective in crayon resist.*

Children's art is the happy result of seeing, knowing, and imagining. Be responsive. Be appreciative. Applaud. The joy of discovery is captured here in the girl's wonder at the central boy's very special hat and hairstyle. The teacher brought to class an assortment of sports equipment for the children to hold as they sequentially posed for the multifigure composition. The upper-elementary-grade artist richly colored all spaces. The shirts, skirts, and cap were enlivened with six areas of exciting stripe pattern.

stages, in which development is much more variable, the early stages of artistic development (up to 5 to 7 years of age for children without developmental disabilities) are universally determined; they are strongly similar across different cultures and times. The young child's natural graphic responses are instinctive, spontaneous, and intuitive.

Children's Variability

While universal patterns of development govern the early stages of expression, as children mature, forces of the specific culture and its educational and enrichment programs play greater roles. Some fortunate students may have had abundant experiences in working with art materials, whereas others may have had limited creative opportunities. Some inquisitive youths may have developed a keen interest in a particular area, for example, in horses, cars, bikes, birds, kites, dolls, rockets, planes, insects, model building, shell collections, miniature models, sports, and electronic games. Consequently, their observed knowledge will often distinguish their art from that of their classmates, standing out because of its complexity and richness of detail.

No two children are alike. Even twins, who may confuse their teachers with surface similarities, have different personalities, different feelings and reactions, and different mental and creative abilities. Children's uniquely individual characteristics present teachers with some of their most critical guidance challenges. Teachers of art soon learn that they cannot expect the same responses, skills, or art interpretations from any two children, even those of identical ages and backgrounds. Those who excel in clay manipulation may respond less enthusiastically and perform less ably during drawing and painting sessions. The child who confidently tackles brush and paint may sometimes need more supportive guidance when faced with three-dimensional construction problems. As anyone who has looked at children's art would attest, the complexity of children's graphic imagery varies with the stages of their mental, physical, psychological, and social development.

Since no two children are alike, it is almost impossible to categorize them by grade or age. Students in the same class may come from different backgrounds and economic levels and may have had totally different day-to-day experiences; their problems and needs are not the

The drawings on this page illustrate increasing refinement in drawing horses made by the same girl at ages 7, 9, 10.

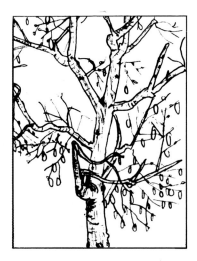

No two children will draw the same tree in the same way. The teacher's role is to challenge them to notice trees and their varied parts. ("Describe in your art the trunk, bark, knots, branches, leaves, roots, twigs, buds, blossoms, and fruit.") Let them touch the trees, perhaps climb them, and pretend to be a tree swaying in the wind, feeling the rain, the snow, and the warm sunlight.

same. Yet to understand them and help them grow through art, the teacher must be aware of those characteristics that have been identified with certain age groups by researchers in art education, educational psychology, sociology, and child study. The following detailed, sequential description of children's growth and behavior patterns and art learning needs should give helpful lesson planning clues.

But a word of caution is indicated here. Stage theory should be used only as a descriptive device, not a prescriptive device. Stages are "external" not internal. A person doesn't "have" a stage. Rather, a stage is a commonly available structure of thought. Stage theory doesn't take into account how cultural influences can shape development. Lowenfeld's stages (the scribbling stages; the preschematic stage (first representational attempts), 4–7; the schematic stage (the achievement of a form concept), 7–9; and the gang stage (dawning realism), 9–12 years) have been criticized for these reasons. Stage theory overlooks cultural differences. In school the child is taught culturally approved systems of drawing and is taught to ignore those which that culture doesn't approve or value. In older children, a wider variety of graphic expressions are manifested and development becomes less universal, more relative. Chance and choice can occur. Stages may be skipped and even reversed. Even within one drawing, indications of several stages may be found.

Art Development

Artistic expression is not a driving force seeking improvement, nor is it an unfolding of predetermined abilities. Instead it is bound to the time and place of its creation and reflects the creative options available at that time and place. It is not the case that "later is higher is better." A younger child's work may appear to show more giftedness than that of an older child. The spontaneity, beauty, and naiveté of a child's artistic expression at age 10 may never again be seen, in that unique form, in the child's work. Like fine art from past times in history, work from earlier stages in a child's life is not inferior to later work. Instead, the work from each time shows the distinctive characteristics of that time.

How and why do children draw? Do they draw what they know? Or do they they draw what they see? What guides the drawing process, knowledge or vision? Perhaps it is a third element, feelings, which guides children's drawings. Or is it a fourth, their cultural context? Developmentalists have made the case for the connection between children's drawings and their intellectual growth. Perceptualists have instead emphasized the tie to children's ability to see, and especially to see differences. Others have emphasized the emotional and psychological basis for art expression. And contextualists maintain that development does not move toward a specified end; rather, the pro-

Left: Reproduced by permission of Jimmy Morris, Athens, Georgia.

"Later is not higher is not better." At each stage of artistic development children have unique awarenesses and capabilities. The special character of the art of differing ages is shown in these still-life arrangements. **Left:** *A first-grade crayon design is filled with spontaneity and assuredness.* **Middle:** *A fifth-grade found-materials collage shows calculated design decisions.* **Right:** *A sixth-grade watercolor shows careful observation.*

cess is one of making choices within a given context. For example, some cultures have not been concerned with showing realism while others have.

Young children tend to pay little or no attention to the object, instead using a scheme, a product of individual cognition. After the primary grades, children do attempt to draw objects as they appear. In general, young children draw what they know, and older children in our culture tend to draw what they see. Thus the young child's stubborn use of a consistent scheme is a feature of the young child's quest to depict things as they are known. In other words, young children

The known and the remembered are delightfully combined in this Greek child's depiction of the terraced countryside. It shows the boat pulled up onto the beach, the houses lining the meandering road, and the sun peeking around the mountain.

draw "what they know." The traits and characteristics described here are but clues to understanding children in general and may not necessarily apply to a particular or individual child. For a description of the characteristics of children with special needs—those with significant mental or physical handicaps and the gifted—refer to Chapters 13 and 14.

Need for Sequential Curriculum across the Grades

For the teacher who has the chance to teach children over a span of years, the sequential teaching of art is a richly rewarding and highly fulfilling experience. When it is undertaken with conviction, purpose, imagination, and love, it is a privilege, a revelation, and a joy to observe and guide children as they create, to witness this fascinating aspect of their personalities emerge. Their designs and configurations are excitingly unpredictable. Their naiveté delights us. No wonder, then, that their spontaneous and intuitive visual expressions have influenced noted artists such as Jean Dubuffet, Juan Miro, Paul Klee, and Karel Appel.

In no other subject area in the elementary and middle schools is continuity of learning so misunderstood and so neglected as it is in art. In other subjects, most classroom teachers are familiar with the specific content to be mastered at each grade level and can help the students build with confidence on previous years' learnings. In elementary and middle school art classes, however, it is a different story. Teachers in the upper elementary grades are, in most instances, unfamiliar with the content of the primary-grade art program, if in fact such a program exists. Middle school instructors of art are often unaware of the art skills mastered during the elementary school art curriculum. In too many elementary schools, art projects are a medley

Grade 1 girl

Grade 1 boy

Grade 2 girl

Grade 2 boy

Grade 6 boy

Grade 7 boy

Children's development in art is sequential. In our culture it moves toward showing more realistic proportion, more muscles, gender characteristics, and detail. However, there are numerous exceptions to the "typical" sequence. After leaving the scribbling stage, at first children draw tadpolelike figures, in which single, stright-line limbs protrude from the head. By first grade most children conceive of the head as a separate circle, from which hangs a body drawn with a triangle or square. Attached to this are straight limbs, with two sides, rather than just being a stick (grade 1 girl). Then the phenomenon of bending limbs becomes graphically realized and curved, sausage-type limbs are drawn (grade 2 boy). Joints develops, and knees and elbows are then

Grade 3 boy

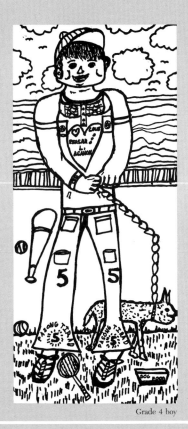

Grade 4 boy

Grade 5 girl

Grade 6 girl

drawn as the locations of the bending (grade 3 and 4 boys shown here). The limbs become progressively more fused to the body (grade 3 boy and grade 5 girl). Overlapping of limbs over the body can be seen (grade 2 and 4 boy, grade 6 girl and boy). Proportions change from the three-heads-high figure (grade 2 boy) to the five-heads-high figure (grade 6 boy). The form of the neck, arising from the torso, becomes more clearly realized. Hips and muscles become more clearly represented (grade 6 girl and boy). Foreshortening appears (grade 8 girl's writing arm), and three-quarter views may appear (grade 8 girl's face). Grade 1 girl courtesy of David Harvell, Athens, Georgia. Grade 7 girl courtesy of Baiba Kuntz, Glencoe, Illinois.

Grade 7 girl

Grade 8 girl

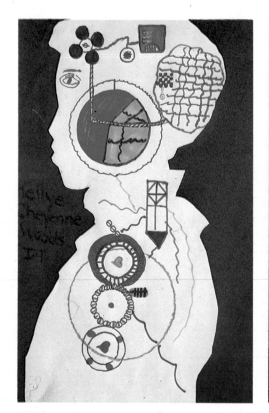 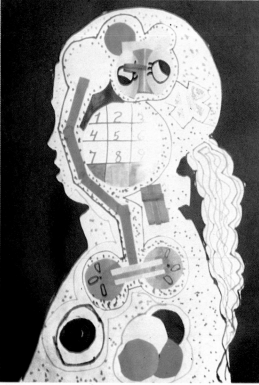 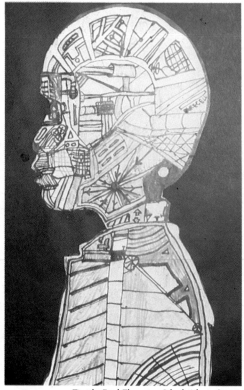

Timothy Road Elementary School, Athens, Georgia.

Fifth-grade students, whose knowledge about perception, evaluation, and aesthetics is increasing, created these X-ray silhouettes. They show how the opportunities and challenges of technology—for example, radio transistors, motors, battery watchworks, cameras, computers, and television—have affected them. Materials employed were 18- × 24-inch white construction paper, watercolor markers and crayons, wallpaper samples, scissors, pencils, and paste. A film projector lamp was used to create the student's shadow, and the silhouette was drawn by outlining the student's profile in pencil on the white paper. The completed drawings were cut out and mounted on dark-colored construction paper.

of one-shot, spur-of-the-moment activities unrelated to one another or to the children's earlier art experiences. Often these token art lessons are hastily concocted to fit into, but not exceed, the 30- or 45-minute period allotted to art once a week, or once every two weeks. Very often they are squeezed in on a late Friday afternoon when the children are exhausted by the long day's activities and certainly not at their creative, physical, and mental best.

Due to a paucity in the planning of sequential art experiences, children from grades one through eight are often provided with a monotonous diet of endless crayon lessons, usually seat-work assignments, supposedly designed to illustrate some aspect of social studies, literature, or science. It is only natural for students to lose interest and become bored when they realize they are not growing in fundamental art skills. Too much art class time is spent on the insignificant, the peripheral, and the frivolous, on the "instant" activity. "All right, children," says the classroom teacher at the close of the art lesson, "put away your crayons now and let's get down to something serious" (such as math, science, or language, perhaps?).

In today's art education, two forces have converged to produce a call for a clearly spelled-out curriculum. One is competency-based education's mandates for clear instructional objectives written in terms of what skills the student will be able to demonstrate (see Chapter 12). The other is teachers' uncertainty about how to implement the call for a more scholarly approach by proponents of discipline-based art education.

Confronted by conflicting mandates, some teachers feel that their difficult jobs would be easier if the art curriculum were clearly spelled out. But what if a systemwide curriculum proves to be too structured? To what degree should the school system direct the teacher in the goals and objectives for each grade? Already there is a constraint on elementary classroom teachers, who must attempt to fit their art teaching in between meeting grade-level goals on the standardized reading and math tests. A top-down art curriculum may further hinder teachers from carrying out the specific art projects they personally would like to carry out. Some teachers will feel that their autonomy in directing their students' instruction has been taken away, making them feel like mere tools in the school district's hands.

Another force working against a top-down curriculum is due to developments in cognitive theory that have caused a shift from the curriculum-centered instruction of the 1970s to learner-centered instruction. These new approaches engage students at their level of understanding and require them to examine their own knowledge to come up with solutions. Another force opposing a sequentialized curriculum in art making and art criticism is the intrinsic cumulative nature of art learning itself. Art learning follows more of a spiral course than a clearly delineated sequence.

The development of districtwide standards needs to be balanced by the honoring of teachers' individualized differences. It is important that the content of art instruction develop from the essential strengths of the teachers themselves and their passions about art. In observing a class where art is taught purposefully, seriously, imaginatively, and knowledgeably with an emphasis on the continuity of art learning, the observer will see education at its finest, a total education of the whole child. He or she will witness students absorbed in making hundreds of decisions: sharing, evaluating, comparing, revising, growing in language skills, and adding to their development as perceptive, discriminative, and aesthetically aware human beings. Teachers who use the following sequential, developmental quality art program will see children grow yearly more confident in self-expression, verbal and visual literacy, and self-worth.

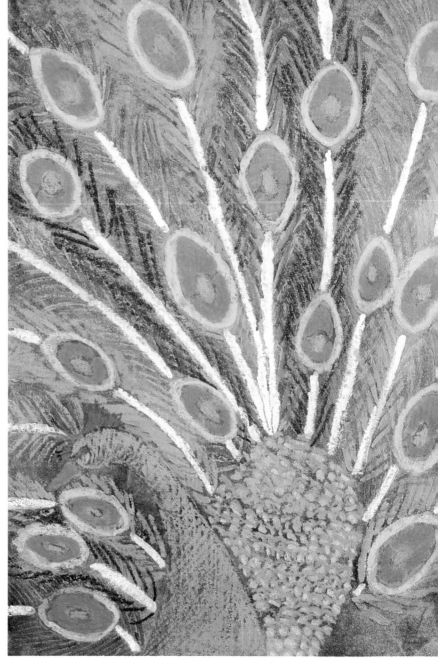

Courtesy of Nancy Elliott, Athens, Georgia.

The teacher's strength in teaching about color is evident in this picture. The peacock is crayoned mainly in green and its variations, along with strong, pure accents of blue, red, and yellow. White crayon is especially effective with the dark grey crayon resist.

CHAPTER 4

A Sequential Curriculum for Grades 1 and 2

Developmental Characteristics

The left-hand column of the following chart lists some of the developmental characteristics of first- and second-grade children. The right-hand column gives some implications of these characteristics for art teaching.

Developmental Characteristics of First and Second Graders	*Implications for Art Teaching*
Are active and easily excited.	Use most any topic as motivation.
Enjoy working with their hands.	Use hands-on art activities as vehicles for correlated learning.
Take great pride in their work.	Display work in the hall.
Exhibit strong feelings of possessiveness.	Be aware that some children may cry if work is kept for an exhibit.
Are eager to learn.	Teach them many ways to see and draw. Do not underteach.
Want to be first.	Assign special responsibilities; for example, "You may be the scissor monitor today."
Have a limited span of interest and are easily fatigued.	Give a series of objectives *throughout* the lesson, rather than all at the beginning.
Have feelings that are easily hurt.	Point out several alternative ways to draw something, with each conveying different qualities, not just one right way. Praise when students have arrived at their "own way" of drawing something.
Developmental Characteristics of First and Second Graders	*Implications for Art Teaching*
Are alternately cooperative and uncooperative.	Give "road signs" to foreshadow how long each phase will be, when the phase will stop, and what the next phase will be.
Usually can grasp only one idea at a time.	Give instructional objectives throughout the lesson, instead of all at the beginning.
Delight in imaginative games, dances, stories, and plays.	Use psychomotor games and role-playing exercises.
Like to pretend and engage in make-believe.	Use puppet plays and made-up stories about the characters in their pictures. ("What would this character in your picture say?")
Desire the approval of classmates and teachers.	Encourage them to tell about their pictures at sharing time.
Often live in their own secret world.	Use fantasy as a motivation. ("If I were a . . . , what would I be like?")
Are interested in new things to touch and taste.	Use tactile motivations, for example, rabbits, toys, turtles.
Are fascinated by moving and mechanical devices.	Arrange wind-up toys as still lifes. Use visual-perception devices such as kaleidoscopes.
Enjoy TV, illustrated books, movies, picnics, school field trips, new clothes, pets.	Ask them to do art criticism of book illustrations. Have children draw after field trips, draw pictures of pets.

34

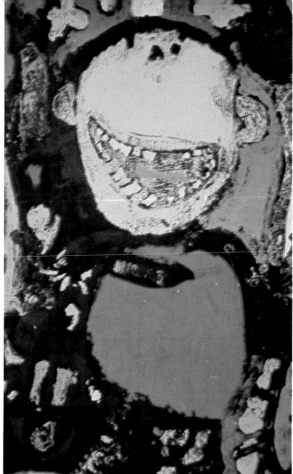

In these attractive first-grade tempera and India ink portraits can be seen the characteristic features often seen in very young children's art. These include *circle heads, the figures from 2½ to 3 heads high, the bodies comprising circles, squares, and triangles, and the sausage limbs.*

This chapter and the following chapters treat students' development at each two-year period: primary grades 1 and 2, intermediate grades 3 and 4, upper elementary grades 5 and 6, and middle-school grades 7 and 8. Each time period is discussed in three parts. First, characteristics are listed in the left side of a table, and in the right-hand side, some implications of the developmental characteristics for the teaching of art. Second, children's artistic development is described in terms of their use of shape, size, color, space, shading, ways of drawing objects, the human figure, and favorite subject matter. Third, teaching procedures for the four areas of art criticism, art history, aesthetics, and art production are described.

Art Development

This next chart shows how many children ages 5 through 7 employ various art elements. The left-hand column shows early development, and the right-hand column shows later development. At these stages, enormous variability and change in children's art development occur. Although the chart is written in the form of instructional objectives, it is not meant to be prescriptive. Beauty and expression can be achieved in many ways, not just one teacher-prescribed "right way." Representations consisting of scribbles can be as expressive as representations depicting houses, if not more so. Later is not better.

Geometric shapes of circles, squares, and triangles are used by a 7-year-old from Colombia. The shapes compose the figures and boarding school of Colegio de Cuento. The intuitive necessity to distribute the red, yellow, and blue colors throughout the composition takes happy precedence over any regard for naturalistic coloration. The symmetrical composition has as its center the child's boarding school with its strong design.

	Early Art Development: Ages 5 and 6	Subsequent Development: Ages 6 and 7
SHAPES	Student will draw the geometric symbols of the circle, square, triangle, oval, and rectangle. Student will employ a basic symbol, such as a circle, to depict varied visual images—the sun, the head of a person or animal, a table, a flower blossom, a tree, a body, and even a room. Students will use combinations of symbols that are very often different from those of their classmates. Student will depict simplified representations and are not too concerned with details.	(Because child art develops so rapidly during this period, this column deals with the development of some six-year-olds but especially seven-year-olds.) Student will change slowly from geometric, symbolic interpretations to more specific characterization and delineation. Student will use more details in depictions—hair ribbons, buttons, buckles, eyeglasses, necklaces, rings, shoelaces, purses, fingernails, patterns, and wrinkles in clothes.
SIZE	Student will use emotional exaggeration of size. Students will enlarge things that are important to them and omit features that are not important. For example, children may draw themselves bigger than their parents or omit arms and hands if they are not needed in their depiction. Size may also be determined by the need to fill an empty space or the desire to show a clear relationship.	Student will approximate more representative proportions, although figures may still be three heads high (the proportions of the *Peanuts* cartoon character, Charlie Brown) rather than the subsequent five heads high.
COLOR	Student will use color in a personal or emotional context without regard to its local use or identity; for example, a face may be painted blue or green.	Student will use color used in a local, stereotypical way; e.g., tree trunks are brown, the sky is blue.
SPACE	Student will employ a baseline as a foundation on which to place objects such as a house, tree, or figure. Sometimes the bottom of the page substitutes for the baseline. Later, student may use a second or third baseline higher on the page.	Although distant objects are often drawn the same size as those nearer them, student will begin to place distant objects higher on the page. Student will draw both the outside and inside of a place, a person, or an animal as if in an X-ray or transparency. Students will use a foldover technique, turning their paper completely around as they draw, to show people on both sides of the street, diners around a table or picnic lunch, people at a swimming pool, or players on a baseball field.
SCHEMAS FOR DRAWING OBJECTS	Students will draw things intuitively as they know them: the sky as a band of color at the top of the page; the sun that appears in part or whole in an upper corner of almost every picture; the railroad tracks that seldom converge; the leaves that are wider where they attach to the branch or stem; the tree with a very wide trunk to make it strong; the eyes high up in the head, and the mouth as a single, curved, happy line.	Students will draw objects as they know them to be, rather than how they see them at the moment, for example, a table with four legs when only two are visible from their vantage point, a house with three sides when only one side is visible from their sketching station.
THE HUMAN FIGURE	Students will devise a variety of interpretations or schemata of the human figure, house, tree, animal, and so on, depending on their experience.	Student will begin to use characteristic apparel and detail to distinguish sexes, such as skirts and trousers, and differences in hair styles.

This busy child is not a slave to realism. Four eyes are called for, two to keep track of the hair brushing and two to keep track of the simultaneous teeth brushing. What could be more expressive! Figure schemes are energetically explored. This Picasso-like black crayon self-portrait, 12 × 18 inches, is by a first-grade girl.

Art Criticism, Art History, and Aesthetics

"Do you like this painting? Why?" This kind of art criticism can be done at this early age. For children at this time, subject matter is most important. If they like the object portrayed, they'll like the picture. For example, in responding to Albrecht Dürer's drawing of a hare, the

children like it because it's cute or because they like rabbits. In their speaking, children do not differentiate between the world of pictures and what the pictures represent. They like pictures of things they like and reject pictures of things they dislike and fear. A grasp of the difference between appearance and reality develops slowly. For example, one first grader, needing to assure himself that he had not created a frightful lion, told the class, with some uncertainty in his voice, "It's not a real lion."

Children this age like pictures that are clear and vivid. Clarity of perceptual cues and an orderly organization of elements are very important. They look through the visual rendition; they do not see the style, or the composition, or the multiple meanings. Their perceptions are limited to a single interpretation. Talking about art reproductions helps to develop their skill in drawing inferences. They can scan and take in whole scenes to figure out situations, characters, and narration. They can predict what a scene would be like if they were there and how they would feel about it. They can't imagine the scene in an alternative way, and art inquiry is thus limited to what is shown, rather than how what is shown could be changed. By the second grade their preferences grow beyond like or dislike of a subject to include personal experiences as important factors.

Children between the ages of five and seven are particularly drawn to the effects of color. From the very first day of school, begin teaching the perception of the art elements, especially color aware-

Photo courtesy of Eastern Airlines.

A child's aesthetic awareness is at work in thinking about the patterns and pentagonal symmetry of a starfish echinoderm.

ness, with emphasis on the child's everyday surroundings: the classroom, clothes, books, and paintings and posters on display. ("If you have anything turquoise around your desk, maybe a notebook or a bracelet, hold it up.") Help them to identify the primary and secondary colors. Introduce the warm, sunny colors, such as yellow, orange, pink, and red, and the events associated with them—the circus, county fairs, parades, Mardi Gras, autumn harvest, and shopping malls. Talk about the deep, cool colors—green, turquoise, blue, and blue-violet—and the images they evoke—the mysterious night, the ocean depths, the rain-wet jungle, and the deep, dark forest.

Take advantage of the many stimulating games, toys, and devices available for developing color awareness: the prism, paint chips, the color wheel, and the kaleidoscope. After a rainfall, if a rainbow can be seen from the schoolroom window, use this natural phenomenon as the basis of a discussion of the spectrum. Encourage color matching and color sorting exercises, using found materials such as scraps of art paper, wallpaper, magazine illustrations, cloth, and yarn. Store the color collection in shoe boxes, one box for each color. When the children are using paints, encourage them to create new colors by mixing colors on wet or moist paper and naming their new color inventions.

Have the children explain the meaning and contribution of the following terms: color, shape, line, pattern, repeat, scribble, and texture. Encourage them to describe pattern and texture in clothing, in school surroundings, and especially in nature's bark, fur, fish scales,

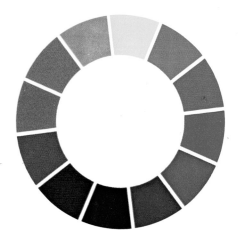

Complementary colors are those opposite each other on the color wheel; analogous colors are those side by side.

and plumage. Just as talking about art helps promote their artistic creativity, artistic creation helps them talk about art.

Teachers should exploit all means at their disposal, including the chalkboard and bulletin board, to call the child's attention to art-project-related vocabulary. Children of this age should know the following basic art terms: black, blue, bright, brown, brush, cardboard, chalk, circle, clay, coil, construction paper, crayon, dark, dot, drawing, easel, eraser, fingerpaint, glue, green, grey, hammer, ink, kiln, light, manila paper, mural, nail, newsprint paper, orange, oval, overlap, paste, pastel, pen, pencil, pink, pinch pot, purple or violet, rectangle, red, ruler, scribble, shape, square, stripe, tempera paint, tissue paper, triangle, watercolor, weaving, white, yellow.

Designing, Drawing, and Painting

> Something big, something small.
> Something short, something tall,
> Something dark, something light,
> Helps to make your drawing right.

This rhymed stanza helps remind young children to add variety to their compositions. In most instances the *more* images, shapes, or ideas the students incorporate in their compositions, the more unified their drawings become. Say to them, "Who else was there? What else might have been on the ground?"

As children join the community of picture makers, they begin to understand the demands of representation. They like to paint simple images, of themes such as a favorite toy or "What I like to do when it rains." For children who have developed beyond the scribbling stage, discourage rushing to finish or scribbling haphazardly. Children love to use their pictures to tell stories, and both pictures and stories can change from time to time. They often make several representations of the same subject, for example, dealing with a new baby in the family. Some can write their own titles and stories; in other cases, help is needed.

Introduce your children to various tools for making linear images. These include pencil, ballpoint and felt-nib pens, crayon, oil and chalk pastel, small brushes, school chalk, a nail for crayon-engraving projects, a stick in stand, or the fingers (for finger painting). Promote discovery of various line patterns: stripes, plaids, circles, stars, spirals, radiating lines, and zigzags.

Some children will make the delightfully charming foldover drawings (see page 223). They will show figures arranged in a circle or

Ann Arbor, Michigan.

A primary-grade youngster uses the circle-square figure schema. Figures are shown with no elbows and no shoulders, which would distract from the figures' crosslike forms, but the cat has well-defined elbows and shoulders. Pattern in clothing is depicted by stripes, plaids, and even a floral design. The

multicolor crayon engraving technique requires considerable patience. Because it calls for the application of several layers of crayon, use a small size of heavy oaktag. Begin with a light hue such as yellow or pink and build layer on layer through darker colors to a final brown, dark blue, or black.

on both sides of the street, upside down on one of the sides. Games such as ring-around-the-rosy can be used to stimulate these charming representations. Foldover is to the children quite a satisfactory method of design representation, since it very clearly tells what is occurring.

Children this age like their pictures to show clear relationships. One way they do this is to draw objects against an empty background. Still another is to use an outline, such as a ¼-inch or ½-inch brush

would give. During this period, floating objects will gradually diminish, to be replaced by figures on a stand line or baseline. Later the children may move to the use of multiple stand lines. At this time it is too early to introduce overlapping.

An interesting representational device that appears in some of the drawings at this stage is X-ray drawing or transparency—seeing the figure through the clothes and seeing what's inside the house through the walls. As children grow older, this way of representation

Courtesy of Jimmy Morris, Athens, Georgia, and Mary Sayer Hammond, Fairfax, Virginia.

In this drawing, shown in process and completed, "flowers short, flowers tall, flowers large, flowers small, flowers dark, and flowers light" help to make this young child's broad-nib marker drawing right. Here, the word "right" means artistically organized and delightfully varied. Small-size background paper (9 × 12 and 12 × 12 inches) is recommended when children use small, fine-nib markers.

Here, the walking figures and cabin cruiser are seen as if from the side, while the rowboats and sidewalk are seen as if from the top. Showing both the top and side views in one scene is called mixed-plan-and-elevation drawing. This and foldover drawings, which show the events upside down on the other side of the street, are charming ways by which artists represent what is known rather than what is seen. Conception and perception work together in this Taiwanese primary-grade child's telling about events at the water's edge.

For this first-grade oil-pastel mask on colored construction paper, the teacher emphasized thick and thin lines. Also emphasized were how linear repeat patterns can be created from circles, stripes, and stars.

"On our street" was the subject of this colorful colored construction paper collage by a first-grade child. The class first discussed shapes of houses, garages, churches, synagogues, and stores, then trees, bushes, hedges, fences, sidewalks, telephone poles, traffic signs, billboards, mailboxes, pets, cars, and trucks.

diminishes and children say that they don't do it that way anymore. Transparency does not mean children think that clothes are transparent. Instead it comes about because they draw the figure first and then dress it, just like using paper dolls. The representational device is used in some other cultures, for example, Australian aboriginal art, which can be used as motivational materials.

Introduce the children to line drawing, variety of shades, light and dark value, color, and pattern. Encourage drawing based on personal experiences and observations, but welcome and praise imaginative expression as well. Provide many opportunities to draw from real objects. These might be plants in and around the school, pets brought to class, flower arrangements, toys and dolls, classmates as figure-drawing models, self-portraits, depictions of the family in various settings, community helpers, and subject matter observed on field trips. Give large-size paper or newsprint so the details they consider important can be shown. In figure drawing, the size of the drawn head often determines the size of the body. Encourage the children to fill the page.

Collage (Cut and Paste)

Encourage students in scissors-cutting skills. Invite them to create simple, basically geometric shapes out of construction paper. Make sure to have scissors available especially designed for children who are left-handed. Provide opportunities involving pasting little shapes onto big shapes. Point out how contrast is achieved by pasting a light-colored shape over a dark-colored shape and vice versa. Demonstrate how to use paste and glue economically and effectively. A felt board can be employed to introduce children to the countless possibilities of cut-out shapes and how they can be juxtaposed. Cooperative murals employing the cut-and-paste technique in which each child contributes one or more parts to the whole are very satisfying projects (see Chapter 20, "Mural Making"). Almost any theme lends itself beautifully to collage making at this stage: flowers in a garden, animals in the jungle, fish in the sea, birds in a tree, and butterflies in flight.

Printmaking

Simple repeat prints will result in colorful allover patterns. These can be made using vegetables, found objects, clay pieces, erasers, cellulose scraps, and hands and fingers. In most instances colored construction

For primary-grade children, delightful prints can be created by using discarded plastic foam meat trays as the printing plates. Trim off the curved part of the tray. A preliminary drawing with a felt-nib pen or soft lead pencil is recommended. Make the impression by pressing a blunt-pointed pencil into the tray. Water-base black printing ink, rolled out on the engraved tray with a brayer may be used.

paper is recommended for the background printing surface. Other possibilities are colored tissue paper, newsprint, wallpaper samples, brown wrapping paper, and fabric remnants. Printmaking activities at this age level are somewhat limited, because young children do not possess the necessary skills for complicated techniques. Certainly worth trying are plastic foam meat-tray prints with incised relief created by pencil pressure.

Ceramics

Provide exploratory experiences with clay. Sufficient clay must be available; a ball of clay about the size of a grapefruit is recommended for every child. The clay must be of the proper plasticity—malleable,

An animal with a figure or with its young is a popular ceramic theme. Additively constructed pieces can come apart in drying and jostling. Therefore, emphasize heavy legs, firmly attached with roughening and smearing of the clay at the points of attachment.

not too sticky, and not too hard. Allow the children to discover clay's potential; encourage squeezing, pinching, poking, and stretching the clay. Show them how to make coils and form the clay into small balls or pellets. Guide the children in the creation of simple and familiar forms. Suggest that they hold the ball or lump of clay in their hands as they manipulate it into the desired shape. This procedure discourages the tendency of some children to pound the clay flat on their desks.

This girl sketching outdoors knows that the sun's rays fill the sky.

overlapping pinches. Caution them not to make the wall or bottom of the pot too thin. Since the marks of their fingers and thumb often add an attractive texture, minimize their use of water to smooth their clay.

Suggested Subjects or Themes

The following topics are suitable for children of ages 5, 6, and 7 (grades 1 and 2):

Playground games	Skipping rope
Fun in the snow	Our community helpers
Fun in the fall leaves	Butterflies in a garden
A flower garden	Farm animals
My pet and me	Noah's ark
Animals in the zoo or jungle	Fish in the sea
What I like to do when it rains	Land of make-believe
What my parent and I like to do together	My favorite toy

A 5-year-old from St. Petersburg, Russia, shows a favorite toy tiger in this tempera painting on paper. Notice how the exciting square patterning fills the space.

Primary-grade children can control the relatively simple sculptural forms of an elephant, hippo, cow, horse, rabbit, turtle, pig, dog, cat, whale, or resting bird. They enjoy manipulating the clay in either an additive or subtractive way. Teachers prefer the subtractive (pulling features out) way, since it results in a form less likely to fall apart.

Children at this stage can also construct simple pinch pots from a lump of clay the size of an orange, and the pots may be bisque-fired if a kiln is available. Ask them to hold the clay ball in the palm of one hand and insert the thumb of the other hand in the middle of the clay about half-way down. As they rotate the clay, they should push and pinch thumb and fingers along the inside and outside of the ball in

CHAPTER 5

A Sequential Curriculum for Grades 3 and 4

Although children's art at all stages has a unique beauty, some people refer to children's art of grades 3 and 4 as the "golden age of child art." Just as roses are most beautiful at the moment halfway between bud and full flowering, during this time children create art reflecting the charm of newly discovered representational concepts, along with signs of a move toward realism. Abstraction and realism are in a state of happy coalescence, and children's belief in their expressive powers is not disturbed by the anxiety about "not looking right" that comes later. By this time most children have developed methods of drawing that satisfactorily communicate their meaning to adults. Their schemes may be based partly on concepts and partly on perception. Early forms, such as a lollipop tree, which once seemed okay, yield under increasing perceptual input to become more novel, fresh forms; yet beneath the surface the conceptual model still has an influence. Teachers should not be content with having students rely on stereotypes but should help them take pleasure in putting visual discoveries into representational forms. The teacher might say, "Does anyone see anything around the mouth that we could draw? Juan says he sees half-circle lines at the edge of the mouth. How can we draw these?" However, the child who uses a conceptual scheme should not be made to feel inadequate, for this child's vision may be driven more by intuitive design decisions.

Developmental Characteristics

In the left-hand column of the next chart are listed some of the developmental characteristics of third- and fourth-grade children. The right-hand column gives one or more related art instructional objectives for each characteristic.

Developmental Characteristics of Third and Fourth Graders	Some Related Art Instructional Objectives
Have improved eye-hand coordination.	Students will draw from peers posing as models.
Have better command of small muscles.	Students will draw details of clothing and features.
Are becoming aware of differences in people.	Students will show differences among figures and objects in their artwork.
Are gradually learning to become responsible, orderly, and cooperative.	Students will share, distribute, and collect art material.
Begin to form separate sex groups.	Give art motivations for both boys' and girls' interests.
May start to join gangs and cliques.	Students will depict their friends in their art. The teacher can use peer approval to modify behavior.
Enjoy comic books.	Students will create their own comic characters and superheroes.
Are growing in critical skills, self-evaluation, and evaluation of others.	Students will use instructional objectives to evaluate their work.
Are now able to concentrate for a longer period.	Projects may span more than one period, if new objectives are brought forth.
Are developing an interest in travel.	Students will describe how historical artworks relate to a culture.

Developmental Characteristics of Third and Fourth Graders	Some Related Art Instructional Objectives
Are interested in the life processes of plants and animals.	Students will draw from life, taxidermy models, and pictures of flora and fauna and describe how their drawings show the specific features of plants or animals.
Are developing a sense of humor.	Students will discuss aesthetic issues raised by art cartoons.
Are becoming avid hobby fans and collectors.	Students will discuss their collections in terms of art criticism. "The picture shows his batting strength."

A major developmental issue of this time is whether the child develops feelings of competence or inferiority. While regular classroom activities develop children's skills in reading and math, children may develop inferiority feelings about their drawing ability if they are not instructed.

An intermediate-elementary-grade boy, who was incidentally in need of braces, did this fantasy oil pastel resist of an imaginary creature, part animal, part bird, part fish, part insect. The white shapes of the head and ears are repeated in the spirals of the tail and hind legs. Star, flower, and leaf forms fill the background.

Art Development

Once again, later is not better. The stages described below are descriptive and not prescriptive.

SHAPES	Students will draw and compose with more conscious deliberate planning, and will show more naturalistic and realistic proportions.
	Students will select and arrange objects to satisfy their compositional design needs.
COLOR	Students will mix and experiment with an expanded range of colors including the tints and shades.
	Students will discuss the mood and effects of warm and cool colors, within a painting and in the environment.
	Students will use related colors, those adjacent to one another on the color wheel.
	Students will neutralize (dull a color) by mixing a color with its complementary hue (opposites on the color wheel).
	Students will describe the effect of subdued colors next to bright, intense colors.
SPACE	Students will create space and depth through employment of vertical placement, diminishing size, and overlapping shapes.
	Students will describe how the horizon line can be used to show distant space.
OBJECTS	Students will select and arrange objects to satisfy their compositional design needs.
THE HUMAN FIGURE	Students will show action in their drawings of people and animals.
	Students will draw with more naturalistic and realistic proportions; more will use the five-heads-high figure.

Art Criticism, Art History, and Aesthetics

This is the stage of beauty and realism, the golden age of child art. The child believes the purpose of art is to represent something. The children yearn to make objects look real, and they strive for clarity and good definition. The more real and clear, the better the artworks are

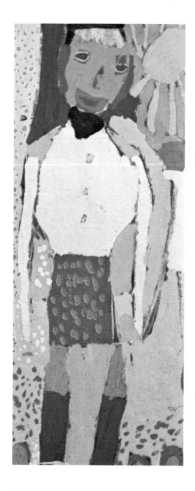   

Courtesy of David Hodge, Oshkosh, Wisconsin.

Grade 3 youngsters show their individuality in these large (12 × 24 inches) tempera self-portraits. Notice especially the spirit and wonderful complementary and analogous colors in the third self-portrait. It has orange and purple eyes, purple and green fingernails, and green lips and eyelashes! Beautiful!

Here again, qualitative, in-depth teaching strategies are the key to such successful artworks. These strategies include mixing a varied range of tempera hues, making sure the children devote time to doing preliminary sketches, and encouraging the imaginative use of color.

liked. In responding to realistic art, children comment, "I wish I could draw like this." This hankering after realism is so strong that when confronted by abstract artworks, they try to find a specific image in it.

By this time, children are beginning to try to figure out what an artwork is about, to make their first interpretive efforts. They take a longer time to look at art. Children now have the linguistic skills to express the concept that artworks are different from the thing itself. ("It is a picture of a rabbit" rather than "It is a rabbit.") Students can identify events depicted in artworks. They can describe likenesses and differences between pictures. They can accept their peers' differing

representations as being valid art expressions. They can recognize style in each other's works. They can tell about the colors, shapes, lines, and textures in an artwork. Children this age can recognize different media and the forming processes in different works of art. They can identify the forms of artwork, for example, sculptures, ceramics, landscape, portrait, architecture. They can describe some criteria for art. They can plan an art exhibition.

The following words can be added to the children's growing art vocabulary: background, balsawood, batik, brayer, cellophane, ceramics, collage, collograph, color wheel, complementary colors, composi-

Courtesy of Baiba Kuntz, Glencoe, Illinois.

This self-portrait is a contour drawing. An upper-elementary-grade child from Iowa City patiently delineated what she observed. Guide children to look carefully, to see freckles, collar stitchery, and patterns in the hair. This portrait reveals once again what drawing skills youngsters are capable of when they are encouraged to become aware, to observe details, and to draw slowly and deliberately.

tion, cone, contrast, contour line, crafts, cube, cylinder, engraving, foreground, form, found material, hue, India ink, inking slab, intensity, landscape, linoleum, linoprint, masking tape, monoprint, mosaic, negative shape, papier mâché, plaster, plywood, positive shape, poster, pyramid, radiation, rasp, scoring of clay and paper, shade, sketch, slab, slip, spiral, staple, still life, stitchery, tie-dyeing, tint, unity, value.

Drawing, Designing, and Painting

Children like to depict clothing—their favorite outfit, or occupational clothing, like a police uniform. Group projects comprised of students' individual works can demonstrate the power of working together to create projects of large size and scope. Continue to call attention to

the immediate and visually stimulating subject or image for drawing. On sketching excursions, scout for the unusual site, the pictorially exciting vista with multifaceted structures and interesting towers and spires, with varied foreground and background breakup. In representing distance and overlapping, children often change color and size to show space, and they like to show vastness of space. Suggest new directions in design:

- Overlapping shapes
- Achieving distance through diminishing sizes and placement of objects higher on the page
- Creating pattern and textural effects contrasted with quiet or plain areas
- Drawing the lines with varied weights and in varied ways

Children at this stage, by the fourth grade certainly, can be introduced to observational drawing and basic contour-drawing techniques. For an immediate visual stimulus, begin with simple, easily recognizable everyday objects: a fruit, vegetable, shoe, glove, helmet, cap, cowboy hat, baseball mitt, football, or water pitcher. When the students' skill and confidence in contour drawing increase, introduce a combined arrangement of several objects in which the items overlap. Guide the children to look carefully and intently at the object and draw it very slowly and deliberately.

Explain about inner contour lines. For example, with a flower, suggest that they begin in the middle with the core, adding a petal at a time, rather than with a hasty general outline of the entire flower. In other instances, for example with a banana or okra, begin with the outer contour line and then add inner contour lines to clarify the form. A few children can even draw oblique planes and use overlapping.

A soft lead pencil is best for contour drawing. Kindergarten pencils are recommended. Erasures should be discouraged. A second corrective line more carefully observed is suggested. The students may stop at critical junctures, reposition the drawing tool, and then continue drawing.

Direct the children's attention to the environment, to nature and its variety of lines, shapes, textures, colors, patterns, rhythms, and contrasts, and help them to see examples of radiation, emphasis, and unity in natural forms. Urge students to bring in interesting natural objects (taxidermy specimens, roots, weeds, fossils, honeycombs, bird's nests, pods, pinecones, seashells, and coral), to be used in discussions about artistic perception and for inspirational still lifes.

Color Awareness

Introduce art projects that demand multiple color choices:

Making collages using colored construction paper, colored tissue paper, wall-
   paper samples, paint chips, and assorted color fabrics and felts
Weaving with colored papers
Coloring with crayon or oil pastel on colored construction paper
Making mosaics with colored tesserae on a colored or black background
Creating a color environment or happening in the classroom, combining, for
   example, crepe paper, balloons, beach towels, hula hoops, fans, colored
   cellophane, ribbons, scarves, umbrellas, posters, and fabrics

Encourage students to mix and experiment with an expanded
range of colors including the tints and shades. Discuss the mood and
effect which warm and cool colors give within a painting and in the
environment. Call attention to the related colors, those adjacent to
one another on the color wheel. Students are now often ready to
tackle the intricacies of color neutralization (dulling a color) by mixing
a color with its complementary hue (opposites on the color wheel).
They can appreciate the subtle contrast of subdued colors next to
bright, intense colors.

Collage

Introduce cut, tear, and paste projects that require the creation of
texture and low-relief effects. These can be accomplished by folding,
crimping, pleating, fringing, weaving, braiding, and curling the paper.
Direct attention to positive and negative shapes. Suggest how the positive shape, obtained by cutting a motif (star, leaf, heart, cross, diamond) from a piece of paper, and the negative shape, the paper that
remains after the shape is cut out, can both be juxtaposed in a collage

*In these collages by third- and fourth-grade children, both positive and nega-
tive cutout shapes were used. Students chose one color of 12- × 18-inch construction paper for the background and several smaller scraps of construction
paper of different colors (approximately 4 × 6 inches). They drew motifs with
pencil in the center of the small sheets and cut them out. They then pasted both
the positive shapes and negative shapes onto their large background paper,
placing the pairs some distance from each other. They continued this process,
overlapping some shapes, until the composition filled the page.*

Courtesy of Jimmy Morris, Athens, Georgia.

design. Introduce colored tissue paper, either cut or torn, as a collage medium. Urge the use of light-colored tissues first and only later build up to the sparing use of darker colors as accents. Encourage color discovery by suggesting that students build several tissue layers. Collage projects in tissue lend themselves beautifully to nonobjective designs and to depictions of dreams and moods. Children can make collages interpreting sounds: whisper, shout, swish, rattle, squeak, roar, and thunderclap.

Printmaking

The vegetable, clay stamp, and found-object print media, introduced in the primary grades, can now be augmented with oil pastel as a final, rich embellishment. A variety of printmaking processes, explained fully in Chapter 22, are now manageable. These include the glue-line print; the collograph or cardboard relief print; and the string or cord print in which string is glued to a cardboard plate, inked, and printed. An excellent medium for greeting card designs is the plastic foam meat tray print in which lines are indented into the tray with a pencil and the plate is inked and printed so lines will appear white in the completed print. In the monoprint technique, a sheet of plastic laminate or of glass (its edges taped) is inked with a brayer. The composition is then created by scratching through the paint with a stick, Q-Tip, edge of cardboard piece, eraser end of pencil, or wood chopstick. Then a sheet of paper is placed over the inked surface, pressed down, and pulled off carefully.

Ceramics

At this stage, review the knowledge children have gained in earlier school years about clay: where it comes from, its properties, such as plasticity, its possibilities, and its limitations. Describe the importance of ceramics in the everyday life of ancient and contemporary cultures. An exploratory session in clay manipulation is again recommended to help students recall that:

- Hardening clay is difficult to model.
- Clay that is too moist sags if the supports of clay or rolled paper, or the "fifth leg" under the stomach of an animal, are not sturdy enough.
- Appendages break off when the clay piece dries unless they are securely joined to the main structure with clay-scoring or slip-cementing.
- Textures, patterns, and details can be made in clay with fingers, pencils, and assorted found objects.
- Solid clay pieces over a half inch thick may explode in the firing kiln unless openings are made through which the air inside can escape.

In pottery making, children can make the basic, simple pinch pot into a larger container or an animal's body by joining with clay slip two pinch pots of the same size. Cut out openings and add feet and spouts for more complex pots.

Suggested Subjects or Themes

These topics are suitable for children of ages 7, 8, and 9 (grades 3 and 4):

Inside me (imaginative X-ray)	Totem poles
Fun on the jungle gym	Soapbox derby
The circus parade	A tree house
The merry-go-round	Tree of life
The house where I live	Imaginary animals
Rare birds	Prehistoric animals
Animals and their young	The insect world
Autumn leaves and trees	Playing a musical instrument
The pet show	Still life of interesting objects
A magic forest	Flower market
The wedding	The toy store or Santa's workshop
Here comes the clowns!	The circus in action
Washing the family car	Space voyage
Boarding the school bus	Sunken treasure
A quiet activity at home	Design in nature: radiation

If I were a balloon seller, a juggler, a tightrope walker, a ballerina, a scarecrow, a skydiver, an astronaut, a clown.

CHAPTER 6

A Sequential Curriculum for Grades 5 and 6

After the powerful beginning in the primary- and middle-elementary grades, when almost all children feel that they can do art, a period of plateau or decline may occur during the upper-elementary grades. It is not known whether self-doubt about drawing is the cause of this decline, or whether the decline is the result of self-doubt. To be sure, the best art, whether realistic or abstract or primitive, is characterized by assuredness and verve, and this confidence seems to be shaken in the upper-elementary grades. Children's criteria of what is good in art outrace their abilities. They come to feel that their drawings are "not good enough," and they decide that they are "no good in art." These attitudes underscore the importance of discussions of aesthetics, on what makes quality in art, and whether realism is the only goal.

We believe that the guidance and encouragement of a sympathetic, knowledgeable teacher can prevent students from lagging on the same creative plateau for years. Without a teacher's guidance and encouragement, children's cognitive and affective growth in art, their employment of visual resources, their command of the vocabulary and language of art, and their use of formal elements may remain static or may even retrogress. This may lead eventually to discouragement, frustration, and apathy. If children are not taught art skills and are left to their own devices, many of them develop into adults who feel limited in their ability to make and discuss art.

On the other hand, under the guidance of a teacher who helps them to create and to appreciate the beauty they create and who gives them good reasons to try, children will grow in their ability to be careful delineators, to represent overlapping and receding spatial planes and to use these concepts in their contour drawings, in their drawings of buildings in nature, and in their imaginative drawings of the fantastic.

Developmental Characteristics

In the left-hand column of the next chart are listed some of the developmental characteristics of fifth- and sixth-grade children. The right-hand column gives one or more related art instructional objectives for each characteristic.

Developmental Characteristics of Fifth and Sixth Graders	Some Related Art Instructional Objectives
Begin to concentrate more on individual interests.	Students will depict their individual collections, their clothes for special occasions, for example, baseball uniforms, ballet costumes, scout uniforms.
Are now interested in activities that relate to their gender.	Students will use art criticism methods to describe and interpret artworks showing preadolescents.
Vary in maturity, with girls more developed physically and emotionally than boys.	
Are becoming more dependable, responsible, self-critical, and reasonable.	Students will use their own evaluation of their artwork—describing both strengths and weaknesses—as a guide toward making changes in it.
Are interested in doing and making things "right"; try to conform to ideals of "good" behavior.	Students will explore using the methods of realistically showing deep space. Students will be able to conform to their group's behavior policies.

Iowa City, Iowa. Courtesy Baiba Kuntz, Glencoe, Illinois.

Developmental Characteristics of Fifth and Sixth Graders	Some Related Art Instructional Objectives
Develop interests outside of home and school—in their community and the world at large.	Students will describe how the arts are incorporated into their community.
Begin to criticize grownups and anyone in authority.	Students will debate art judgments of experts.
Are undergoing critical emotional and physical changes.	Students will depict their physical appearance and emotions in their art and writing.
Become more involved in hobbies and collections.	Students will create an art display or representation of a hobby.
Begin a phase of hero and heroine worship.	Using examples from art history, students will describe a favorite artist's life.
Often enjoy being by themselves, away from adult interference.	Students will create a personal art notebook-diary, showing one's inner life.
Enjoy working on group projects.	Students will cooperatively work with a group of peers in planning and executing a group project.
Are developing a sense of values, a sense of right and wrong.	Students will debate issues in art ethics. ("Who should own and display Native American art, big city museums or tribal museums?")
Are increasing their interest and work span.	Students will work on an art project for three or more hours.
Tend to form separate gangs or cliques according to their interests, sex, ethnicity, neighborhoods, and family status.	Students will identify and interpret historical art exemplars representing groups with which they identify.

Fifth- and sixth-grade youngsters created these sophisticated self-portraits with an animal or bird. The drawing was first done in gold or silver crayon on black construction paper. Then oil pastel was used to create the complementary and analogous color areas. Notice the perceptive and sensitive handling of the eyes, eyelids, hair, and face planes.

The principal developmental focus beginning to come into play around this time is of identity versus role confusion. Can the child find a meaningful place in the world and in the world of work? Promote the development of a sense of identity through group art projects focusing on community occupational roles, including the many occupations that artists have.

Art Development

The level of mastery which individuals achieve in the development of expertise is largely intertwined with the effectiveness of instruction. Without a teacher's guidance, children's growth and interest in art and in the use of formal elements, in the way they perceive artistically, and in how they discuss art may remain static. Yet some unique abilities appear at this stage of development, to which the illustrations throughout this chapter attest.

The following table gives some general stage-related descriptions of children's art development at this age.

Art Development	Instructional Objective
Become increasingly critical of their drawing ability and are often so discouraged with their efforts that they lose interest in art class unless they are wisely and sympathetically motivated and guided.	Students will describe well drawn and expressively drawn parts in each others' artwork. Students will describe and use design principles in creative crafts items. Students will show more interest in art history.
Develop a growing curiosity to experiment with new and varied materials, tools, and techniques.	Students will use specialized tools and techniques, for example, linoleum cutting tools, plaster carving, weaving, and stitchery.
Experiment more with value contrasts, neutralized colors, patterns, and textual effects.	Students will neutralize colors and create pattern and texture effects.
Begin to use rudimentary perspective principles in drawing landscapes, buildings, streets, train tracks, fences, roads, and interiors.	Students will use vanishing area perspective, as well as appreciate other ways to create depth.
Become more interested in their environment as a source for their drawings and paintings.	Students will draw scenes of historical interest and natural beauty in their community.

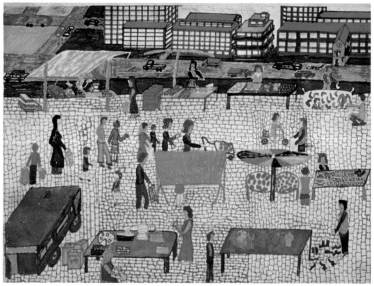

Courtesy International Children's Art Collection, Illinois State University, Normal, Illinois.

The perspective lines (lines receding into depth) of tables, trucks, and buildings in this 11-year-old student's drawing of the Bilecik, Turkey, market do not go to one vanishing point. Instead, the lines head to a general area in the upper right corner, in a method called isometric perspective. *The technique in which the perspective lines diverge as they go back in space is called* inverse perspective. *It also appears in this drawing and in much Near Eastern art.*

Art Criticism

At this age students will be able to identify the major compositional features of an artwork. They can suggest alternative ways that something could be made and to make critical judgments about artworks. For example, one student said, "It needs to have a black dog in the painting." They will be able to compare and contrast works in terms of both form and expressive meaning. They can describe how the elements work together to convey the ideas. They can learn to see beyond the subject matter and use terminology to identify the style and mood. They can describe what things are like in art, though they do not use metaphors (e.g., "icy person") until later. They can identify symbols used in artworks. They will be able to describe artists in their community, and they have a growing multicultural awareness, in that they can analyze works from a wide variety of cultures.

They like to know about illustrators' tricks of the trade, such as zoom lines and ways of depicting muscles, and are interested in studying how artists and illustrators use such conventions. For example, students might brainstorm about what is necessary to make a good depiction of a villain or a princess. A bulletin board, onto which students pin up examples they bring in, can show symbols for power, violence, speed, and motion.

Students should be able to use art terms such as the following in discussing artworks:

Design: harmony, motif, gradation, symmetry, asymmetry, emphasis, balance, composition, repetition, rhythm, simplicity, unity, variety
Shape: concave, convex, conical, pyramidal, exaggerated, geometric, biomorphic
Representation: foreshortening, proportion, symbol
Color: analogous, monochromatic, shading, harmony, spectrum, neutralization, transparent, opaque, translucent
Eye movement in a picture: circular, straight, spiral
Size: microscopic, telescopic
Space: narrow, wide, horizon line, perspective, vanishing point, vanishing area
Texture: granular, pebbled, regular, irregular

Art History and Aesthetics

In art history, students will be able to identify major figures and masterworks. They will be able to explain how two styles of art differ. They will be able to arrange examples of historic styles into chronological sequence. Encourage their thinking more deeply about experiences, about the motives that underlie behavior. For example, ask them, "Why did the artist do it that way?" They will be able to explain different art criteria, those based on aesthetics and those based on nonaesthetic criteria, such as money or subject matter. Since students of this age tend to value things according to size, expense, complexity, and power, the teacher can present reproductions of artworks that are especially large, costly, or complex, or artworks that depict powerful individuals.

Their art preference is for "super" realism and realism, a preference which peaks at age 11. In response to realistic artworks, students will say, "I wish I could draw like that." They are puzzled by pictures showing objects as they aren't or as they "should not" be. They call these depictions "weird" or "ugly." They feel that the things in pictures should be recognizable and valuable, neat, and interesting. At the same time, they are beginning to comprehend on an intellectual level, though often not on an emotional level, why an artist might show something other than a realistic rendering.

At this age students are sensitive to the idea of system, of a right way to do things. They try to adopt the rules and the codes necessary to survive in society. They want to know the right ways to do counting, reading, and math, the proper ways to play and to work, codes of right and wrong. Because of the firmness of their convictions and their awareness of rules concerning the way things are supposed to be, their language contains many "shoulds." ("That's not what a good drawing of a car should look like.") The teacher of aesthetics can use these "shoulds" to raise contested issues about the nature of art. ("Should good art take a lot of time to make?") Encourage them to come up with questions about meanings and values. Ask them to clarify their statements, to give reasons to support them, and then to examine the reasons given.

Drawing, Designing, and Painting

Students now can be careful, expressive, observational delineators. They begin to include shadows and receding planes in paintings. Scout out challenging sites to draw, such as building constructions and demolitions, Victorian-style homes, shopping malls, harbors and marinas,

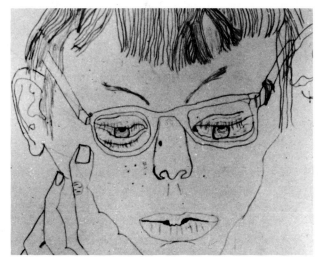

Iowa City, Iowa. Courtesy Baiba Kuntz, Glencoe, Illinois.

The self-portrait of this upper-elementary-grade boy is a contour drawing, patiently delineated.

bridges, museums, botanical gardens, aquariums, zoos, fire stations, and farm buildings. Students can be guided to create variety, space, and movement in their compositions by imaginative placement of images, objects, or motifs within the picture plane. Encourage them to put figures or buildings on different foreground levels and to terminate them at varying heights in the background. Shapes can be juxtaposed or overlapped to create unity and space-in-depth.

Inability to achieve satisfactory realistic results sadly leads some children mistakenly to conclude, "I am no good at art." Challenge this now. Continue practice in contour drawing, but introduce new approaches such as fantasy, nonobjective, and optical-art themes. Interest in the surreal shows up in the use of macabre and bloody images. They can use metaphoric images, for example, an isolated tree for loneliness and despair. Lead the students to discover the many different ways they can use line as pattern to enrich surfaces and vitalize backgrounds. Students become absorbed in the tricks of the trade; they like learning the conventions of comic book illustration, such as thought bubbles, clearly defined muscles, and stars and steam to depict violence.

In painting with color, reinforce learning about complementary, monochromatic, and analogous color harmonies. Discuss tints and shades, the directions for neutralizing colors, the color spectrum, and the color wheel. Continue to build color awareness by calling the students' attention to color usage in their everyday world—billboards, magazine and recording covers, athletic uniforms, storefronts, and automobiles. Use mood music as a background for free, expressive painting.

Collage

Recapitulate previous learnings such as the use of positive and negative shapes. Recommend using partially three-dimensional effects through paper folding, fringing, pleating, spiraling, and curling. Introduce paper scoring to students who are ready for more skillful challenges. Demonstrate the scoring technique: placing paper to be scored on a thick pad of newspapers; using the blunt point of scissors,

---

Discuss tints and shades. Help the students gain knowledge of the artistic power of complementary and analogous colors. Color photos of fish and seaweed were the topic for these oil pastels on colored construction paper by upper-elementary-grade children.

the pointed end of a wood popsicle stick, or a similar tool to indent the curved line into the paper; and then carefully folding along the indented line. To enrich students' collages, encourage them to scout for found objects such as wallpaper and rug samples, fabric and ribbon remnants, yarn, old greeting cards, and discarded building materials.

Printmaking

Although the various printmaking processes introduced in previous grades (vegetable and found-object print, collograph, glue-line-relief print, polystyrene print, and monoprint) can be repeated successfully

Courtesy of the International Children's Art Collection, Illinois State University, Normal, Illinois.

Maori chief by a New Zealand student, age 10.

This woodblock print of a child model playing a recorder is by an upper-elementary-grade student in Japan. It shows carefully delineated fingers, and lines around the mouth to indicate the blowing. Removing the background created an attractive texture.

at this age level, the maturing students will now respond to more complex, more challenging print techniques. Linoleum printing is a favorite because of the opportunity to use a variety of gouges. Since more tools, materials, equipment, and time are required for advanced printmaking, see Chapter 22 for guidelines on inking, printing, and using cleanup stations.

Courtesy of Baiba Kuntz, Glencoe, Illinois.

Mirrors help students achieve success with projects like these life-sized clay-relief self-portraits. Upper-elementary-grade students are concerned with realistic portrayals showing correct proportions and details.

Ceramics

Popular subject-matter themes for this age level include animals and their young, animals in combat, portraits and self-portraits, clowns, acrobats, and mother and child. Students now place a strong emphasis on realistic portrayals and on the achievement of correct proportions and characteristic detail. Toward these ends, the teacher must be prepared to offer sympathetic and supportive guidance when called upon. In most instances, recalled images alone will not supply the child with sufficient visual data. Direct the students to the original, inspirational source of the subject matter—to the figure or animal itself or to photographic resources. Build a library of photographs and slides of exemplars of ceramic art through the centuries. Neither overpraise the purely realistic approach they admire nor harshly criticize it; instead, introduce students to a variety of styles and interpretations.

Suggested Subjects or Themes

These project suggestions are suitable for children of ages 9, 10, and 11 (grades 5 and 6):

At the airport	Cities in outer space
At the gas station	Self-portraits
On the subway	Portraits of classmates
At the train depot	Traffic jam
A view from a plane	Landscape, cityscape, seascape
Bicycle race	Nature study
Horse show	The marching band
Warriors in armor	Track meet or scout jamboree
Undersea marine life	Amusement park
At the swimming pool	The shopping mall
Still life of musical instruments	Disneyland, Six Flags
County fairs and 4-H competitions	Motorcycles
Winter carnival	Renowned sports figures

CHAPTER 7

A Sequential Curriculum for Grades 7 and 8

Middle-school students move into a changed academic world. For the first time they may have a different teacher for each subject they take. If they come from the typical elementary-school situation where the classroom teacher taught art, it will be their first contact with a specialist art teacher. In American schools, just a little over half of the students this age participate in visual arts classes. In some schools, students involved in band or orchestra programs cannot take art. Also regrettable is the fact that, in general, students draw less as they grow older. However, for a fair number of adolescents, a new synthesis occurs. Their newly developed technical facility is joined to their vision of what needs to be expressed.

Middle-school students are experiencing a renaissance of intellectual inquisitiveness that in some ways may never be matched again. They are less inhibited than upper-elementary-grade children, but they are still highly critical of their own performance. They are more willing to tackle new processes and new materials. They are technically more proficient. Their ability to capitalize on suggestions is heightened, and they can enter into critical discussions on art design and structure with a keener sensitivity and with sharper argumentative skills. They are highly impressionable. Their cultural horizons are expanding, and they may carry with them the preferences and prejudices regarding art they develop in these middle-school years for the rest of their lives.

This middle-school student is intent on his ceramic creation. For many youngsters, there is no greater satisfaction than hand building structures out of clay. The simple, basic pinch-pot form has been enriched by the addition of a foot, neck, handles, and an embellishing relief pattern.

Courtesy of David Hodge, Oshkosh, Wisconsin.

Developmental Characteristics

Developmental Characteristics of Seventh and Eighth Graders	Implications for Art Teaching
Want to be accepted by their peers. This acceptance is often more important to them than the teacher's approval.	Students will work in small groups to plan and carry out group projects.
Are often more inclined to daydream, to watch rather than to perform.	From a study of art history books, students will describe an imaginary day in the life of an artist.
Begin to place a new emphasis on their appearance, grooming, and popularity.	Students will create a clay head in three dimensions, showing their own appearance and hairstyle.
Are becoming more self-conscious regarding their changing physical characteristics.	Students will be able to draw caricatures of their prominent features.
Possess varying degrees of physiological and sexual maturity.	Students will interpret artwork showing persons of this age.
Are in constant communication with their friends on topics of dates, parties, TV shows, movies, recordings, classmates' doings, teachers' and parents' foibles.	From a personal record of phone doodles, students will describe the design variations and use these design ideas as the basis for a T-shirt design.
Boys and girls frequently model their behavior and their appearance after sports stars, television personalities, rap singers, recording artists, movie stars.	Students will be able to draw from photos persons whom they admire. Students will express through art their interest in sports, music, or other arts.
Are often unusually sensitive to other people's problems but do not know how to help.	Students will create a work of art to share with another person and give empathic feedback to another student about art.
Are trying to develop a code or sense of values.	Students will interpret a work of art in terms of the moral dilemmas of the persons represented.
Form status groups and cliques, using "accepted," "tolerated," and "rejected" categories.	Students will interpret artworks by diverse groups, and, looking at pictures of alienation, explain what the artists were trying to communicate.

Painting a design for a record cover may reveal that middle-school students' opinions about the quality of rap music are different from the teacher's. Nevertheless, the teacher can lead them to consider how the artistic solutions of artists such Wassily Kandinsky and Max Beckmann may be applicable to their own designs.

Developmental Characteristics of Seventh and Eighth Graders	Implications for Art Teaching
Have a growing desire for new and exciting experiences.	Students will be able to depict exciting, imaginary adventures through art.
Fluctuate between childhood and adulthood in their interests, insights, abilities, and judgments.	Students will describe art careers in the community.

Emotional Vulnerability

Teachers of art should remember that young adolescents are vulnerable emotionally. Direct criticism of students' artwork in front of their classmates can be humiliating. Avoid sarcasm and belittling remarks at all costs. Writing as an adult, Georgia O'Keeffe recalled the painful humiliation she felt when, at age 13, her art teacher criticized her in front of her classmates for drawing a plaster figure's hand too small. "At the time I thought she scolded me terribly. I was so embarrassed that it was difficult not to cry" (O'Keeffe, 1988). Teachers may also embarrass students by praising their work too lavishly in front of their peers. To avoid public embarrassment in correcting or praising students, give individual, in-process critiques.

Emotional swings and moodiness are not unusual, and some students may reject their own excellent artwork. Drawings of teenage clothing, sneakers, and hairstyles considered contrary to the adult culture's norms can express adolescents' need to be separate from the dominant adult culture. Especially if their art experiences in elementary school were limited, unsatisfying, or unrewarding, middle-school students may be apathetic or cool in their response to art. But once they become caught up in the excitement of a creative, productive, and qualitative art program, they become enthusiastic converts to art's adventures, challenges, and personally satisfying rewards.

In the middle school, teachers really begin to see the personalities and idiosyncrasies of the students reflected in their behavior and their art. While the students can be conformists, they can also be fiercely independent. Roles are tried out: the extrovert, the loner, the risk taker, the methodical planner, the procrastinator, the idol seeker, the plodder, the perfectionist, the maverick, the dreamer, the braggart, the idealist, and the quiz whiz. One week one role is tried; the next week, a different role. Personalities depicted throughout art history (such as Albrecht Dürer's knight on a horse and Renaissance depictions of David and Hercules) can be related to some students' fantasy interests. Rites of passage are acted out in real fights, mock fights, and challenges to authority. This is a time of increased awareness and self-consciousness, of sensitivity to differences in others, of identification with the peer group, and of heightened emotional responses. Possibly as a means of self-searching, preadolescents like to draw portraits and capture their changing self-image.

Going steady, having crushes, engaging in sexual activity, and being subjected to physical and sexual harassment and abuse are emo-

From "Middle School Expressions," by Teddy Oliver and Robert Clements, *School Arts Magazine,* September 1983. Courtesy of Davis Publications, Wooster, Mass., and Teddy Oliver, Blairsville, Georgia.

A 12-year-old has expressed his pain and humiliation in his oil pastel, My Mother Just Spanked Me.

Red Barn, Lake George, New York, 1921 (oil on canvas, 14¼ × 16¼ inches). Georgia Museum of Art, Eva Underhill Holbrook Memorial, Gift of Alfred H. Holbrook.

Georgia O'Keeffe distastefully remembered for decades when her middle-school teacher publicly rebuked the realism of her figure drawing in front of her classmates. Her paintings are acclaimed for their bold shape patterns.

Courtesy of Fay Brassie, Athens, Georgia.

In a design for a jacket, this middle-school student has expressed yearnings for love, joy, and the banning of rules.

tionally charged situations in which some older students may find themselves. Other events fraught with the potential for creating guilt feelings are the divorce of parents, an abortion, or the death of a loved one. Feelings of worthlessness, incompetence, ugliness, anger, guilt, and complicity interfere with development of students' positive self-concepts. Teachers used to say that the schools' biggest problems were talking in class, chewing gum, making noise, running in the halls, and getting out of turn in lines. Nowadays, more serious problems are endemic. By being a friend to the student and expressing personal concern, you may play a pivotal role in the student's life at a critical time. The art program may provide the vehicle for students to express their conflicts or to come up with positive responses.

When students are going through emotionally trying situations, you may see a decline in ability to concentrate on art expression. In their behavior, you may see a shortness of temper or, contrariwise, a lack of affect. Art expression may serve as a warning beacon, announcing that a person is in trouble. Students' verbalizations during art criticism and art interpretation often provide a forum for other students to speak out about what is on their minds. Very general and wide-open art topics such as "crying" or "oppression" may provide a way to express through art what formerly seemed unmentionable. The teacher of art may be able to help the young person cope with problems, not by being a psychologist, but by being a friend, someone with whom significant events may be shared. The art teacher, through the school counselor, may be able to help the individuals or their parents get in contact with agencies skilled in dealing with serious problems.

Not only can art announce to the sensitive perceiver the individual's distress, but it can play a major role in restoring a person's balance after a traumatic situation. Art creation and discussions about art can help students to feel better about themselves. Problem solving through art provides an opportunity for the "person within" to emerge. Applying the principles of good design (balance, proportion,

dents will talk about the expressive qualities of the artwork. They can recognize style, and they can contrast the treatment of theme in two or more artworks. They understand metaphor and mystery, and can identify multiple meanings in represented objects.

Accompanying the rapid changes in their bodies and their own search for identity is a shift in understanding. Students can now understand that the expression of the experiences of others and of one's self is subjective. Expression characterizes this stage. There is less concern about realism and about the beauty of a subject. Pictures can now be seen as metaphors for ideas and emotions, and valued for their ability to inspire feelings. Students can speculate on the artist's mood. Students can imagine alternatives to what the picture shows, speculating on different scenarios. This allows them to feel an identification with accepted, mature artists.

Students will be able to discuss the aesthetic quality of an artwork or a utilitarian object. For example, students can judge the effectiveness of the designs of athletic shoes, T-shirts, and motorcycles and analyze how these objects suggest ideas and feelings.

The emotional side of middle-school art is shown in this soft firebrick sculpture and in this driftwood sculpture. Here are seen the creators' sensitivity to others, their forming of significant relationships with others, their heightened emotional responses, and their self-searching.

variation) seems to foster those same qualities in the individual creator. In art creation, the individual may find help through being able to share visually, at whatever level is comfortable, the event needing expression. Likewise, through talking about the art of others, the individual may be able to give voice to personal feelings and break out of one's aloneness and grief. Art accomplishment by a student can help others see that person as an individual of worth. In turn, the achievement helps that individual, despite the outrageous blows that fortune has inflicted, to acquire a sense of pride and self-worth.

Art Criticism

A new and genuinely different way of thinking about art now comes into being. The criterion of realism is replaced by the criteria of intention and message. Given artwork containing expressive themes, stu-

Art History and Aesthetics

Adolescents' ability to think abstractly and to reason about ideas increases dramatically at this time. They can consider the logical possibilities in a problem. They make guesses about what might be going on behind the depicted scene. They can discuss symbolism, deeper meanings, and double meanings.

They have the ability to conduct inquiry from several vantage points. They can role-play different parts, such as art critic, artist, disgruntled client, or government official. In individual or small group reports, students can give reports on artists' careers. They can stage mock debates between artists, pointing up contested issues in art, such as whether paintings should show realism or emotion. Some terms to discuss are expressivism, realism, aesthetics, anatomy, judgment, value, art critic, censorship, metaphor, spontaneity, craftsmanship.

During this new stage of aesthetic response, students can investigate questions of content and social significance. Since art is an expression of its creator, ask them to talk about how the artist uses color and design to show emotion. Students are also able to consider more abstract aspects, like style and composition. They understand that other students' perspectives can be different from their own.

To tap their interest in expressive works of art, expose them to Van Gogh's life and letters. Show them works about the suffering of women and children during wartime by Kaethe Kollwitz, Francisco Goya, and Max Beckman. Expand their knowledge and appreciation of master drawings and paintings by artists such as Leonardo da Vinci, Albrecht Dürer, Rembrandt Van Rijn, Rosa Bonheur, Paul Klee, Henri Matisse, Pablo Picasso, Louise Nevelson, Andy Warhol, Katsushika Hokusai, Georgia O'Keeffe, William Hogarth, Romare Bearden, Peter Breughel, and Mary Cassatt.

Call their attention also to the cave drawings at Altamira and Font du Gaume, to Benin bronzes, and to the tribal-huntsmen renditions of African and Australian native cultures. Show them the sumi-e ink drawings of China and Japan, and the expressive graphics of the Eskimos and Native Americans.

Middle-school students, coming as they often do from different elementary schools, will bring varied backgrounds in art vocabulary. Students should be able to match artworks to styles. One appropriate task is to identify the artwork that doesn't belong in a group. Words that have been suggested in previous grades should be reviewed and new vocabulary words added as they are introduced:

Art history and criticism: expressionism, neo-expressionism, op art, pop art, African sculptures from Yoruba, Benin bronzes, Zaire nail art, Chi Wara antelope sculptures, surrealism, cubism, Renaissance art, impressionism, symbolism, double meaning

Drawing and painting: conte crayon, sienna, spectrum, stipple, umber, montage, ochre, watercolor wash, distortion, encaustic, fixative, foreshortening, gesture drawing, hatching, converging lines, crosshatch, caricature

Printmaking: baren, bench hook, burnish, etching, intaglio, printing press, proof, relief print

Photography, film, and video: negative, fixer, plate, tone, daguerreotype, cibachrome, playback, wipe, fade, establishing shot, zoom shot, soft focus, montage, slow disclosure, low angle shot, freeze frame, long shot, pan, superimposition

Sculpture: armature, assemblage, bas relief, solder, sandcore, sepia, stabile, incised relief, repoussé, patina

Courtesy of David Hodge, Oshkosh, Wisconsin.

Through drawing classmates modeling, students can express indirectly something of their own emotional nature. Here, a middle-school youth captures in a contour line drawing a quality of openness and searching. The drawing also conveys an understanding of the human form, the chair, and folds of clothing.

Art Development

Art Development	Instructional Objective
Choose subject matter for their art expression that relates to human-interest activities, community and worldwide events, and current projects in ecology, medical research, space, and undersea exploration.	Students will use current events as the setting for their art expression. Students will explain the art principles they used in depicting the sociological, artistic, or scientific event.
Attempt shading and crosshatch techniques to make their drawn forms appear solid, cylindrical, and believably realistic. Experiment with perspective drawing.	Students will use shading and crosshatching to create the appearance of three-dimensional form. Students will be able to apply some perspective concepts.
Are self-conscious and self-critical about their drawing ability. Supportive instruction and contour and gesture drawing helps them become increasingly skillful in figure and animal drawing.	Students will use gesture and contour drawing to capture the feeling and dynamics of the posed human figure.
Are ready to interpret complex compositions such as richly orchestrated still lifes and multifigured events and celebrations.	Students will apply design principles of repetition and variation to draw an organized composition from a complex still life or from many figures in action.
Are mature and skillful enough to handle a variety of challenging crafts: photography, glazed ceramics, repoussé, plaster reliefs, sculpture in hard materials, and woodblock printmaking.	Students will use craft processes for personal art expression.

Circle self-portraits in oil pastel on colored construction paper by middle-school students. By using a circle format and emphasizing imaginative use of color and form, the teacher created a new artistic design challenge. Flags, flowers, camouflage, and birds serve as auxiliary ways the artists have conveyed their interests.

University of Wisconsin, Oshkosh Campus Laboratory School.

Perspective is shown in this 10-year-old girl's street scene from Tehran, Iran. Diminishing sizes are seen in the street vanishing around the bend, its dotted centerline, the curved fence, and the street-side buildings.

This direct yet sensitively drawn model of a seated adolescent was created by a middle-school youngster in a U.S. Defense Dependents School in Manila, Phillipines.

Drawing, Designing, and Painting

Students like their work to have expressive content—to convey a mood and to have a message. They are interested in finding a powerful means to convey an experience or an idea. Whereas younger students showed scenes, adolescents now use scenic natural forms to communicate their attitudes toward life. They can study symbols, and work motifs for peace, freedom, evil, or envy into their designs.

Most students this age have a love-hate relationship with drawing; they seek realism but are often frustrated by their inability to attain it. Elaborate still-life setups with a model in expressive apparel stimulate their interest and hence their desire to accurately represent the model's positions and clothing. Line drawings of cartoon characters, mythical animals, and sports events are popular, as are cartoon portraits. Using shading, stippling, hatching, crosshatching, and washes, they can begin to comprehend and depict the effect of spotlights on models. They will need guidance and reassurance, however, in handling color values and using cast shadows and reflections.

Students interested in creating depth in their pictures will begin to realize the importance of creating avenues into the composition. This is done by using lines and shapes that terminate at the boundaries or borders of the paper. They lead the viewer into the picture. A bonus is that the more avenues created, the more opportunities the student has to employ a variety of colors, values, and pattern in the resulting shapes. Perspective may be introduced as just one of many ways artists create the illusion of depth. However, only a tiny fraction of students can work out realistic perspective showing space and depth. Thus, unless a student specifically requests help, it is wiser not to introduce regimented perspective rules or foreshortening techniques at this stage.

Inverted perspective sometimes appears, and the beauty of this method should be pointed out, for example, as in Persian art. Some students will want their drawings to "look right" and will request specific assistance in making their toppling, meandering fences stand straight. They want their sidewalks to lie flat, and their roads to disappear believably over a distant rise or hill. To help them achieve these effects, show them that fence posts are drawn parallel to the sides of the page, division lines in sidewalks are drawn at angles directed to a distant vanishing point, and roads or highways diminish in width as they move away from the viewer toward the horizon.

Older middle-school students are often enchanted by the mechanical, mathematical aspects of perspective drawing. The illusion of space gives some students, especially those who do not like to draw, a feeling that they have done something of note. Their enthusiasm should not be dampened, but the teacher should enlighten them regarding the compositional limitations of rigid reliance on perspective. Similarly, although it is all right for students to strive for "right" proportions in their figures, the instructor must help them realize that drawing something "realistically right" does not necessarily make it "artistically right." Especially now, when expression of feelings is so important, students can be shown that many artists throughout time who either did not know of or ignored the rules of perspective and proportion produced art of great impact and beauty.

Middle-school students are mature enough to respond to the many subtleties and complexities of color harmonization. Review the processes for making tints and shades and the techniques for neutralizing colors. Challenge the students to use color principles in designing album covers, monograms, posters, logos, book jackets, store-window displays, room decor, and stage designs. Call attention to how color is used in artworks for conveying emotion. Discuss the psychological effect of color on people; the colors emphasized in packaging and advertising; the colors of ceremonies, celebrations, rituals, and rites of passage. Analyze how various countries and cultures use differing symbolic color meanings.

Taking ideas from contemporary color and light shows, students can be encouraged to construct their own color "happenings." They can use found materials such as ribbons, yarn, wrapping paper, kites, cellophane, balloons, hula hoops, confetti, crepe and tissue paper in assorted colors, giant paper flowers, fabric samples, and beach towels. Other exciting projects to stimulate color awareness can be motivated by such artists as Victor Vasarely, Richard Anuskiewicz, Marc Chagall, and Judy Pfaff. For example, students can construct toothpick and box sculptures painted in bold tempera or fluorescent colors, and make miniature stained-glass windows using scrap colored glass, colored tissue paper, or stage gels.

Printmaking

The simple prints that the children enjoyed in earlier grades—vegetable and found-object prints, glue-line-relief prints, collographs, monoprints, and linoleum prints—can be done with satisfaction and success in the middle school. More complex subject matter and themes can now also be employed in a variety of printmaking pro-

Mixed media, 113 × 192 × 72 inches. Courtesy Holly Solomon Gallery, New York.

Exciting color projects to stimulate color awareness can be motivated by showing the work of Judy Pfaff, such as her 1986 Apples and Oranges.

cesses. As always, the organization and monitoring of inking, printing, and cleanup are of special importance. At this grade level, sophisticated printmaking techniques such as woodblocks can be undertaken if teachers are experienced in supervising advanced printmaking techniques. Use nontoxic water-based inks rather than oil-based inks.

Ceramics

Since students may come to middle school with varying backgrounds in clay experimentation and creation, provide for several sessions to review clay exploration. Discuss the importance of clay in the lives of people of other cultures. Discuss art visuals of ceramic pottery and sculpture from ancient as well as contemporary cultures. Include Greek vases of the Hellenic period; Chinese Tang figurines; the outstanding life-size ceramic warriors and horses unearthed at Xian; Japanese Haniwa creations; and clay vessels in the form of human figures from Mexico and Peru. Copies of *Ceramic Monthly* from the library can bring the students up to date on the newest developments in the field of ceramic pottery and sculpture. Put up a "potter of the week" display on the art-room bulletin board so the students will become familiar with pioneers and innovators such as Shoji Hamada, Andy Nasisse, Dan Lucero, and Peter Voulkos.

Above and below: Courtesy of Mary Sayer Hammond, Fairfax, Virginia.

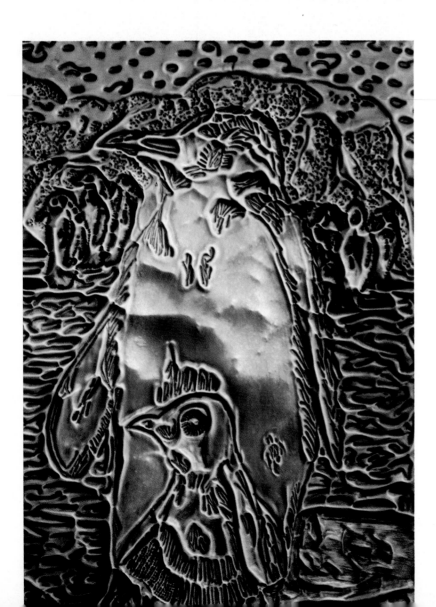

Larger-than-life clay portraits from Japan capture the human figure's expressive potential. Observe the heavy supporting neck and the free application of dabs of clay to create the form.

Students can now engage in more complex and challenging clay construction and modeling. If glazes and adequate kiln facilities are provided, students can experiment with safe ceramic glazes to give their ceramics glowing color. Chapter 26 gives suggestions on staining ceramics. Remember, however, less is often more in ceramic decoration and embellishment. Encourage restraint in their color choices by showing them exemplars of ceramic craftsmanship.

Crafts

Little has been included about construction projects or crafts such as weaving, stitchery, papier-mâché, puppetry, and simple jewelry. Yet all of these hands-on activities should be included in a qualitative, progressive, elementary and middle-school art program. For example, weaving can progress from simple paper weaving in the primary grades to sophisticated hanging woven panels in the middle school. The story quilts of Faith Ringgold and of Harriet Powers can motivate exciting sewn appliqué banners and quilts. Mask construction, simple puppets, and stitchery can be offered at all levels. Papier-mâché, paper sculpture, leather and metal tooling, marionettes, and jewelry are best reserved for upper elementary grades and middle school. Then many students are also ready for challenging subtractive sculpture projects in soap, balsa wood, sandcore, leather-hard clay molds, plaster-of-Paris blocks, and soft firebrick. They will enjoy additive sculpture employing toothpicks, wood scraps, wire, metal, driftwood, and found objects. Specialized craft vocabulary terms such as the following should be taught: glaze, gouge, greenware, grog, leather-hard clay, mat, mat knife, mixed media, mold, raffia, reed, tesserae.

Collage

The collage process, with its related family of montage, frottage, mosaic, collograph, and assemblage, provides middle-school students with a host of opportunities to use art principles. These include variety in shapes, contrast in values and color, and overlapping to create unity. Collage allows them to express through art their personal concerns about attractiveness and intimacy and their social concerns about such world problems as ecology, hunger, drugs, and war.

On facing page: *Metal repoussé. Metal embossing or tooling is an art craft that upper-elementary- and middle-school youngsters will enjoy. The teacher should provide visually stimulating motivational resources so the students can create their own designs. Discourage the use of ready-made stereotyped patterns. Recommended subject themes are animals and their young, tropical fish, butterflies, birds of fancy plumage, and denizens of the jungle or zoo. All of these ideas provide excellent opportunities for the use of detail and texture. Preliminary drawings for this project may be made on newsprint, manila paper, or notebook paper. The size should be limited to 6 × 9, 9 × 9, or 12 × 12 inches. The copper repoussé examples illustrated here are 9 × 12 inches. Heavy-duty aluminum foil or commercially available sheeting (36-gauge) can be used. Tape the preliminary drawing to the metal sheet with masking tape to guide the initial embossing. To make the relief indentations, use a blunt-pointed pencil, the end of a round watercolor brush, or a commercially produced embossing tool. After the basic preliminary outline is completely indented (students can lift their papers to check), remove the paper and work directly on the metal. Emphasize detail, designs, veins, and textures. When the piece is completely embossed, embellish it by applying black shoe polish and then wiping it off the raised surfaces. If the budget allows, obtain copper sheeting, emboss it, and give it a beautiful patina employing liver of sulfate, which is strong-smelling but safe.*

Courtesy of David Hodge, Oshkosh, Wisconsin.

Vehicles are a popular topic with middle-school youths. Students created collages from detailed drawings of an open-doored van parked on the school's premises. Gas pumps and logos were added to enhance the compositions.

Review with the students the fundamentals of the collage process: how to identify and exploit positive and negative shapes and how to create subtle space through overlapping. Show them how to achieve three-dimensional effects through paper folding, scoring, pleating, fringing, and curling. Preliminary drawings or sketches are recommended for collages when subject matter deals with landscapes, figure studies, or still lifes. In themes from the imagination or in purely nonobjective interpretations, the direct cutting, tearing, and application of the shapes to the background may be encouraged. However, in both approaches, the pasting or permanent adhering of materials should be delayed until the students, with the teacher's guidance, can make those compositional changes—additions, subtractions, and revisions—necessary to enhance their creations.

New materials and found materials have expanded the range of collage creation immensely. Explore the possibilities of colored tissue on white or colored cardboard, colored sections from magazine ads, wallpaper samples, and fabric remnants. Incorporate nature's store of colored and textured wonders: bark, leaves, seaweed, sand, feathers, butterfly wings, dried flowers, seeds, and snake skins. The collage is an excellent first project of the year for middle-school art classes. It does not put as much pressure on the students as an assignment in drawing or painting would. It is not stressful to cut out elements and put them together to make a whole design. Every student in class can succeed in collage making.

Suggested Subjects or Themes

These project suggestions are suitable for children of ages 12, 13, and 14. Visual resources are absolutely necessary. For additional ideas, refer to themes recommended earlier for grades 5 and 6, which can be adapted to the middle school. Middle schools may be composed of grades 6 to 8, or even 5 to 8, and this variation will affect the suitability of topics. Some themes, such as a bouquet of flowers, self-portraits, and animal pets, can be recommended without reservation for all grades, 1 through 8.

Environmental problems and
  solutions
The Olympics
I wish
Great moments in music, ballet
Great moments in theater,
  literature, science
Great moments in sports
I would like/I would not like
Customs and costumes
  of the world
The weather's mood
Sadness in the world
Legendary heroes and heroines

Helicopters, planes, air balloon
  races
Bicycles, dune buggies
Landscapes
Illustrations of selected stories and
  poems
Dream cars, motorcycles, and boats
Historical costumes
Flying trapeze act
The electronic game arcade
String quartet
Fashion show
Wrestling match

PART II
Teachers and Teaching

CHAPTER 8

The Role
of the
Dedicated Teacher

Wherever art programs of quality and promise exist, whether in elementary or middle schools, in crowded cities or quiet farm communities, in the United States or abroad, one always discovers in the wings an enthusiastic, resourceful, knowledgeable, imaginative, and gifted teacher. The teacher of the successful, productive art class is invariably a planner, an organizer, an expediter, a counselor, a dreamer, a goal setter, and, most of all, a lover of children, life, and especially art.

Without a well-prepared, creative, and dedicated teacher at the helm, an art program can founder in a sea of hasty, last-minute decisions, in trite and stereotyped activities, or in chaotic, pseudotherapeutic play sessions. The school that boasts a modern physical plant, a generous budget, and an administration sympathetic to art is fortunate, but if it does not attract teachers who are prepared to teach art confidently, enthusiastically, developmentally, and qualitatively, it has little chance of establishing and implementing an art program of excellence and stature.

Dedication is, and always will be, a vital teaching strength in a democratic society. It transcends teaching expertise. Nothing is written in the teaching contract about dedication, nor is there anything explicit in that agreement about the requisites of love, patience, and sympathetic support that go hand in hand with good teaching. But unselfish dedication and enthusiastic involvement are freewill gifts of a devoted teacher and cannot be measured except in terms of the inner fulfillment and satisfaction they bring.

The best teachers of art, whether classroom teachers or special art instructors, believe wholeheartedly in art's unique, spirit-enhancing, and rejuvenating power. In every project, they seek to perfect the critically important motivations, the technical intricacies, and the evaluative strategies. They organize materials, tools, space, and time schedules to produce exemplary working conditions. They search for inspirational art stimuli to renew the children's interest in a project whenever initial excitement wanes. In their enthusiasm, which they display openly and generously, they encourage the students to open their eyes to the design, color, form, rhythm, texture, and pattern in the world around them. They identify with their students and are elated when one makes a discovery or masters a skill. Conversely, they are genuinely concerned when students encounter difficulties that defy resolution. A creative, confident, enthusiastic teacher with a love of children and an understanding of art fundamentals is the prime catalyst in a productive and qualitative art program. The successful teacher is responsible for constant planning, organizing, experimenting, motivating, evaluating, and resource building. Yet the privilege of sharing the contagious, exuberant, magical world of students as they explore, discover, and invent compensates beyond measure for the extra effort required.

Who Teaches Art
and In What Kinds of Situations?

Some teachers of art feel handicapped by a limited background in art fundamentals. One reason for this inadequacy is the minimal art experiences that these teachers have had during their own elementary-, middle-, and secondary-school years. Another may be the lack of an art education course in their college preparation and inservice work.

Who teaches art, regular elementary classroom teachers or art teachers? Most teaching of art is done by elementary classroom teachers. Three-quarters of regular elementary classroom teachers teach all

Middle row, left and center, courtesy of David Hodge, Oshkosh, Wisconsin; bottom row, courtesy of W. Robert Nix, Athens, Georgia.

The ever-renewing cycle of life is all around us in exquisite and radiating forms. Teachers of art should turn to design in nature for constant motivational inspiration. Be alert for opportunities to guide students to notice the subtle variations in the leaves and petals of a flower, the feathers of birds. Lead them to examine the interstices of a spider's web, the scales of a fish.

or part of the art their students receive in school. The classroom teacher has flexibility in scheduling, and can have small groups of students work on certain phases of art projects while others in the class are engaged in different subjects. Since only one group of students is involved, storage of materials is not a major problem, and there is little chance that elaborate still-life materials will be stolen.

A second situation is when art is taught by an itinerant art teacher. The nickname "à la carte," misappropriated from the restaurant industry, is often used by those who do this mobile type of teaching. Usually, such teachers see 500 to 800 students per week, in twenty different classrooms, in two to five different schools. Supplies, and what passes for an office, are in a closet. While the regular classroom teachers may or may not be supposed to remain in the room, in practice the art teacher is usually left alone to handle discipline. Often the art teacher has little opportunity to know how the regular teacher handles disruptive incidents.

The third type of art teaching situation is when art is taught by an art teacher with an art room. More elaborate facilities, such as hot plates, looms, and sinks, are possible in the specialized art room. Elaborate still lifes can be set up. While this situation prevails in the middle school, it is the case in only a fraction of the elementary schools. The middle-school teacher usually sees 125 students a day. The elementary art teacher with an art room sees 600 to 800 students each week. The teacher has one 45-minute art period in which to motivate the students, distribute supplies, monitor the lesson, clean up, evaluate the lesson, and store the artwork if the project is to go on for a second week.

Need to Guide Students to Create and to Appreciate

To appreciate their students' developmental possibilities and limitations, teachers must have a basic understanding of the children's natu-

The teachers of these students were well rewarded for their planning and motivation when the students completed these artworks. **Top:** *A child from Japan did this watercolor painting of insects in a prehistoric forest.* **Middle:** *An 11-year-old's crayon illustration of the fable "The Old Man, His Son, and Their Donkey," Tunceli, Turkey.* **Bottom:** *A 10-year-old's story illustration showing sophisticated use of analogous colors and spatial divisions, St. Petersburg, Russia. Middle and bottom courtesy of International Children's Art Collection, Illinois State University, Normal, Illinois.*

 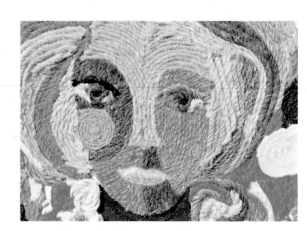 

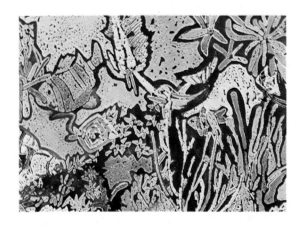 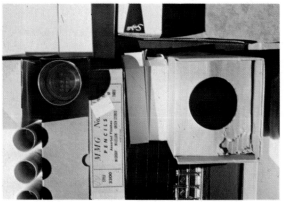 

Illustrations from the author's university classes. Bottom right illustration courtesy of Jimmy Morris, Athens, Georgia.

ral art-making abilities. However, the elementary- and middle-school qualitative art program demands more of the students than what they do naturally. While some students do perceive, draw, and compose sensitively, the majority of students require guidance and motivation. Since the teacher is the prime catalyst, it is the teacher's responsibility to establish a positive learning climate in which inquiry, creativity, and individuality thrive. Teachers of art may ask their students to set higher standards of performance for themselves or demand greater effort than the children have been accustomed to making. The best art is, in most instances, the result of perseverance—of purposeful, consistent, and time-consuming effort. The results are not accidental, the product of undemanding, trivial, or thoughtless activity. To teach that art is undemanding is to create a false impression.

Experienced teachers do not assign a new, untried technique to their classes. The teachers' confidence and effectiveness are heightened immeasurably if they have explored ahead of time the art materials and tools available to their students and created successfully using those tools.

Students should be guided toward a fuller aesthetic awareness of their environment, for example, to see such things as droplets of morning dew glistening in a moisture-laden spider's web. Students are highly impressionable and susceptible to visual influences over which teachers and parents have little control. Television and MTV, the movies, video games, musical recordings, makeup, magazine illustrations, recording covers, posters, cars, clothes, and package design clamor for their attention, shape their developing taste, and help shape their cultural values. While students' discriminative choices often differ from those of adults, the teacher can help guide students to consider aesthetic choices. In teaching art criticism, art history, and aesthetics, top-notch teachers of art use as many audiovisual aids as possible. These include original works of art, reproductions, films, photographs, slides, video recordings, magazine articles, colorfully illustrated art books, and examples of student work. (Chapter 10, "Art Motivation," discusses still-life arrangements; Appendix E lists some audiovisual sources.)

*College and university students preparing to teach art should explore varied art materials and techniques. The knowledge they gain will build the confidence they need to guide children's art endeavors. **Top row:** Oil pastel, plaster relief, tempera batik. **Middle row:** Oil pastel, yarn collage, crayon engraving. **Bottom row:** Crayon resist, box construction, and vegetable print.*

The Teacher's Positive Personality, Rapport, and Respect

A positive, cheerful, and outgoing personality is a major asset for teachers of art. Teachers must learn in sometimes difficult and trying situations to be patient, calm, and resolute. Children want to believe in their teachers. They need the security of a teacher's abiding confidence in the worth of the subject being taught. Students come to rely on their teachers for help with important choices in resolving perplexing problems. They become skeptical of those teachers who confuse them with vague generalizations and who place all the responsibility for decision making in their hands.

Teachers of art should learn to listen to the children's descriptions of their experiences, both real and imaginary, with sympathetic interest. They should avoid a desultory, keep-your-distance approach. Instead, their commitment, concern, and excitement for the project in process must be evident in their action, words, and faces. Veteran teachers learn to cultivate a ready sense of humor, which can help alleviate many a tension-fraught situation. Teachers who really care about children do not talk down to them; neither do they underestimate their potential to excel.

A teacher's success in the art class is often based on the empathic rapport that can develop between instructor and students. Getting to know the students is especially important because of the one-to-one relationship demanded in creative atmosphere. Name tags and a seating chart (with movable tabs to expedite changes) will hasten memorizing the students' names. Once teachers establish a climate of cooperation and mutual understanding, their ability to challenge their charges becomes the cutting edge of their teaching strength.

One can immediately sense the electric involvement, the purposefulness of endeavor, and the genuine rapport that exists between students and teacher when one visits a classroom where qualitative art learning is taking place. The special quality that distinguishes high-quality teachers of art from average instructors is their ability to respond intelligently, sympathetically, and purposefully to the children's creative efforts. They can communicate with the students knowledgeably and honestly regarding their progress in art. The best teachers evaluate their students' work seriously and objectively; their critical attention gives the work importance and significance in the students' eyes. These teachers show sincere respect for what the individuals are trying to do as they strive to give form to their ideas. Most important, they take the students seriously as artists.

Athens, Georgia. Courtesy of Mary Sayer Hamniond, Fairfax, Virginia.

Qualitative art learning is evident in the seriousness, deliberation, and confidence shown in this sixth grade girl's oil pastel on red paper.

CHAPTER 9

Teaching Strategies

The Art Room During the First Week of School

The first week of school, the first art class, the first art project, and the first motivation are especially important in establishing a qualitative art program. The appearance of the classroom or art room is especially critical, reflecting as it does the teacher's art convictions and awareness of design as a vital environmental influence and conditioner. Indeed, the room's impact on the students on the opening day of school is, for all purposes, the teacher's first art lesson. The classroom should be orderly yet inviting and, above all, visually stimulating. Artwork by children, attractively mounted, should brighten the walls. Hanging mobiles of fish, shells, birds, or butterflies created by preceding classes add a surprising element of color in motion. The creative teacher relies on a variety of eye-catching resources, including attractive bulletin-board exhibits, found-object displays, living plants, animals, or birds, art-book displays, hobby collections, antiques, and selected original works of art and craft. These make the classroom or studio into a perpetually changing world of wonders.

A word about maintaining a productive atmosphere in the art class: Experienced teachers know there is no single solution to the varied behavioral problems they must cope with. Veteran instructors of art generally find it expedient to begin classes with a serious, organized approach, which can be modified later if the situation warrants it. This is better than allowing so much uninhibited freedom that it is impossible to bring the class under control when necessary. If the students suspect that the teacher is unconcerned when they waste time in idle chatter or horseplay, they will develop a self-defeating, laissez-faire attitude in art class.

Using Nonverbal Instructions

The best teachers do not rely on verbal instructions alone. For example, teachers of art can enhance their instructional effectiveness by using the chalkboard to emphasize their motivational presentation and to outline the specific objectives of a project. Students entering class can read the instructions on the chalkboard and proceed to their work without wasting time. The chalkboard provides a ready format for the identification and clarification of the various possibilities and process steps of an assigned project. Evaluative criteria in the form of questions posted on a chalkboard or bulletin board allow students to make their own evaluations of their in-progress work (see Chapters 11 and 12). Using the chalkboard minimizes students' dependence on their instructor and discourages the "am I finished?" refrain. All of the written and display materials should be reinforced as necessary by the teacher's spoken, personal interaction with each student.

Planning the Distribution, Collection, and Organization of Materials

Crucial to an art project's ultimate success is housekeeping. The teacher must organize classroom or art-room facilities so there will be adequate working space, a sufficient supply of art materials and tools, varied storage facilities for both projects in process and those retained for exhibition, a diversity of display spaces, and effective cleanup facilities (see Appendixes A and B).

So that valuable time is not wasted, the distribution of student work in process, art supplies, and tools should be planned carefully

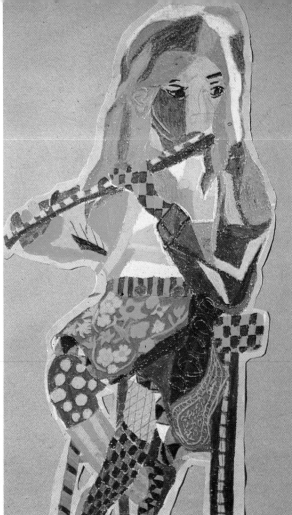

Campus School, University of Wisconsin, Oshkosh. Courtesy of David Hodge, Oshkosh, Wisconsin.

The art room was decorated with these colorful figures to stimulate other classes (see page 165). They were drawn from class models on large 24- × 36-inch colored construction paper, and colored with oil pastels. Then they were *cut out and mounted on a sheet of construction paper of a complementary color. Two eighth-grade students cooperated on the coloring of each figure.*

before the class begins. To expedite the return of artwork, have students put their names on their work at an early stage. To avoid the bottleneck of students waiting their turn at the paper cutter, paper should be cut to size before class begins. Materials can best be distributed through a student-monitor system or by having students come up by tables or rows to a central supply area. Since disciplinary problems can arise when supplies run short and students have time on their hands, the teacher must be sure the supply of art materials and tools is adequate for the project in process.

Beginning the Lesson: Getting Attention and Keeping the Motivation Brief

Getting the class session off to a good start is a major step in creating a productive studio atmosphere. When students come to an art room for class, the teacher should meet them at the door at the beginning of the period. A positive, cheerful greeting by the teacher can start the class off in the right mood. If some of the incoming students are boisterous, the problem can be resolved before it gets out of hand. Experienced

Courtesy of Baiba Kuntz, Glencoe, Illinois.

Attractive bulletin board displays help stimulate students' achievement. The color chart over the board is used to suggest why certain colors go together. It shows the beauty of related colors combined with accents of others. Some of the most sophisticated color usage reproduced in this book was done in view of such a display.

teachers usually wait until they have the attention of all before they provide motivational material or give demonstrations.

In striving to be certain the students understand the project's objectives, sometimes the motivational session is mistakenly prolonged beyond the point of effectiveness. The teacher must be alert for the unmistakable signs of disinterest: the shuffle of chairs, the tapping of pencils, the whispered conspiracies, and the far-away looks. Teachers must learn to stop before students reach their response fatigue point. Students need information, but they also want to get into their work. Perceptive teachers can detect when students are only half listening, or are more intent on some distracting gadget they possess than on the teacher's remarks. When expert teachers spot wandering prodigals, they may bring them back with a pointed question, a reprimand, or simply a pause and a meaningful look in the offender's direction. When having a discussion before studio activity, it is recommended that materials and tools not be distributed until the discussion is over. This is because students are naturally tempted to explore the materials on hand instead of giving their full attention to the teacher's presentation.

Getting the Design Off to a Good Start

The first few minutes of creative work are critical. Here the parameters of a successful work are laid down: The main compositional features are put into place. Just as a push is needed to set objects into physical motion, an extra push may be needed at the initiation of the art working period. The first three minutes immediately following the motivation, when the students pick up their art media for the first time, is a crucial period. While most students will be eager to do art, some students may be overcome by uncertainty or fear. Students who do not feel secure about their own creativity may not be able to get started. Some may sit perplexed, overcome by waves of confusion, self-doubt, and inadequacy. One way to spur such students into creative action is to give them one specific task to do. For example, the

"Make the clown's hat touch the top of the page and his feet touch the bottom edge." This statement helped the children create a composition which effectively filled the page, one with sufficient room to show important details. Making the figures large helps to eliminate the problem of filling up empty background space. Crayon encaustic was then used for the paintings.

teacher may say to a student who requires direction, "To begin, place a line for the head at the top edge of the paper and a line for the feet at the bottom edge."

Another task is to prevent bad starts. Left to themselves, some students, perhaps those who have not listened well to the instructions, will get off to a poor beginning, perhaps making procedural mistakes that threaten their ultimate success. For example, some will draw tiny, tiny figures which cannot be painted or cut out. Others, instead of getting the overall picture put into place, will use too much time and worry in drawing one small part. They will insist on erasing one small object repeatedly trying to "get it right." Still others may set an unrealistically high goal. Try to forestall such problems by giving instructions or materials that will prevent their occurrence. For example, to prevent fussing with and erasing timid pencil lines, have the students draw big outlines with chalk. Instead of criticizing the negative, focus on the positive. On seeing a problem, hold up as a model a student's artwork that avoids the mistake.

Strategies for Fostering Perseverance

Perseverance, which probably contributes as much as anything to a successful artwork, is central to the qualitative method. In this age of jets, rockets, computers, video games, and space exploration, it is difficult for students not to be caught up in the desire for instant gratification. Too many students race through their assignments, and their art reveals a lack of sustained effort. It is a mistake to equate speed of execution with freedom of expression, for a genuinely spontaneous and sparkling quality in a work of art is not achieved easily.

One of the major problems an art teacher has to face is lagging student interest once the initial excitement of a new project or technique has waned. This is especially true in those situations in which students are satisfied with only a superficial effort, or when the children do not develop a real concern for the subject matter involved. In almost every art class there are some children who find it difficult to persevere in a project. They insist that they are through with their work sooner than the others. They feel that they have exhausted the

Nurturing Creativity during the Working Period

During class, the teacher should not only keep students focused by calling attention to the instructional objectives, but also be on the lookout for creative uniqueness, for work that shows imagination, elaboration, and new variations. Use these exemplars to stimulate others to arrive at their own individual solutions. Holding up a student's work, call the class's attention to the particular creative inventiveness in evidence. ("Look at how this composition has filled up the paper; four dancing figures are repeated and the arms and skirts of several touch the sides of the paper, to give the design a feeling of unity. I wonder in what ways other artists are giving their designs unity?") Two words of caution are in order. The teacher should be careful not to embarrass the student who is singled out. Also, while the class is seriously at work, the teacher should not interrupt constantly with calls to "look at this." However, when attention flags, then the teacher can use students' exemplars, as well as reproductions, to rekindle the fires of motivation. (See Chapter 14 for additional ways to stimulate the creativity of students.)

Perseverance contributes much to the quality of an artwork. Too often students stop short, when extra effort could make the difference. Here, in contemporary artist William Sapp's 1992 piece Dogpack, *approximately 8 × 10 feet, are not one, but a thousand clay figures.*

possibilities of the project while their classmates are still busily involved in their creations. In this situation the challenge for the teacher is to find the right balance between what children may be willing to settle for and what they are capable of if they are given sensitive teacher guidance.

If at the outset of the project the teacher, in collaboration with the students, stimulates their interest in setting and reaching objectives in expression and design, children will be less likely to rush through their work. Perseverance is reinforced when students are internally motivated. For example, when students want to express something personally meaningful, they will work on it for a long time. This is why developing instructional objectives to encourage the expression of feelings is so important. For upper-elementary-grade and middle-school students, posting the process and evaluative criteria on the board allow the teacher to function effectively both as a classroom manager and as a facilitator for individual students. When questions arise, the teacher can clarify and resolve them for the entire class by referring to the posted criteria rather than by repeating them to each student in a time-consuming procedure.

Encourage the students to go further—to "weave in" the figures in their pictures, to tuck some objects behind other objects, to create rhythm. Encourage them to make their pictures swing, to have rhythm through repeating forms. One way to encourage a child to go further is to combine praise with suggestion. For example, a teacher may say, "Now Mandy is starting to put in the children; I wonder how many are in the line at noon?" Mandy is likely to respond to the teacher's expressed faith by putting in many figures.

A suggestion offered to one student will often trigger fresh ideas for others who may have reached a creative impasse. Using students' work in progress, call attention to compositional requirements as well as variations in expression. To the child who says, "I spoiled mine," reply, "The only way that a picture is spoiled is not to do it in your own personal way." Another way to stimulate extra effort is to have students anticipate having a special show of their work. For example, ask

The teacher encouraged these students to go further and to add more figures. Then students were encouraged to break up the empty background space in inventive, beautiful ways. Illustrations on this page are by upper-elementary-grade children. They took turns modeling with sports equipment and musical instruments in the center of the room.

Middle picture reproduced by permission of Jimmy Morris, Athens, Georgia.

the kindergarten teacher if she would let your class come in for a few minutes to show their artworks.

At the upper-elementary-grade and middle-school levels, the practice of writing brief, constructive remarks on the back of the student's work or on slips of paper attached to the work, has proved beneficial in promoting perseverance. Although time-consuming, this strategy for evaluation can help the conscientious teacher give individualized instruction. It gives the teacher a chance to evaluate studio performance at a time relatively free of distractions and other responsibilities. It strengthens the possibility that every student in class will receive specific, individual help at some time during the project. It provides the students with a definite working direction for the ensuing studio period.

Cleanup and Evaluation

Cleanup procedures should be planned in advance to ensure that enough time has been allotted and that the process will take place in an orderly fashion. Because cleanup comes at the end of the lesson, when students are ready to do something else, and often requires several students to be out of their seats at once, planning is necessary to avoid problems. For example, the teacher can prevent confusion and possible disruptive behavior at the sink by sending students from one row or table at a time to that facility. The time needed for efficient cleanup will vary with different projects and should be allocated accordingly.

If there is time remaining after cleanup, the teacher should use it to good purpose and not let the period end in idle chatter. The after-cleanup period can be used for a summing-up or evaluation session. This is a time to come around full circle and to demonstrate how the instructional objectives have taken form in the students' work and produced positive results.

Classroom Management

A common complaint of students is that the teachers have eyes in the backs of their heads. Yet it is vitally important that the teacher be aware of what is going on in the room and be at strategic stations at critical times. During materials distribution, the teacher should be

Courtesy of David Harvell, Athens, Georgia.

In this elementary classroom are posted five rules: (1) Listen. (2) Respect others. (3) Be polite and helpful. (4) Follow directions. (5) Take care of the room and materials. The first offense results in a warning; the second and third offenses result in varying lengths of time out.

near the supply area. When lecturing, the teacher should avoid facing the chalkboard or standing against a window, since this forces the students to face the glare of light. Effective instructors move among the students during the studio activity rather than staying at the teacher's desk. Experienced teachers do not let themselves get beleaguered by the demands of a bevy of questioning students when they should be monitoring the class as a whole, especially during the opening minutes of class and at cleanup time. Teachers should be sure that students know that they will advise students one at a time, and remind the students to take turns when conferences are necessary.

The quality of art expression diminishes as the amount of talking and socializing increases. Unless given permission by the teacher to move about, children should ordinarily remain in their assigned seats during class. In large classes, students should take turns obtaining and returning materials and tools, either by tables or by desk rows. Excessive talking, laughing, whistling, running, throwing things, gum chewing, propping of feet on desks, table hopping, and crowding at sinks should not be tolerated. Students eager to test their power will act out in disruptive mock fighting, challenges to authority, and subversive tactics. Problems of student apathy, disinterest, and errant behavior are heightened by insufficient lesson planning, meager motivational material, too little visual stimulation, insufficient knowledge of the technique, weak rapport between teacher and student, and a lack of conviction by both regarding the worth of the art experience.

Explore all possible avenues of motivation and persuasion, of reasoning and strategic reconciliation, before resorting to chastisement of any sort, whether it involves moving students to other seats or sending them to the principal. As a rule, do not act hastily in the matter of disciplining students. Never mete out punishment during the heat of a crisis. Admonish the errant students and tell them you will discuss the infraction with them after class. Once you have stipulated a punishment for a student, put it into effect. Students learn to take advantage of the instructor who makes idle threats but fails to carry them out.

Teachers realize that students have a need to communicate and that talking in class can be a common, natural occurrence, especially during studio activities. However, when the talking becomes so loud and disruptive that it prevents concentration on the project, teachers must take action. How they respond to this situation is critical. If they shout "Quiet!" or "Settle down!" or rap a desk with a ruler, ring a bell, or clap their hands, they may be successful in calming the class for a few minutes. Experienced teachers use a more positive, constructive approach. Calling the class to attention, they emphasize some aspect of the project that needs amplification. They also might hold up a student's work in process and point out specifically creative solutions achieved. By using this positive strategy, teachers achieve the objec-

Students can appreciate the seriousness of their endeavors when their work is arranged in attractive, eye-catching displays. These interlocked fish and birds combine into chainlike mobiles that are suggestive of the interrelationship of the species.

tive of restoring order and at the same time avoid being seen as martinets in the eyes of their students.

In art sessions in which the teacher builds respect for serious endeavor and in which excessive, boisterous socializing is minimized, the students' performances are consistently of a higher caliber than those of students in highly permissive situations. A class is less likely to be bored or cause disturbance when it has been guided to see the many possibilities of the project and when it has been richly motivated. Motivation is the subject of the next chapter.

CHAPTER 10

Art Motivation

Most children need some form of stimulating motivation, visual or verbal, to achieve high-quality results in their studio-art endeavors. Students must have something to say in order to give it visual form. The introductory phase of an art lesson should kindle the spark that ignites the curiosity and interest of the students. It is unfair to expect students to be challenged or excited by the teacher's saying "Draw what you want today" or "Paint the way you feel." The many successful ways to begin an art project include:

- Showing visual materials on the theme selected
- Viewing examples of previous work
- Guiding a class discussion in recalling a past experience
- Conducting a field trip to enrich the students' knowhow of the subject selected
- Playing recordings or tapes to create the mood of the particular visual theme
- Demonstrating the technical process with student participation
- Calling attention to a bulletin board or chalkboard presentation prepared for the project
- Having a guest speak, perform, or model for the students
- Using poems, stories, songs, and music as motivational enrichment

Inspiration for children's art expression comes from a variety of sources. It may spring from their experiences at school and at home; from their playground activities; or from their visits to special places such as a nearby barbershop or bakery or fire station. The responsibility, however, for reactivating these motivational experiences and giving them an immediacy to stimulate students into art expression is primarily the teacher's. With motivational procedures planned in advance by the teacher, students can experience art class as a time of purposeful significance and excitement, a unique and rewarding period of the school day.

Personal Experience as Motivation

The most vital and successful art-project motivations are usually the result of vivid and meaningful personal experiences. The teacher's role is to help the students graphically clarify the significant aspects of the experience. There are two main types of personal experiences that can be used for art lesson motivations: recalled experience and direct visual perception.

Recalled Experience

In recalled experiences, the children do not actually see the objects before their eyes, but rather recall them. Teachers must activate the children's store of knowledge and help them to tap into their recall powers. Perhaps students have visited some special place, such as an aquarium or farm, or seen a circus, carnival, parade, dog or cat show, or sporting event. Perhaps they have read an exciting story. Perhaps it is an experience that they experience regularly, such as playing a sport or a video game.

Because some children are not able to recall enough specific attributes of an event or object, they may complain that they do not know how to draw the object or event. Then the teacher must help them to recall their experiences by asking questions such as *Who? What? How? Where? When?* and *Why?*

The "what" is the overall experience the child is being asked to recall, for example, "a bad dream." To revive the "what" and "how" in the child's mind, ask the children to physically act out the experience, using their bodies to re-create what was scary in the dream (for example, spiders, ghosts).

Campus School, University of Wisconsin. Oshkosh. Courtesy of David Hodge, Oshkosh, Wisconsin.

The everyday interests of young adolescents give them motivation to create art. These include sports, bicycling, rock celebrities, TV and movie idols, electronic games, and dancing. In the mixed-media collage by a middle-school youngster, notice how the rider fills the space and how the wheel motif is repeated in the background to create unity. Areas of analogous color comprise the background, and a feeling of motion is created by the bent back of the cyclist and the flowing scarf.

A Philippine child recalls a favorite game, "jumping over the stick." She used her schema for profile and frontal views to depict the figures in this joyful watercolor of an important activity. The figures up front are drawn larger and the figures in the background are drawn smaller. In the small figures in the lower corners, realistic requirements yield to decorative requirements.

The purpose of *Where?* and *When?* is to make passive knowledge active. To continue the dream example, ask the child to describe the room and the setting, its location in the house, who uses the adjoining rooms, the time of day or night, what else can be seen in the room, and the feeling the experience gave the child.

The purpose of asking *Who?* is to give the child the opportunity to express self-identity and relationships with others. For example, a child may say, "I am in bed with my teddy bear in my arms, and Momma has tucked me in." Sometimes the response to Who? will help the teacher decide whether the lesson can be done by a small

Courtesy of Mary Sayer Hammond, Fairfax, Virginia.

Countless motivating questions were asked in this grades 3 and 4 lesson about recalling memories of tree houses. (What is a tree house? How large must the tree be? How will you climb to your tree house? What will you store in your tree house? Who will come to visit you in your tree house?) Children used crayon on 12- × 18-inch colored construction paper to capture these personal memories.

group working together or whether it is more appropriate for the lesson to be done by a student working alone.

The "why" question is for the teacher. Teachers should ask themselves why this particular theme is considered important enough to warrant being done. In the scary dream example, the hope is that, by representing and sharing the frightening event with the group, the individual will gain a feeling of personal control over its scariness. A different purpose might be served by sharing a different kind of experience. For example, the theme of playing on the playground may promote an individual's feelings of integration with the group. Or a lesson topic might be chosen to stimulate a certain type of artistic representation. For example, depicting "my street" and "ring-around-the-rosy" would stimulate the use of foldover drawings, and depicting "what's inside my body" (or "inside my house") would stimulate the representation of transparency or X-ray images.

The power and charm of designs which young children create based upon their experiences is nowhere better illustrated than in Weissa Wassef's project, Weaving by Hands (see page 90). Young children growing up in a small Egyptian town, Hourranie, near Cairo, created beautiful designs and transformed them into utilitarian and aesthetically satisfying weavings of significant economic value.

Direct Perception

Recalled experience is one kind of motivation, another is direct perception. Long before we are cognitive beings, we are aesthetic beings, responding to the world through touch, taste, smell, sound, feel, and sight. One of the teacher's greatest challenges is to turn students into *noticers,* avid observers of color, structure, and design in their environment. Children who note the unique cornice on a door, the intricate latch on a cabinet, the subtle patina on an aged sculpture, the moving reflections in water, the varied cracks in dry mud banks, the shadow of a tree on the snow, and the veins in a leaf or dragonfly's wing can bring deeper insights to their art expression. Help them to

 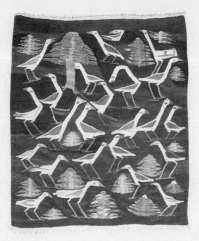 

Children near Cairo, Egypt, create weavings directly from memory. They use no prior drawings and often weave with the image sideways. Weissa Wassef's world-famous experiment in creativity has brought wealth to the villagers. **Left:** *An 8- × 10-inch weaving of village animals, trees, and bird by Amal, age*

11. **Middle:** *At age 16, Amal created this sophisticated 12- × 14-inch design of ibis and trees.* **Right:** *Rowhia Ali, who had been considered the most talented of the child weavers, is now 55 years of age. She recently created the 42- × 66-inch* Bedouins Entering the Village at Night.

take delight in nature's colors, textures, and patterns. Nothing replaces the actually perceived object, the direct contact, or the immediate observation for eliciting a detailed, richly expressive response. Teachers should avoid "draw-anything-you-want" assignments and emphasize drawing experiences based on things that can be directly perceived. Lead your students to look intently at everyday things, to see the unusual in the usual, and they will become inquisitive explorers for the rest of their lives.

Help students see analogies between things. "What does it remind you of?" Our perceived experience of what we see is extended by meanings drawn from what is remembered. The immediate visual experience is supplemented by what can be brought to the mind through the imagination. Let the children's imaginations help them to see, feel, and represent their own reality, sparked by the phenomena which are before their eyes.

Still-Life Arrangements   The elementary classroom or the art room can be the child's first and often most enduring art lesson. Still-life arrangements should be on view for sketching purposes, and, through these exciting eye-catching displays, teachers can create stimulating surroundings. Students should be encouraged to contribute to the store of found objects and nature's treasures in the classroom. There should be a constant display of arrangements. The following motivational resources are suggested:

Hang several colorful umbrellas from the ceiling. They may overlap one another, and the more variety the better. Umbrellas from the Far East are especially attractive. Also display Japanese, Chinese, Indian, and Indonesian kites, balloons, and banners. *Caution:* Don't hang anything from light fixtures.

Arrange still-life objects such as bottles, lanterns, clocks, musical instruments, lamps, and a variety of antique Americana.

Courtesy of David Hodge, Oshkosh, Wisconsin.

Help your students to develop a feeling for their cultural heritage through drawing a still-life arrangement incorporating Americana. When children sensitively capture in their drawings an old coffee grinder, a railroad lantern, a kerosene lamp, a mantle clock, an antique sewing machine, a steam iron, architectural gingerbread, and assorted old musical instruments, these objects take on new meaning. Widen your students' cultural horizons by introducing them to a host of exciting artifacts from many cultures as subject matter for their art expression.

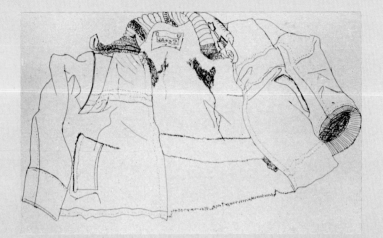

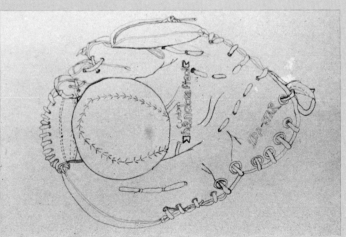

Top: Courtesy of Baiba Kuntz, Glencoe, Illinois.

When nothing else is available for a still-life arrangement, stack several chairs or stools on top of one another—some sticking out at different angles. Weave some drapery or beach towels in and out of the openings. (In middle school, following a contour drawing of the setup, you might suggest that the students paint the negative shapes instead of the positive shapes.)

Drape different kinds of fabric, plain and patterned, against a cork bulletin board. Arrange and pin the material to create bunches of fabric balanced by draped swags. Pin some old hats of many colors against the drapery.

Bring into the classroom a fairly large dead tree branch. Mount it against a light-colored wall area or bulletin board. It provides unmatched subject inspiration for contour and line drawing projects. It is also ideal for display of paper sculpture or papier mâché birds, butterflies, painted eggs, fish, planes, kites, sailboats, and abstract mobiles.

Boots, shoes, shoulder pads, hats, caps, helmets, and gloves provide interesting organic shapes for drawing because they conform to the human form, which is the ideal drawing inspiration. Invite students who are willing to remove their shoes to stack them in the middle of a table, on a chair, or on the floor for a still-life arrangement.

Arrange bottles of different colored glass on window sills or against a light source. Fill some of them with dried flowers or branches, some clear ones with colored water, and others with strips of aluminum foil.

Bleached animal skulls and bones your students find make excellent studies for line drawings.

Have the students participate in building a color environment as a motivation for painting in tempera and watercolor. Make it a class "happening" and incorporate colored tissue paper, crepe paper, fabrics, beach towels, ribbons, colored streamers, fans, banners, balloons, posters, party hats, beach balls, and Day-Glo materials. If near a window, incorporate colored cellophane for a stained-glass effect.

Left: *The most common everyday object is a likely subject for drawing. Objects with special significance, like the warm fur-lined jacket, the sturdy hiking boot, and the professional baseball mitt and ball, stimulate even greater interest. Items which specifically relate to or fit the human body possess unique lifelike qualities and natural contours that lend themselves most beautifully to dynamic, effective drawing.*

Opposite page: *Art and science are two complementary approaches to understanding nature.* **Top:** *Sketching trips to a natural history museum stimulated this handsomely detailed linoleum block print by a fifth-grade Iowa City youngster.* **Lower right:** *A study of fish, their adaptations and forms, resulted in this glowing window fish mural. The bodies and openings were cut from black construction paper and colored tissue paper pasted over cut-out areas.* **Lower left:** *A Japanese upper-elementary-grade child envisions the famous French entomologist Jean-Henri Fabre as a boy pursuing his hobby.*

Above: Courtesy of Mary Sayer Hammond, Fairfax, Virginia.

Large potted plants of assorted foliage and blossoms make ideal sketching, painting, collage, and printmaking subject themes. They also brighten up a classroom, especially when there are few windows.

Use large, colorful bedspreads, quilts, and costume jackets to drape on class models and in still-life arrangements. Set up an exciting still life against a wall or on a counter and then pose a standing, sitting, or reclining student in costume against it. Have students take turns modeling.

Contact travel agencies for large, colorful travel posters and display them in the classroom for color and design inspiration.

Vintage automobiles, bicycles, and motorcycles (with a student modeling as the driver) can be sketched in school parking lots.

Science Correlation Through Still-Life Drawing Correlative interpretation and description should be encouraged in every science and art experience using natural forms. John Dewey wrote that "Art—the mode of activity that is charged with meanings capable of immediately enjoyed possession—is the complete culmination of nature and 'science' is properly a handmaiden that conducts natural events to this happy issue" (1934). Dewey not only reverses the traditional hierarchy that places science over art, but he also denies there is any rigid dichotomy between them. Both science and art are ways of knowing, both provide students with a grasp of new similarities and contrasts, and both go beyond traditional categories to yield new visions about our world. Help children sense what these fields have in common by calling attention both to the design structure and to the scientific explanations of nature's phenomena.

Tactfully discourage the student's dependence upon visual stereotypes. Instead, urge careful observation in creating the artwork. Enthusiastic artistic responses can be evoked by bringing to class live animals, as well as materials such as the following:

Fruits, vegetables, gourds	Driftwood, bark, rocks, minerals
Live and dried flowers and plants	Mounted birds, fish, animals
Indian corn, locust pods, fall weeds	Fossils and skeletons of animals
	Ant farms
Aquariums and terrariums	Insect and butterfly collections
Birds' nests and birds in cages	Pets, turtles, rabbits, guinea pigs
	Coral, seaweed and seashells

The millions of varieties of insects have unlimited possibilities as illustrated in these crayon engravings by intermediate-elementary-grade youngsters. All of them have been enhanced in the final stage by an application of oil pastels on the background areas. Bordering lines of black should be preserved to unify the composition.

Still lifes of plants and taxidermic specimens can be used to call attention to the ecological devastation faced by plants and animals, for example, the fact that 250,000 of today's plant species will vanish by the year 2000.

Devices to Enhance Visual and Aural Perception

Assorted devices and equipment to help expand the students' awareness and visual horizons: microscopes, prisms, kaleidoscopes, touch-me kinetics, magnifiers, liquid light lamps, telescopes, microscopic projectors, computers, mirrors, and black lights.

Recordings of music, dramatizations, poetry, sounds of geographic regions— city and country, nature's forces, forest and jungle—and sounds of machines, planes, ships, trains, circuses, and amusement centers.

Still-Life Material for Multicultural Awareness and Social Studies

Artifacts from other cultures and countries can be displayed. Masks, wood carvings, costumes, textiles, ceramics, toys, dolls, fans, puppets, kites, and armor can be correlated to the study of other cultures. To meet multicultural goals, we must not just draw an object from another culture, but also discuss how the culture treated groups such as children, women, captives, and the elderly. Discuss who had power and who was dominant and subordinate (see Chapter 1).

Mexican, Columbian, Indian pottery
Colorful paper umbrellas from Japan
Kites, fans, and bells from the Orient
Masks: African, Indian, Malaysian, Indonesian, Mexican, Chinese opera, Mardi Gras, clown, Japanese Noh or Bugaku, Greek drama
Eskimo sculpture in soapstone or whalebone
Indian kachina and Japanese kokeshi dolls
Navaho rugs and San Blas Indian molas
Musical instruments from around the world
Puppets, toys, dolls, and wood carvings from around the world

Sketching Trips Correlated to Social Studies

Resource and sketching trips are wonderful art motivations in themselves or they may be correlated to the study of careers, history, and science. Visit the sketching site beforehand, if possible, to check on hazards and procedures.

Science, natural, and historical museums	Fair or arts festival
Construction site	Bus and train station
Manufacturing facilities	Shopping mall
Zoo or observatory	Local art studios
	Farm or dairy

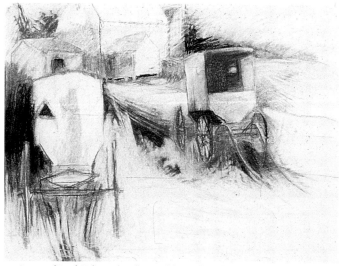

Courtesy of David Hodge, in the collection of the Neville Public Museum, Green Bay, Wisconsin.

Take the students on sketching trips to places where different cultures may be studied. Here, Amish wagons are captured by art professor David Hodge.

Fire station	Park or greenhouse
Historic monument, building, or statue	Bridge and dam sites
Art museum	Boat marina or wharf

Other Materials for Still Lifes

Teachers will find many occasions during the school year to use the following resources in still-life arrangements to enrich their art programs:

Fluorescent paint and papers	Model cars and airplanes
Fish netting and glass buoys	Plastic foam wig holders
Window-display mannequins	Old fashioned hats, shoes, purses
Wallpaper sample books	Texture table, felt board
Theater costumes and makeup	Spotlights for illuminating still lifes
Tissue paper in assorted colors	Bicycles, motorcycles, helmets
Full-length mirror, face mirrors	Stained glass
Sports equipment	Acetate or acrylic plastic in varied colors
Contemporary posters	
Duck decoys	

Bulletin-Board Dislays

Plan exhibits and bulletin-board displays that relate to the art objectives. Bulletin boards and displays should be changed regularly and often to allow students to appreciate completed projects and to whet their interest in further art endeavors. The students should be invited to contribute to designing and mounting displays and exhibits that help make the classroom attractive and colorfully stimulating.

Art History
Reproductions of paintings, sculpture, prints, and crafts that illuminate and intensify the objectives of the lesson
Color slides of art, crafts, and architecture; of design elements in nature and constructed objects; of creative work by children worldwide; of examples illustrating technical stages in a project; of people in active work, in sports, and in costume; and of animals, birds, fish, insects, and flowers
Filmstrips and cartridge tapes on artists, art history, and art techniques
Films, videos, and tapes that relate to the art project undertaken
Books (stories, plays, poems, and biographies) and periodicals that can lead to a richer interpretation of a project

(See Part III for an in-depth discussion on incorporating art history, art criticism, and aesthetics.)

Models
Invite guests and parents with interesting occupations and hobbies to art class to model while they chat. The following can stimulate wonderful pictures that provoke thinking about careers: police officers, firefighters, and nurses; performers such as clowns, dancers, pantomimists and musicians with their instruments; scuba divers, airline personnel, and athletes in uniform. The students themselves can take turns wearing special hats or jackets and serving as models, posed in a still-life arrangement.

Combining Recalled Experience and Direct Perception

A general tendency is to use recalled experiences more often in the primary grades and to use direct perception from still lifes, nature, and models more often in the later grades. However, both methods effectively supplement each other. Students can be encouraged to add things from their memories or from their imaginations to the background of a picture derived from direct perception. Mature artists often blend the two methods. Artists doing a scene from memory often turn to the use of real objects or photos to acquire supplemental information. The French painter Marc Chagall did still-life paintings from bouquets of flowers and then, from his memory, added simply drawn human figures to the background.

The Art Medium as Motivation

The materials, tools, and techniques of the various art projects can themselves be the special catalyst that fires the students' efforts. The teacher's demonstration of a technique can challenge the students. In the primary grades the introduction of new, vibrant colors in oil pastel, tempera paint, watercolor felt-nib markers, crayon, and construction paper elicits enthusiastic response. Tissue paper in a host of colors delights upper-elementary-grade children who can handle it confidently in collage projects as they discover new colors through overlapping. In the upper grades, the teacher can stimulate the students' interest by introducing them to melted crayon for encaustic painting, discarded tiles for mosaics, waxes and dyes for batiks, plaster for carving sculpture and bas reliefs, glazes for ceramics, and wire, plastic, wood, and boxes for construction projects.

In recent years, critics of current art-education practices have called attention to the proliferation of media and techniques in the school art programs, citing their deleterious effects. Although some of this criticism is justified, it is usually not the new materials and techniques per se that are to blame. Instead the fault lies in how the material is used: as the sole motivation and purpose of the lesson. The solution to the problem is to teach for qualitative art excellence and to incorporate a range of valid lesson objectives (see Chapter 12). Any teacher can testify that a poorly motivated student equipped with the newest and most expensive art materials may produce a careless, nonartistic monstrosity, whereas another student using only discarded remnants from a scrap pile may create an art object of singular beauty.

Amount of and Timing of Motivation

Because most children can absorb and retain only a few ideas at a time, don't overwhelm them with an avalanche of suggestions. Motivations should be provided in small doses, introducing, if possible, a new and exciting attention-getter each time the art class meets. Strategic timing is of utmost importance in successful motivations. The teacher must sense when students have reached a fatigue point and need richer incentives to ensure progress in their work. Because students are most receptive at the beginning of a period, this is usually the best time to introduce new motivations, materials, and techniques. Teachers should not interrupt a busily engaged class to point out something that could have been handled at the outset of the lesson. Time allotments for motivational sessions should be budgeted so the children will not feel cheated out of their studio or activity period. Gauge the listening and interest span of the students. Plan out the entire sequence of motivation, discussion, demonstration, studio time, and evaluation imaginatively and economically.

Exhibitions as Motivation

Having one's work put on exhibition is exciting. As teachers we can provide the students' introduction into this important aspect of the art world: exhibiting. Exhibition criteria should be both on aesthetic grounds and on the grounds of students' educational growth and motivation. A principle is that the further away from the classroom, the more selective the exhibit needs to be. In the self-contained classroom, every student's work might be exhibited. Each student might assume ownership of a designated place, identified by the child's large name label. Even high places and very low places can be assigned. In the school hall only the most significant works of a child need be exhibited.

At some time during the term, every child should have his or her artwork on exhibit. Some teachers save each student's work in a folder, from which they select pieces for exhibition. They then send all the works home at special times of the year, such as Mother's Day or the winter holiday. Multiarts exhibits can combine the art display with student performances, musical or dramatic, and actually demonstrating in the hall or gym. School arts festivals can be made more special by having students wear costumes or bring special theme-related food to be served at the opening, or by having a joint exhibition of parent and child art.

*Sharing one's artwork with the community and with the larger public provides valuable social interaction. Teachers of art can help children to develop such interests, which can provide life-long leisure satisfaction. **Top:** Observe the high degree of artistic organization in this elementary-school art bulletin board. It contains sunflowers by grades 3 and 4 and tulip paintings by grades 5 and 6. **Middle:** Notice the colored mats and aligned arrangements in this elementary-school art display. **Bottom:** Middle-school art exhibit at annual Art Education Conference, University of Iowa, Iowa City.*

Top: Courtesy of Baiba Kuntz, Glencoe, Illinois. Bottom: Courtesy of David Hodge, Oshkosh, Wisconsin.

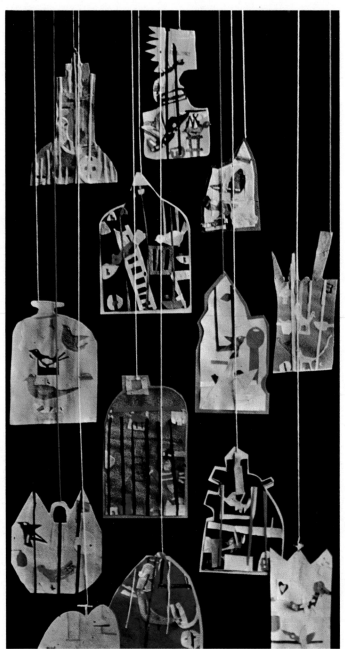

University Elementary School, Iowa City, Iowa.

A second-grade class made caged birds from cut paper and yarn. Each cage is mounted on paper of a complementary color, hung from strings (suggestive of movement, air, and flight), and displayed in the school's entrance hall.

To avoid displays that look disorganized, align the pieces horizontally or vertically. Traditionally, artworks are mounted with a border that is 3 to 4 inches wide on three sides and about ½ inch larger on the bottom. Check with school administrators for school policies on how work is to be hung on the walls. Can tape be used, which might pull off the paint when removed, or are tacks or staples preferred, which will leave tiny holes? Another consideration is the audience. Should the work be hung at the eye level of the teachers and adult visitors or of the students?

Although a permanently installed hanging strip limits the level at which the work is hung, any type of fastener can then be used in it. Another solution is permanent display panels of composition board. Tacks and staples can be freely used in these, although excess use of such flammable boards may conflict with fire codes. A few 4- by 8-foot foam-core display boards can be taped together along the edge with duct tape to make a lightweight temporary folding display area suitable for school open houses.

Move out into the community for even greater motivational power. Tell the students that some of their work from a project will be exhibited at a store or a branch bank or a parent's restaurant. Children's art is charming displayed in the local post office at holiday time. Attention-catching exhibitions can be hung in unusual places. Works can be displayed in the windows of an unused store, or murals can be painted on fences or walls.

Though commercial exhibitors usually pay a fee, school art can often be exhibited free at community events, such as fall festivals, county fairs, and arts and crafts exhibits. Middle-school students can take part in the local museum's exhibitions by serving as junior docents for children's tours. A hospital may underwrite the production costs for a full-color calendar of children's artwork advertising the hospital's departments. A newspaper can have a design-an-ad contest at Halloween. Sponsoring businesses might pay to have students' artwork framed.

Not only do exhibitions serve as a way to motivate your students but they are also prime ways your art program is evaluated. Motivation and evaluation go hand in hand. While motivation is usually thought of as being at the lesson's beginning and evaluation at the lesson's end, the two processes are better when each is integrated throughout the lesson. The next two chapters discuss in depth the topic of evaluation.

CHAPTER 11

Evaluation

This chapter describes evaluation in three ways. The major part of the chapter deals with how the teacher, through in-process evaluation, can help students in their thinking about how to achieve a qualitative result. (Student project evaluation using instructional objectives, the topic of the following chapter, is also introduced here.) The second part of the chapter discusses evaluating student performance for grades and arriving at an overall evaluation of the effectiveness of the program. The third part of the chapter discusses tests and performance assessments used to evaluate the teacher.

In-Process Evaluation of Student Work

Among the many questions that teachers of art seek to answer, the one most commonly repeated is: "How can I help those students who rush through their projects, who so often exclaim, 'I'm finished!' when they have barely begun to tap their expressive potential?" There is no doubt that the quality and promise of the school art program depend in great measure on how teachers meet this particular challenge. There is no miracle formula, no surefire panacea, for dealing with those students who have a short interest span, deficient school preparation in art, and minimal self-motivation. Every teaching strategy and stimulative approach will meet with varying success, depending on the students' backgrounds, personalities, and readiness. Some students simply need personal encouragement, some demand specific help, and others require only a clue, but all students are entitled to more than vague generalizations. They are entitled to assessment of their learning. The best evaluative criticism provides the students with

guidance they can understand, store, and then use over and over in succeeding art projects.

Evaluative strategies are most vital during the studio phase and the final stages of a project. A highly productive procedure is for the teacher to sit down with a student individually and discuss the student's work at various stages, perhaps using a framing mat to set off the work.

The most positive evaluations always take into consideration the personalities of the children themselves. Children at all stages have individual styles in art expression and diverse imaginative and inventive capacities. Thus, the teacher might say that one student's piece shows his or her "energetic personality through the dynamic shapes and the way the colors fly out of the shape borders." The teacher may comment on a contrasting piece by a student with a different personality by saying that the work shows "a calm, determined, and thoughtful way of working, by the way each shape is carefully drawn all the way around."

The subtle strategies of high-caliber teaching are evident in the words, action, sincerity, and confidence that teachers exhibit when they help students evaluate their art efforts. What instructors say, how they say it, how much they say, and what they leave unsaid are vitally important.

If the students are engaged in a multilesson crayon-engraving project, for example, the following self-evaluative questions written on the chalkboard or as a mimeographed handout will provide working criteria for each stage:

1. Did I use enough pressure in applying the crayon so the paper is completely and solidly covered? With padding under my paper, did I apply the crayon heavily and smoothly? Did I vary the sizes and shapes of the many crayoned areas?

  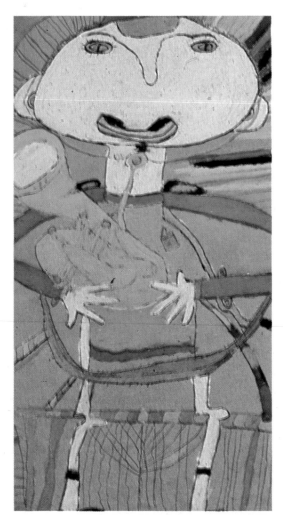 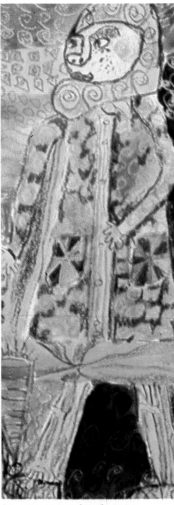

Third picture: Courtesy of Mary Sayer Hammond, Fairfax, Virginia.

The teacher can help students to evaluate their work in terms of the lesson's instructional objectives. Instructional objectives may be the use of analogous and complementary color. Here, in these works by intermediate-elementary-grade children, the human figure is interpreted through a variety of challeng- *ing art materials and techniques. These include mixed media, tempera, oil pastel, and crayon-watercolor resist. The bent knees of the posed seated musician, third from left, are depicted in a highly original way.*

2. After coating the drawing with black paint and transferring the sketch to it, ask: Does my preliminary line-drawing composition for my engraving fill the space effectively? Have I employed a variety of lines, shapes, and sizes? Have I emphasized detail, pattern, and textures that are especially effective in the engraving process?

3. During the engraving process, the main part of the lesson, ask: Did I engrave the basic outlines of the shapes in my composition first? Did I make variations of lines, thick, wavy, jagged? Did I take time to engrave details, vary patterns, and create textural effects as contrasts against plain black areas? Did I create some bold contrasts by scratching away solid areas of black to reveal the crayoned surface underneath? Have I used all three methods fully: engraved line only, detailed and patterned areas, and scraped-out, solid crayon shapes?

4. During the subsequent enrichment lesson, ask: Did I enrich the composi-

Instructional objectives are beautifully executed in this multicrayon engraving.

tion by applying oil pastel over some of the remaining black areas and repeat the oil pastel colors in different parts of my composition to achieve unity? Did I engrave lines, details, or patterns through the oil pastelled areas for even more subtle embellishment?

Evaluative questioning can be effectively employed in every art project to give purpose, direction, and continuity to the students' efforts. Although the specific instructional objectives will vary with different projects and at different age levels, the important, recurring design criteria will be echoed in project after project. In any one session, however, choose only one, or at most only a very few, to emphasize.

Composition and Design

One or more of these questions may be asked to evaluate composition and design:

Are the sizes and shapes of objects (people, buildings, cars, trees, and so on) varied? Do they produce interesting negative spaces?

Is informal balance employed (as opposed to formal balance) to create a varied, more flexible composition?

Are the shapes or objects drawn at different levels to create varied space breakup in foreground and background?

Do objects or shapes overlap each other to create unity and subtle space-in-depth?

Do some lines converge to create space-in-depth?

Do some lines or shapes touch or intersect the borders of the picture plane to create movement in depth into the composition?

Is contrast achieved by juxtaposing light areas next to dark ones, patterned or detailed areas next to plain ones?

Color

Depending on the students' ages, one or more of these criteria may be used in an evaluation of color use:

Are colors repeated throughout the composition to achieve movement and unity?

Has pressure been used in coloring with wax crayons or oil pastels to achieve rich, glowing colors?

Does the picture lack excitement because of too rigid a dependence on the use of local color?

Are bright, high-intensity colors employed for emphasis wherever such emphasis is needed?

Are the intensities of the colors varied for compositional diversity and subtle effects?

Is the color scheme limited or monochromatic to achieve a chromatic unity?

Are the values of the colors (tint and shade) varied for compositional interest and contrast?

Is the color employed based on one of the color-wheel schemes: complementary, split-complementary, analogous, or triad?

Are the neutralized colors in the palette (umber, ochre, sienna, and so on) employed for their special subtle effects?

Are colors employed to achieve a feeling or mood: warm and cool colors, colors with psychological impact?

Line Drawing

Another important area for evaluation is line drawing. Three criteria are used. To introduce the subject of instructional objectives, which will be the topic of the next chapter, a chart showing the three criteria and the instructional objectives derived from them is presented. As shown, the questions which are spoken or written on the chalkboard for students to apply in judging their own artwork can as easily be written as lesson-plan instructional objectives.

Courtesy of Mary Sayer Hammond, Fairfax, Virginia.

Evaluational Questions to be Asked or Written on Chalkboard	Instructional Objectives from Lesson Plan
Are the lines varied from thick to thin to create interesting linear movement and subtle space-in-depth?	Students will draw lines varied from thick to thin to create interesting linear movement and space-in-depth.
Is the line on opposite sides of a shape or object (body, tree, vase, fruit, and so on) drawn more heavily on one side and lighter on the other side to create tension and space?	Students will draw lines on opposite sides of a shape or object more heavily on one side and lighter on the other side to create tension and space.
Do the lines drawn complete a shape instead of floating in space?	Students will draw lines to complete a shape instead of floating in space.

Grading and Summative Evaluation

The second focus of evaluation is on grading and summative evaluation. One of the most difficult evaluative tasks any teacher must perform is the periodic grading of students. In a content field such as art, which is so subjective and so colored by expressive diversity, and in which many varied interpretations are acceptable, the problem is compounded. Reporting of students' art progress varies from school to school, from primary and intermediate through upper elementary grades to the middle school. Some institutions employ separate evaluations for behavior and subject mastery; some simply indicate that the student has performed satisfactorily or unsatisfactorily. The majority of report cards in the middle school use the letter-grade system.

In some elementary schools the teachers write a report in the form of a letter to the parents or guardians describing the child's growth in art. They take into account improvement in art abilities as well as behavioral factors. When letter or numerical grades for art are

These colored-tissue-paper collages show several criteria put into practice: varied shapes, informal balance, multilevels, and border touching. **Top:** *Colors moving from a red area in the upper left corner to white in the lower right corner give this grade 1 tissue collage movement and unity.* **Middle and bottom:** *A fifth-grade youngster applies colored tissue onto an 18- × 24-inch white construction paper drawing.*

given, teachers often take into account the students' classroom deportment and working habits as a factor in their evaluation. This procedure has sometimes been questioned, but if students have been forewarned that their behavior and conduct will affect their grades, such action is defensible. For, in almost every instance, the student's prudent use of class time will result in higher-quality work.

The grading of a variety of art projects should not prove difficult if the students are advised in advance about the specific instructional objectives. In the approach recommended in this book, the teacher and students discuss the project's several criteria. For greater emphasis, the teacher writes these suggestions on the chalkboard or on a specially prepared chart or may even ask the students to take notes.

Summative evaluation is used to diagnose, to revise curricula, and to determine if objectives have been met. It summarizes the students' learning and the teacher's effectiveness. Save the students' work in portfolios and periodically go over the work to determine if your goals are being met. Through photos and video, document three-dimensional work and exciting art events. Older students might keep journals to document what they are learning. One good time to have the students help you, through questionnaires or class discussion, to do summative evaluation is when portfolios are handed back to be taken home. Is the program leading students to understand art? Are the students finding satisfaction in the process? Is the language the students use in discussing aesthetics and writing to justify their ideas about the nature of art becoming more advanced?

Some evaluative questions the students can answer are these:

Did you learn any new words or art ideas this year? What?

What was good about art this year?

What was not so good about it this year?

If anything did not work out for you, how would you handle it in the future?

What did you learn this year about how to make art?

Did we do anything in art that helped you to learn about science, math, or social studies? What?

How is art different from other subjects?

How could the teacher be better to the students?

When you are older, how will you ever use anything like what you did in art this year?

How would you change what we did this year?

Do you have any ideas about how we could make art more real and not just like school?

How did you like it when the class talked about art and thought together about art?

To achieve a chromatic unity, the color scheme is limited to analogous colors, yellow through green. What concentration the fifth-grade girl displays as she colors her sunflowers! She is using oil pastel on black construction paper; a preliminary sketch was made in silver.

Outside of school and on your own, did you do any things that were like art? What was it? Did you do it by yourself or with someone?

Outside of school, did you talk with anybody about art ideas? What was the discussion about?

Do you have any ideas for ways to make art class better?

Did anything good about art happen in the community that you knew about?

Why do you you think students should study art in school?

From the following list of what we did in art this year, mark those activities which you really liked or from which you learned a lot. Write if there was anything special about it that made it especially good.

Evaluation of the Teacher's Knowledge and Performance

Evaluation is not just a procedure used by you to plan and assess your students' work. It is also a procedure that may at some time be per-

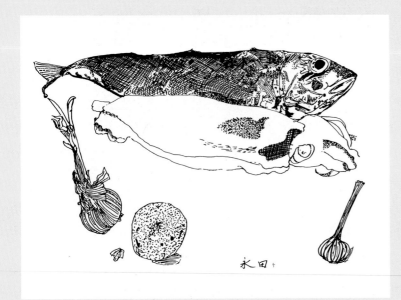

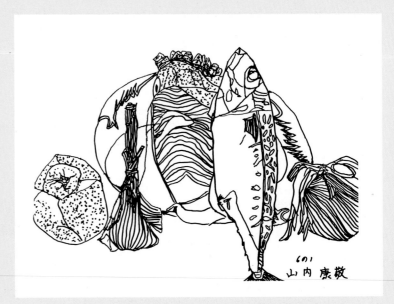

Line is used to reveal interior and exterior form in these detailed and skillfully composed still-life drawings of fish and vegetables created by talented upper-elementary-grade children in Japan.

formed to measure your teaching effectiveness by your principal, department head, or supervisor, or by state education department assessors. While doing student teaching, preservice teachers are assessed by college field supervisors and by their critic teachers. In many states, first-year teachers are also assessed by the local school system or by state evaluators. In some states, even experienced teachers are periodically assessed when they apply for a more advanced level of certification. The first way your ability to teach art may be assessed is through a test about art education knowledge by means of a standardized test, such as the National Teacher Exam or its art education component or a similar state-developed test. For individuals seeking regular elementary-school classroom teaching certification, almost a third of the states have certification tests that include art items. For individuals seeking art certification, more than a third of the states require a test in art education.

The second type of teacher evaluation consists of assessors' judging your lesson plans and/or actually watching and scoring your teaching performance. Several states already have performance assessment as part of their requirements for beginning teachers. Many other states are testing or plan to use competency-based tests of teaching performance. Fortunately, most school systems view these assessment procedures less as "weeding out" and more as diagnosing and remediating weaknesses. They usually give teachers several opportunities to retake the exam and improve other scores.

Some suggestions for doing well on this on-site evaluation are the following:

Develop your lesson plans using a variety of instructional objectives. Each time the lessons are repeated, seek to make the plans and lessons richer.

Be able to show how your lesson plans meet both your goals and school system goals.

Be alert to the art needs of your school, for example, its needs for displays and such public presentations as pageant backdrop designs.

Be alert to the art needs of your school district and network with other teachers of art through district curriculum-development committees.

Be alert to how your art program can interface with the community. Involve the community, for example, through displays of your students' works at banks and libraries and at the dedications of new community buildings.

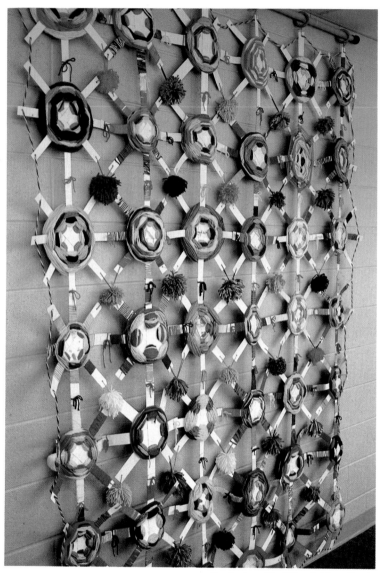

Top: Courtesy of David Harvell, Athens, Georgia.

What evaluator would not be impressed by the art program of the teacher who so ingeniously combined children's works into such fine displays? These displays of God's eyes (above) and beetles (right) also quietly convey another lesson. The lesson is that through cooperation, we can achieve greater goals than anyone can achieve individually.

To maintain evidence of your overall teaching ability, write down laudatory comments you get from peer teachers, supervisors, and parents. Seek out ways for your students to be recognized and keep good records of their achievements and the publicity these achievements receive. Through the above summative evaluation and through photographs and videotapes, document your program's effectiveness and the quality of the art produced. Be active in your state and local education and art education associations and share what you have done through the newsletters of these organizations. The teacher who has done these things, and has done a good job of planning lessons with valid instructional objectives, will do well and the program cannot help but be evaluated favorably.

CHAPTER 12

Writing Instructional Objectives for Lesson Planning

Need for and Form of Instructional Objectives

Clarity of education is greatly promoted when instructional objectives are clearly spelled out both in the teacher's own mind and for students, who gain satisfaction when they know what they are expected to do. In education, the principle of *expectancy* emphasizes the need to inform the learners in advance about the objectives of the task they are to perform (Gagné, 1975). Using instructional objectives can help novice teachers of art incorporate their ideas about teaching into the competencies that the students are expected to demonstrate. To do well in the critical first year of teaching, to keep their enthusiasm and dedication high, new teachers must acquire a growing confidence and pride in their work. Being fully prepared for each class meeting helps develop this necessary confidence.

The best teachers of art plan their motivation, demonstration, and evaluation sessions well in advance. They do not rely on last-minute inspiration. They prepare a written outline of their objectives and refer to it during the class session, knowing that they may otherwise forget to emphasize critically important aspects. They are continually aware of the long-range objectives of the project. Experienced teachers plan the motivating question-and-answer session, the preliminary show-and-tell segment, and the discussion period with special care and attention.

Being able to write lesson plans in terms of instructional objectives is a skill that is absolutely necessary to graduate from many teacher education programs and to receive teacher certification in an increasing number of states. Concerns about the quality of education and about teacher accountability have motivated proponents of the *competency-based* education movement to mandate teachers' writing clearly defined instructional objectives. State or local systems using a competency-based system usually set broad goals and then let the individual teacher focus on specific instructional objectives that will allow the students to achieve those goals. For example, a system-mandated goal might be: "Students will appreciate the art of diverse cultures." One of the instructional objectives through which a teacher believes a class can attain that goal might be: "Students will identify pre-Columbian, Mississippian American Indian, and Greek Cycladic sculptures." By directly setting clear, attainable objectives, teachers can then readily evaluate the extent of overall success in meeting broad goals.

Indicative of this same accountability trend, two-thirds of our nation's school districts with elementary schools have art curriculum guides that specify instructional goals and student outcomes. Sets of required or recommended textbooks, often written in instructional objectives, are used in over a third of elementary-level art programs.

Writing instructional objectives differs from stating goals in terms of what you, the teacher, will do. Instead, you must carefully examine each goal and figure out what specific competencies the students will demonstrate as evidence of mastery. One widely accepted way of writing instructional objectives has four features: subject, verb, conditions, and standards of quantity or quality (Mager, 1975).

1. The *subject* of the sentence is the student or the learner. It is not what the teacher will do.
2. The *verb* should indicate some demonstrable behavior, such as to identify, list, match, or depict. It should not be a broad, vague, or difficult-to-assess goal, such as "to understand" or "to appreciate." Goals typically cover a

Instructional objectives to break up the space into small areas, to leave the space of the chalk line unpainted between forms, and to imaginatively use colors helped the sixth-grade artist of this tempera–India ink resist to create this "bouquet with owl."

whole curriculum or course, whereas instructional objectives deal with one lesson.

3. *Conditions* are the supplies and motivational resources available and the time allotted for each phase of an art project.

4. *Standards* of quantity or quality should be spelled out. (Some example are: "Must meet at least four out of the eight criteria listed on the chalkboard." "Must bump the edges of the paper." "Must show several very large objects and many very small objects.")

An example of these four features in an objective is:

The student (or students) will sketch the main shapes of the model in the still life using chalk on colored paper in 20 minutes showing the floor plane, the ceiling plane, the figure's general shape, and background's spatial breakup.

The subject is "the student"; the verb is "will sketch . . ."; the conditions are "using chalk on colored paper in 20 minutes"; and the standards are "showing the floor plane, the ceiling plane, the figure's general shape, and the background's spatial breakup."

Some Types of Instructional Objectives

Just as there are many ways to teach, there are many different types of lesson objectives. From the several kinds of objectives teachers select those which they believe should be emphasized. Major factors affecting which are appropriate for you are your teaching style and beliefs and the ages, ability levels, and learning styles of your students. However, school administrators and supervisors may require that certain types of objectives, perhaps in a certain order, be used in plans to be submitted to the school's central office.

To make art itself the central focus, five types of art objectives are discussed first, then three nonart types of objectives that are widely used in schools:

Eight Categories of Instructional Objectives

1. Art production	5. Art history
2. Artistic perception	6. Affective
3. Art criticism	7. Cognitive
4. Aesthetics	8. Psychomotor and multisensory

Remember that these categories are not totally separate entities. Instead, like ingredients in a well-cooked stew, they blend into one another. In writing an objective, you must determine which one of the several categories that it may fit into should be the focus.

With many objectives planned that will convey to your students the importance and purpose of the art activity, you can pick and choose among them to meet individual students' needs. The teacher of mainstreamed classes will be working with students of different ability levels and learning modes. Gifted students may very well al-

ready know the concept, and some mainstreamed students facing significant mental challenges might never fully master the concept. The experienced teacher of art has the insight to know what specific art skills are within the general grasp of a given class of students and can tailor the general objectives to address the special needs of individuals. By using several categories of objectives, you can create a powerful motivation which will sustain the learning activity for all your students. It is better to have extra plans—which might be carried out should time permit or perhaps only with a few of the students—than to exhaust the plans for a lesson early and "try to fill up time."

Art Production Objectives

As art teachers, we must teach first about art. In too many instances we find art teachers apologizing for making suggestions to children, for initiating projects, and for emphasizing art fundamentals. Let the truth be known! Where promising, sequential, imaginative, and qualitative elementary- and middle-school art programs exist, the classroom teacher or the special art teacher is on the job organizing, coaching, motivating, questioning, demonstrating, evaluating, approving, and advising—in other words, teaching. The importance of actively

Stress only a few objectives each lesson. During the first lesson in this Japanese classroom, line was used to delineate every part of the bicycle. Filling the picture plane was also stressed. Later lessons focused on using color to set off the bicycle and background.

helping students learn to apply art concepts in their creation of art cannot be overemphasized.

Instructional objectives must be specific. It is not enough just to write, "Students will draw the still life" or "students will use colors with good design." The vagueness of these statements gives neither teacher nor students a specific goal. Without specific standards, the verbs "draw" and "use" are too vague. Better would be "Students will draw the table plane suggesting depth by overlapping and creating avenues in depth" or ". . . show how at least seven objects and forms overlap" or ". . . compose the design so at least three of the objects go off the edges."

In carrying out a project, stress only a few art objectives each class period. Don't confuse the students with too many directions all at once. In a drawing project, for example, during the first session emphasize the quality of line and the full use of the picture plane. During the second session guide the students in identifying and evaluating the variety of shapes and overlapping planes in their drawing. During the

third studio meeting challenge the students to enrich their drawings through detail, texture, and pattern.

Artistic Perception Objectives

Artistic perception requires identifying art elements in what we see in daily life. If teachers can bring children to notice something they have never noticed before, to become aware, to see with the inner eye, they will have started them on an endless, exciting, rewarding journey toward a thousand discoveries. Three sources for perceptual objectives are (1) the classroom, (2) artworks, and (3) the students' daily life experiences.

Examples of perceptual objectives based upon what can be seen in the classroom are: "The student will identify at least three triangular shapes in the classroom" or "The student will describe analogous color schemes from among the colors seen in classmates' shirts."

Courtesy of W. Robert Nix, University of Georgia, Athens, Georgia.

Perceptual objectives deal with focusing attention in order to see vividly and aesthetically the forms around us in daily life. For example, through study of these photos, the viewer is led to appreciate how beautifully the calyx shelters the flower.

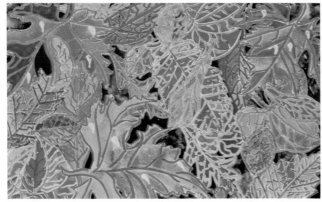

Courtesy of Mary Sayer Hammond, Fairfax, Virginia.

An example of a perceptual objective based upon what can be seen in artworks presented and created is: "From the artwork of a group of classmates, the student will be able to point out instances demonstrating (1) exaggeration and (2) swinging design." (Note that this particular kind of perception is now usually considered as an art criticism objective.)

Perceptual objectives can also be based on what the students have seen outside the classroom. ("The students will be able to recall the order of the colors in a rainbow." "The students will be able to describe and depict the features of insects' homes they have seen and describe why and how the insect's design makes the home effective.") Many perceptual objectives about nature state that the students "will describe verbally" or "show in their artwork" that they have perceived such natural phenomena as, for example,

The intricate pattern of a spider's web
The variety of cracked shapes in mudflats, ice, and cement walks
The blue shadows on fallen snow
The variety of grain pattern in wood
The varieties of green in summer foliage
The varied textures and patterns of tree bark
The shadows of tree branches on building walls
The lines and patterns of bridge girders and cables
The filigree pattern in leaf veins and insect wings
The pattern of frost on a windowpane
The changing formations of clouds
The dew on early-morning flowers and leaves
The undulation of reflections in water
The moody, misty colors of a foggy or rainy day
The flashing colors of stoplights, neon signs, and beacons
The glowing colors of stained-glass windows
The tracks of animals in the snow
The linear grace of a jet's stream
The deterioration of paint on aging doors and old metal

A perceptual objective might be: "Students will observe and be able to draw a variety of leaves." Terms can be taught such as "leaves, opposite and alternate" and "leaves, simple and compound." Other terms include "leaf veins, opposite and alternate" and "leaf margins, entire, serrate, and dentate." Children gathered a variety of leaves and drew them in crayon in a bold contour-line technique, emphasizing the veins but not coloring in the spaces solidly. They filled up the white paper in an allover design, the leaves turning in all directions, some touching, some overlapping. Then using their watercolors and brushes, they applied the transparent colors over and between the leaves.

Art Criticism Objectives

Objectives in art history, criticism, and aesthetics are described in Chapters 15 to 17. Here one form in which these objectives can be written is shown. One way to state an art criticism instructional objective is: "Students will use the language of art to describe qualities in each others' artwork." In the area of feelings, or affect, an example is: "Students will describe how peers have used artistic devices to show different kinds of feelings." In a lesson about depth, an objective might be: "Using artworks of the students themselves, students will describe various ways to indicate that an object appears to go back in space." In a design lesson using art reproductions, an objective might be: "From famous artworks, students will cite instances where an artwork's power might be attributed to the elaboration and variation of a motif."

Objectives in Aesthetics

Aesthetics is about ideas of beauty or the nature of art. Examples of aesthetics objectives are: "Students will discuss varying ideas of what makes a good picture" or "Students will debate whether art which does not realistically represent objects and figures can be considered good art" or "Students will debate whether ugly subject matter can make good art." (See Chapter 17.)

Art History Objectives

Art history performs several important educational roles, and objectives can focus on any of them.

- Study of concepts in art history: "Students will identify different art styles."
- Analysis of famous historical artworks to gain a perspective into the overall development of culture and history: "Students will describe why a theme has been shown differently throughout several centuries."
- Use of artworks from history to give students ideas for their own art: "From examples of Persian and medieval art, students will analyze and apply the concept of overlapping to their own artwork."
- Use of artworks from different cultures to develop multicultural understanding and ethnic pride: "Students will discuss how African-Americans have been depicted in art."

See Chapter 16.

Affective, Cognitive, and Psychomotor Objectives

The last three types of objectives deal with feelings, with knowledge, and with body movement. The affective, cognitive, and psychomotor domains, as they are called, comprise the three major divisions of a system called Bloom's taxonomy of educational objectives. These divisions are widely used in many schools which require written lesson plans. The affective domain deals with emotional factors in learning; the cognitive domain deals with the factual information students learn in school as well as with higher-level skills such as analysis and synthesis; and the psychomotor domain deals with how the movement of the body is involved in learning.

Each domain can be considered as having several levels, ranging from basic to advanced. For example, in the affective domain, the steps are, from lower to higher: receiving, awareness, responding, valuing, and organizing values. In the cognitive domain, the stages are knowing, comprehending, applying, analyzing, synthesizing, and evaluating. When education critics say that too many "low-level objectives" are used and not enough "high-level objectives," they are referring to Bloom's taxonomy.

Affective Objectives

Why bother with feelings in a book about teaching art? The reason is that, for many artists, aesthetic experience is rooted in concerns of life and death, nature and living beings, and the expression of feelings. Feelings often motivate art and sustain art's production over the long periods necessary for its creation. Art gives a voice to our inner needs and desires. It gives shape to our hopes, fears, and ideals, and to our very sense of self. If something is important in an emotional sense, the creation of art becomes a way to take action to share the importance of the experience.

Several variations of affective objectives are described in this section in order to show the wide variety of affective sources the teacher can draw upon to stimulate art learning. The following table gives six affective objectives together with an example, for each objective, of a representative statement teachers or students could make about that particular area.

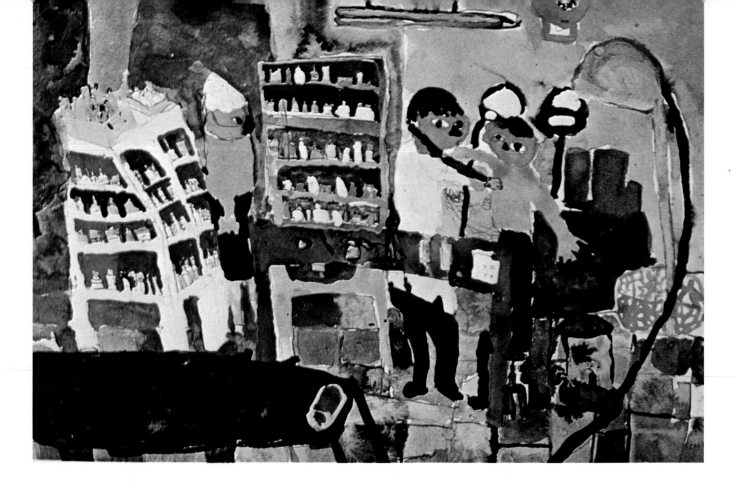

What vivid feelings "a visit to a doctor" must have been aroused in this young Japanese child. One can sense the anxiety by seeing how much was remembered and recorded in this watercolor painting.

Affective Objectives in Art Lessons	Representative Statements by Teacher or Students
Students will express personal feelings in their art production.	The feeling I'd like to put in my mask is one of super power.
Students will express feelings common to their age.	Fear of scary things in the closet was something I felt strongly about when I was your age.
Students will show feelings about external events in their art.	Mary's being in the hospital makes me want to do something to try to make her feel a little better.
Students will express their personal feelings indirectly, via art criticism.	The people in the picture look like they are afraid of the storm that's approaching, like bad things are going to happen to them.

Affective Objectives in Art Lessons	Representative Statements by Teacher or Students
Students will indirectly share personal feelings by peers' interpreting their artwork and through art history examples.	Does anyone get a different feeling from the way the trees and clouds are painted in Bernardo's picture?
Students will express feelings about sharing art as gifts.	What will you say when you give your art to someone special to you? What do you think that person might say back to you?

Personal Emotions

An affective objective might concern one's present personal emotions, one's feelings in school, at home, with one's peers, and with one's family. ("Students will share the feelings of pleasure, fear, and courage they have while playing Red Rover.") Sharing such content usually gives the creator added emotional power to make the art piece. Of course, students should only share what they feel comfortable sharing, whether in discussion or through their artwork.

Developmental Emotional Needs

Each developmental stage presents special emotional challenges (see Chapters 3 to 7). Some instructional objectives related to students' developmental stages, for example, are: "Student will be able to depict feelings . . . about relating to other persons and things . . . , of group belongingness . . . , of pride in accomplishment . . . , of emotionally reaching out to another person to give help or receive nurturance."

Affect Surrounding Events

The affect surrounding events refers to the feelings generated by world and community events, for example, one's emotions precipitated by some natural event (a storm), a war, a civil disturbance, an approaching holiday, or a classmate or family member who has had an accident. ("Through an artistic expression, student will show empathy for a hospitalized peer.")

Interpreting Affect in Peers' Work

A different venue for affective sharing is knowing that one's feelings can be communicated through art to others. ("Students will describe the affect shown in peers' works.") Of course, the teacher should not tolerate unkind remarks and needs to model the type of response desired. For example, the teacher might say, "The expression of this figure looks like he really wants to join the group playing Red Rover."

Sharing Art

It is motivating to make an art object to give to or share with another person. Yet holiday art is notorious for reflecting a nonartistic, nonqualitative approach that involves trite, uncreative, "craftsy" gimmicks. Nevertheless, when pursued with art concepts foremost in mind, pictures, cards, or craft gifts can be appropriate, for example, for Mother's Day gifts. Decorating a jeans jacket for a significant friend can motivate an older student. ("Students will indicate affect through their choice of a gift recipient.")

Courtesy of the Art Education Archives, Art Department, University of Georgia, Athens, Georgia.

The wedding of an older sibling made an emotional impression on this upper-elementary-grade child, who then captured the ceremony's sacred feeling in her tempera painting.

Cognitive Objectives Correlated to Other Areas of Study

The topic of correlating art to the cognitive learning found in other subject areas can be anathema to art teachers in school systems where art learning is considered far less important than social studies, reading, math, or science. Friction can also occur when scarce art supplies and scarcer student art learning time are used solely for another purpose. However, with the current integrated curriculum approach, there is a strong movement to make art "part and parcel" of every school subject.

  An example of an instructional objective that correlates science with art is: "Student will create a design employing repetition of pattern, based upon three different kinds of insects." When the art considerations are serious and are fused to the theme, significant art can result. Teachers of art have succeeded in actually gaining art learning

Courtesy of Shirley Lucas, Oshkosh, Wisconsin.

time and qualitative art experiences for students by doing correlated art projects. Some teachers welcome correlation so long as that activity is not a substitute for formal art instruction.

Making the case that art is an area that should be part of a common, general education designed for the future nonspecialist citizen, the National Art Education Association recommends that there be ". . . one hundred minutes of art class time a week in the elementary school with art taught as a subject in itself." In addition, the NAEA says that "time, space and materials should be provided for supplementary independent and individual art experiences in the regular classroom."

Such experiences will often be correlational:

- Social studies: the study of Native American art and Egyptian art.
- Science: the study of plants, birds, fish, and animals.
- Mathematics: tesselation can be related to Escher prints; Fibonacci series to drawing sunflower heads; and hexagons and octagons to paper sculpture, snowflakes, beehive cells, Chinese lattices, and Moorish mosque tile designs from the Alhambra.

Integrating academic subjects and art helps to sustain students' interest and makes their learning more enjoyable. It lets the holistic power of art knowledge permeate other areas of study. A new form of art today called *conceptual art,* or *systems art,* also does this. Two examples of art used to give insights into nature are the artist Christo's pink plastic floating islands in Miami Bay and Robert Smithson's spiral jetty in the Great Salt Lake.

One successful correlational project, Learning to Read Through the Arts, sponsored by the Guggenheim Museum and New York City Board of Education, helped students to recall with all their senses. It involved art criticism, art production, and field trips, and helped students improve reading scores by one or two months for each month of involvement in the program (Kinder, 1987; O'Brien, 1978). (See Chapter 10, "Motivation," the section on science correlation through still-life drawing.)

Another form of cognitive objective helps focus thinking about economic ideas such as making a living. Occupational value and economic value become of increasing concern to older students as they approach the time when they will begin to consider career options. An example of such an objective is: "Students will describe occupations

---

Science learning and art learning are interrelated in these studies of animals in their habitats. Crayon and oil pastels are by upper-elementary-grade students who were shown color photos, slides, and films.

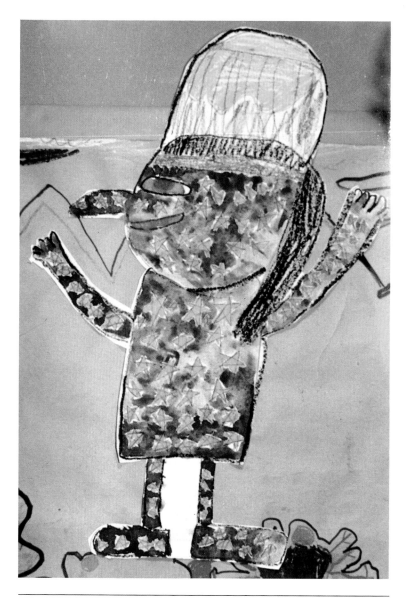

Left and below: Charlotte Country Day Schools, courtesy of Alice Ballard Munn, Anchorage, Alaska, and Diane Barret, Athens, Georgia. Above: Courtesy of David Harvell, Athens, Georgia.

When art considerations are serious, correlated art and culture lessons are of value for both subjects. The study of ancient Egyptian culture comes alive through art expressions. **Top right:** *Life-sized paintings of mummy sarcophagi create a display of grandeur and majesty in the elementary school's entrance hall.* **Above:** *First-grade painting of Nut, the star-studded deity of the night.* **Lower right:** *Glazed ceramic sculpture of the Egyptian ibis-headed scribe deity, Thoth.*

Yung Fu Elementary School, Tainan, Taiwan.

Psychomotor reenactment of catching frogs may have preceded the making of this delightful watercolor painting. One color, blue, predominates. Many tints and shades of green, from blue to yellow, are used for the carefully observed leaves and frogs. The child is fortunate to have an art teacher who appreciates what children can accomplish striving for design excellence.

which use the skills found in this lesson [for example, measuring, designing, color choices]. "Examples of occupation-related discourse the teacher might encourage are: "These cards are more colorful than ones I saw at the card shop selling for over a dollar" or "Many people make their livings by being designers of items like racing automobiles and fashion.""

Psychomotor and Multisensory Objectives

Moving our bodies and using other senses can stimulate art production and art criticism activities. Psychomotor and multisensory approaches can also be used for aesthetic experiences in themselves. Acting out a picture is one way by which kinesthetic awareness can trigger artistic awareness. One objective is that, by using their bodies, students will be able to stimulate awareness of what they have perceived, for example, a cat. ("How do they clean their bodies? How can we show this tongue licking the paw in our drawing?") Olfactory awareness of aromas can be a strong motivator also. ("Sniffing a can of cinnamon, students will show in their artwork the events of which the smell of cinnamon reminds them. Show how the figures looked at they mixed ingredients, did the baking, and ate the baked goods.") A popular auditory stimulation is painting to music. ("Painting to the rhythm of a piece of music, students will represent the music's measured regularity and variation in their paintings of figures in motion.")

Progressive children's programs at museums often use psychomotor methods to arouse interest in artworks. They have children respond nonverbally to the artworks, using their bodies and creative movement. ("Place yourself in the landscape, move like the people shown are moving, intuit the smells.") In the classroom, you can have your students, after viewing an exhibit or art reproduction, represent what they have seen through sounds, impromptu drama, human sculpture, and free movement. ("Students will be able to take the exact pose and facial expression of the portrait, and tell the class something that the person might be thinking.")

A Sample Lesson Plan

As the art teacher uses many of the above criteria in writing lesson plans, students with a wide variety of learning styles, emotional needs, and life needs will become aware of the importance of serious involve-

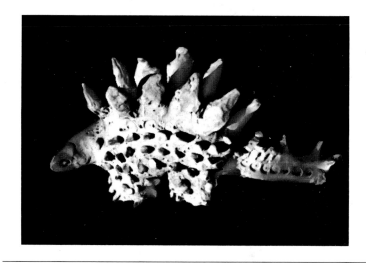

Clay dinosaur, grade 3, Iowa City.

ment in producing quality artwork. Their spirits can be reached. A sample lesson plan containing several types of instructional objectives follows.

Clay Dinosaurs, Primary Grades

1. Art production (specific art skills to be learned)	Students will pull head and leg forms from a ball of clay to construct a dinosaur. Students will form eyes, ears, mouths, and tails.
2. Artistic perception (where we see specific art elements in daily life)	Students will describe similar structural forms in nature, for example, other animals, tree branches, tables, post-and-lintel construction.
3. Art history (interpretation of similar artworks by artists of other times)	Students will describe animal forms shown in reproductions of Aztec pottery, tell how the legs were made, and describe the animal's expression.
4. Art criticism (discussion and interpretations of students' works)	Students will describe differences in each other's creations, identifying those which look delicate, ferocious, or strong.
5. Aesthetics (discussing ideas about art)	Students will discuss whether scary and ugly things can be art, even though some people think art should be only about what is beautiful.

6. Affective (dealing with emotional needs)	Students will describe their dinosaur's personality, how it interacts with friends or enemies that try to hurt it, whether it has any children and what they are like.
7. Cognitive and functional (correlated to important knowledge about our world and our functioning in it)	Students will be able to match their dinosaur to photos of actual dinosaurs. Students will be able to describe how their dinosaur's diet and defense mechanisms relate to those that the students themselves use.
8. Psychomotor and multisensory (dance, music, vocalization, role playing, taste, smell, hearing)	Students will mimic the sounds and movements of their dinosaur and then use these motifs to organize a dinosaur dance.

From Robert Clements and Lawrence Stueck, "Earthworks: A Two-Hundred-Ton Art Educational Media," *Art Education*, July 1983.

Artistic activity can occur in a state of openness, when the objective is unclear even to the creator. Allow for meditation. A mound of loose clay can provide an exciting medium for the unplanned, the unexpected, and that which is full of wonder.

Open Objectives

Open questioning can supplement the use of instructional objectives in evaluation. Rather than focusing exclusively on the instructional objectives given at the beginning of the lesson, the teacher can help the students evaluate problems in their artwork and arrive at their own solutions. For example, ask students questions like, "How do you like your picture?" "Is there some part of your picture you like best?" "Is there something that bothers you about it?" "What could you do to fix the part you don't like?"

A different type of openness has also been advocated. Instructional objective approaches have been criticized for having a hidden attitude of control and domination, and for emphasizing performing rather than thinking. Uncomfortable with the degree of specificity demanded in instructional objectives, especially when it results in describing artistic outcomes of studio activities, Elliot Eisner (1968) has called for a different type of objective, more open-ended, in art. He calls these *expressive objectives* or the objective. "The student will use wire and wood to construct a three-dimensional form" does not specify learning outcomes or standards, only the encounter between student, materials, and goal.

Many school systems today require clearly stated, unambiguous, sequential educational objectives, along with clearly spelled-out standards for evaluation. Nevertheless, as teachers of art, a personal poetic subject filled with wonder and uncertainty, we must also value and leave room for that which is open, indeterminant, and imaginative.

An example of a teacher's statement identifying and reinforcing imagination and poetic interpretation is: "Makeela's picture has a sense of mystery in it—an exciting feeling that we can't quite tell what is going to happen when the figures meet." People learn about art through continually coming back to main concepts in a holistic, contextually sensitive way. Proponents of one-dimensional curriculum goals may need to be reminded of that process.

Much quality art production by artists of all ages occurs in a state of nondirectional "play." It appears that the artist is fiddling around, that the objective is unclear even to the creator. Allow for this "water gazing." Art education has been criticized for trying to force a curriculum with predetermined contents and goals into students. Thus, even though school systems may require goals and instructional objectives to be spelled out, where, if not in art class, will encouragement be given for the irrational and the quirky? Where else will the mysterious, the subversive, and the unexpected be nurtured, the very elements which are necessary for our society's continuing renewal?

CHAPTER 13

Art for Students Experiencing Significant Mental or Physical Challenges

Eight Concepts

Approximately 12 percent of students in U.S. public education are in special education programs. They are entitled by law to art as well as other content areas of instruction. Those with mental and physical challenges (in learning, hearing, and vision, and mobility), and those who use mental health services, are now mainstreamed into integrated classrooms with children without disabilities. Every public school classroom teacher and art teacher will deal increasingly with youths with disabilities. Eight important concepts in the area of special education are: mainstreaming, challenge, developmental disability, normalization, age-appropriateness, partial participation, empowerment, and people-first language.

Mainstreaming

Since the passage in 1975 of Public Law 94-142, the Education for All Handicapped Children Act, *mainstreaming* is being increasingly implemented in regular elementary classrooms and in art classrooms. The law mandates testing, individualized educational plans, parental consent, confidentiality, least restrictive environment, and educational programming for youths with developmental disabilities. Not all students are mainstreamed, but whenever feasible, the procedure is being implemented to the fullest extent possible. For example, in New York City, 40 percent of the students facing significant mental and physical challenges are taught by regular classroom teachers in mainstreamed classes.

"Challenged," not "Handicapped"

The term *challenged* is beginning to replace the terms "exceptional," "handicapped," and "disabilities." Children may be challenged physically, intellectually, emotionally, or socially to such an extent that they cannot function educationally in a mode similar to that of children not so challenged. However, in time and with special instruction and programming, they may learn to cope and to achieve.

Developmental Disability

A *developmental disability* is a severe, chronic disability of a person which:

- Is attributable to a mental or physical impairment or combination thereof
- Is manifested before age 22
- Is likely to continue indefinitely
- Results in limitations in three or more areas of life activity: self-care, language, learning, mobility, self-direction, capacity for independent living, and economic self-sufficiency
- Reflects the need for long-duration, individually planned treatments.

Normalization

Normalization is the use of means as culturally normative as possible to establish personal behaviors which are as normative as possible. It does not mean that all people should be the same. It means that all people in a society should have, insofar as possible, equal opportunity

Illustrations from *Art and Mainstreaming*, a textbook dealing with art instruction for exceptional children in regular classrooms by Claire B. Clements and Robert D. Clements, University of Georgia, Athens. Courtesy of Charles C Thomas, Publishers, Springfield, Illinois.

to live, work, and play. It means that the students with disabilities in your art class should be treated as much like all the other students as possible.

Age-Appropriateness

A concept related to normalization is *age-appropriateness*. Teachers of art have frequently been criticized for having older special education students do activities deemed "babyish." Strive to keep your choice of topics and media age-appropriate. For example, do not have older students do pudding painting but instead use an adult material such as paper pulp. Test whether an activity is too childlike by asking yourself whether nonhandicapped persons of the same age would do the activity. When using art materials such as crayons, which some people may associate with primary school, emphasize how they have been used by famous artists, such as Picasso. (This is a good strategy even for persons without disabilities.)

Partial Participation

Keep in mind the principle of *partial participation*. Is there some way in which the student could participate in the lesson? Perhaps a student who does not speak could hold up the art reproduction which the class discusses. A child without sight could work with another child in cleaning the paintbrushes with soap. Even if a student cannot do all the steps in a process, you or another student can arrange for the individual to do those which he or she can. The child may need longer to do a certain step. Thus, the sequence of the steps may need to be changed.

Empowerment

Another concept is that of *empowerment*. It is very easy for helpers to "overdo" for individuals with disabilities. In fact, many children both with and without disabilities have learned how to get extra services

*Facing page: Drawings depict children in a variety of art activities that build self-worth. **Left to right, top:** Construction with wood scraps from lumber yard; costumes and hats designed for a parade; paper masks. **Left to right, bottom:** Simple cardboard and string mobile; train engines and trucks constructed from discarded grocery cartons.*

from adults, with the familiar refrain, "You draw it for me." By thus disempowering students, teachers do not help them. To foster independent achievement, the less teacher assistance, the better.

People-First Language

In speaking, use *people-first* language. For example, don't focus on disability, a child who "can't draw." Instead focus on capability, a child who can "vocalize about the patterns he or she draws." Do not say "the blind" or "the retarded," implying that these individuals belong in a class set apart; use the more respectful term, "persons with challenges in seeing or learning." "Persons who use a wheelchair for mobility" is preferred to "crippled people." Negative language continues old attitudes of exclusion and a "them vs. us perspective." Positive language promotes positive attitudes and helps to promote independence, self-help, and community integration.

Teaching Approaches

For the majority of children in elementary and middle schools, the guidelines for teaching art proposed in this book should prove adaptable and effective, but for children with special needs, new teaching strategies are called for. The intent of this chapter is to provide some practical approaches to help teachers meet the challenge. First, the good news is that the art class or studio atmosphere is the best of all possible environments in which to work with children with developmental disabilities. Each child is accepted; his or her potential is respected. Each child can excel in some way. Every child can be an achiever.

The importance of the teacher and the teacher's role cannot be stressed enough in the context of teaching children with special needs. All attributes of the dedicated teacher that we have spelled out before—sympathy, knowledge, tact, confidence, resourcefulness, understanding, equanimity, and patience—are doubly important in the successful management of a mainstreamed classroom. Precedence, if any, must be given to the qualities of understanding and patience.

General Strategies

Some general strategies for teachers who are experiencing mainstreaming for the first time are listed on the next page.

1. Accept the children as they are.
2. Familiarize yourself with the handicaps of the special children assigned to your class. Use the student's out-of-school interests as guides for suitable activities.
3. Ascertain if a progress chart has been recorded on the students by a previous teacher. Note the art experiences and projects with which they have been successful.
4. Help the child's parents promote the child's life-enriching recreation and leisure skills by communicating with them concerning what art materials the child enjoys using. Suggest art and hobby materials they might get for in the home, as well as community arts class offerings.
5. If teacher aides are assigned to help you with the special students in your class, involve them appropriately. Don't let the aide sit idle, but also don't let the aide be oversolicitous and do the project for the individuals.
6. Keep your own progress report on every child with disabilities. In a few school systems the art teacher must write and implement individualized educational plans (IEPs) for each student with developmental disabilities.
7. Consider carefully the teaching procedures you will employ in the instruction of your special students. Will you use free-choice projects in which children choose their own subject matter, materials, and time limits? Will you employ the unit or project method in which the same art activity is planned for both students with and without disabilities? The latter format usually calls for individual adjustments to meet the needs and abilities of the student with disabilities.
8. Ask the child if there is something that could be done to facilitate his or her participation in the activity. ("How can we make it easier for you to do the project?")
9. Enlist the aid of students without disabilities in the class, especially those with proven abilities and stable, pleasant personalities, to help their classmates with disabilities.
10. Above all, do not permit the children to participate in copying or tracing artwork. Help them create their own imagery, even though this imagery may differ from the artwork of the students without disabilities. Even when children's graphic expression consists of scribbles, they have feeling for the patterns their marks make. They have made something which did not exist before in the world.

Specific Classroom Strategies

Here are some specific teaching strategies and tactics to follow in working with the student with developmental disabilities. Keep in mind that even if the students with disabilities have above-average IQs, they will probably require some nontraditional teaching strategies and adaptation of materials.

For persons with learning disorders or hyperactivity, try to create a calm, ordered environment. To limit opportunities for choice, keep materials few. Deemphasize group activities. Give immediate reinforcement. Be attentive to when the child may get close to losing control and change the situation before that point is reached. Working with a quiet, mature student or working in a carrel may help the child to concentrate. Try to create seating arrangements and projects that encourage staying in the seat, for example, looking at art history books while seated in a beanbag chair.

At all times proceed deliberately, methodically, and calmly. Give directions or instructions slowly and clearly, using simple language at a rate the children can assimilate. Make sure, if possible, that you have the child's attention when explaining something.

Make eye contact as you address the students. Sit on a chair or stool so your face will be at a level easier for children to see. Don't address the class while facing the chalkboard or standing in the window glare.

Demonstrate more and talk less. Employ visual symbols and models. Speak in a modulated tone of voice. For youths with attention deficits, make the teaching materials colorful.

Printing designs and shapes with potatoes, sponges, and erasers provides an unusual experience in aesthetic discrimination and fine motor coordination. In addition, the decorative patterns which result can then be used for gift wrap, for greeting cards, and for covering boxes.

Prepare lessons to meet specific needs (for examples, hand-eye coordination, fine or gross motor-skills improvement) and to meet identifiable objectives such as color or shape naming.

For students with vision deficiencies, employ media that help them achieve success. For example, for those who supplement vision with touch, use large, contrasting (black and white) sheets of paper. Some students will prefer tinted paper, which minimizes glare. Broad-line markers of vivid colors and brightly colored crayons are preferable to markers and crayons of more subdued values. Some media (for example, glue-line prints) will leave a raised line which can be felt. Black paint can be added to white glue for drawing on white paper, and a raised line will be left when dry. Other techniques, such as printing on plastic foam meat trays and drawing on heavy aluminum foil with a dull pencil, will leave a recessed line. Art media which make noise, such as squeaky brayers and markers, or which smell, like scented markers and paste, can add interest. Wire, pipe cleaner, and clay figure sculptures can be used to emphasize good posture. Topics such as "a call for help" can foster the expression of feelings. Making texture maps and box sculptures can foster the individual's concept of oneself as a person capable of moving around the home and community. Keeping supplies in the same place in the room consistently helps students with vision deficiencies to find what they need easily. For students with partial vision, light shows can use colored gels and projectors.

For individuals with neurological and orthopedic challenges, borders, boundaries, and holding devices may help. Plastic meat trays can serve to contain clay and small objects. Cafeteria trays can be clamped to a wheelchair work surface using a C-clamp. Masking tape and duct tape can be used to tape down water containers and to tape brushes to hands. Individuals with severe limitations in movement can pull a string to move a mobile and make patterns in salt, sugar, or millet on a colorful tray. Carving blocks of balsa wood with a rasp can provide both exercise and an art experience. Papier-mâché can be pressed into a greased mold to create sculptural forms.

For persons with hearing challenges, emphasize projects to help them overcome self-consciousness (self-portraits) and insecurity (working with a buddy on a joint project). Encourage their use of residual hearing (for example, sitting on a wooden floor and banging on a drum, painting to music), and their development of language (staging plays with puppets, masks, model grocery stores).

For students with mental challenges, strive for projects which are both age-appropriate and ability-appropriate. Repeat instructions and procedures over and over again. In a word, overteach!

Plan projects that may be broken down into sequential, manageable, and explainable steps. For example, there are four stages in creating a collage: the drawing stage, the cutting or tearing stage, the pasting stage, and

Courtesy of Knox Wilkinson, Rome, Georgia.

Knox Wilkinson, an artist with mild mental challenge, has successfully shown his work in museums throughout the nation and world. He is involved in efforts to help others achieve through art, and his design of two birds here is an announcement for a Very Special Art Exhibition.

the matting stage. Allow sufficient time for completion of each step, and do not begin a new step until the previous one is completed.

For students with behavior disorders, art media should offer active resistance (linocuts, carving); the project should imply monetary value (glazed ceramics, leather work, crafts); tools should be manual arts tools (hammers, gouges), and the project should have three dimensions. Use unexpected rewards, for example, displaying artwork outside the principal's office. Let the child arrange a bulletin board, or pronounce the art vocabulary words, or sketch a tray of toy figures.

Emphasize experiences that deal with kinesthetic manipulation and multisensory stimulation.

Emphasize the fundamentals of art as critical guideposts in visual expression; for example, identify basic shapes and colors. Emphasize also the awareness of environment and space.

Be cognizant that it may be difficult for students with disabilities to tolerate changes in routines; that some are easily distracted and have short attention spans, and that many will require constant praise and support. Brief, one-session projects that demand minimum memory recall may be suitable for some students. Remember that students with disabilities, like all students, respond more enthusiastically when their art experiences are successful.

Using Art for Community and School Integration

Persons with disabilities are not a separate group from the community at large. They are citizens with the rights of all citizens. Congress has passed the Americans with Disabilities Act guaranteeing these individuals rights to equity in employment, housing, and community services. Some ways the art program can promote positive community attitudes are:

Encourage these students' participation in community activities, so they may see themselves as, and be seen by others as, active members of the community. Especially involve them in activities about their own cultural heritage.

Be alert to opportunities such as art exhibitions for persons with disabilities. A Pilot Club or similar civic organization in your community or state may sponsor activities in which your students could receive recognition. Make arrangements for these students to be taken on trips to community art openings and art festivals.

If a Very Special Arts Festival is held in your community, be sure your students with special needs can participate, either by just attending or exhibiting their work or, even better, by putting on an activity. For information on starting such a festival in your community, talk to your school system's special education coordinator or write to that organization at the Kennedy Center in Washington, D.C.

Display the students' work attractively to show your approval and to elicit supporting response from their peers. Remember that their projects, which may differ from the appearance of the art of students without disabilities, can bring price to the school, delight to parents and visitors, and an enhanced sense of self-worth to the participating students.

Ascertain if the student or the students' parents or care givers are being served by community organizations whose purpose it is to provide support for these individuals. For example, perhaps there is a support group in your community for young people requiring mental health services. Many communities have a quasi-governmental, centralized resource with a name like "help line" or "community connection" that puts people with

---

Projects that may be undertaken successfully with children with some kinds of special needs. **Top:** *Puppet people constructed of characteristic body parts. Wallpaper samples and colored construction paper were provided already cut into arms, legs, body, and head. Children, with the aid of the teacher, pasted them down.* **Middle:** *Three-dimensional animals constructed with folded and cut tagboard.* **Bottom:** *Stabile constructed out of found materials.*

needs in touch with social service agencies and support groups. Certain community service organizations may provide special equipment. (For example, the Lions Club offers services to people with vision difficulties.)

- Be an active advocate for accessibility. In setting up art exhibitions, have certain pieces designated for touching. Have labels for individuals who need large-print formats at the proper height. Be aware of alternative forms of communication such as braille and the Blissboards (boards with pictures to which a person points in order to communicate). Art teachers have helped children without speech to draw their own "talking books."

Experiences That May Appeal to Students Facing Physical or Mental Challenges

Painting
Cutting
Pasting
Beach balls
Opening packages
Toys
Printmaking (with vegetables and found objects)
Big cardboard cartons to hide and play in and transform into vehicles
Construction (wood, boxes, found objects)
Meat-tray boats
Weaving
Balloons
Fingerpainting
"Keep-a-secret" progressive figure drawing
Pets and animals
Flowers and trees
Dressing up, costumes, uniforms
Kinesthetic activities

Decorating the classroom
Puppets
Piñatas
Fanciful hats
Marching, parading
Fish in aquariums
Clowns
Making music with assorted concocted instruments
Bright colors in paper, cloth, yarn, cellophane, ribbons
Noisemakers, horns
Modeling mixtures
Singing
Masks
Face makeup
Drums
Pantomime
Painting to music
Use of mirrors
Mobiles
Kaleidoscopes
Kites

Materials

Be aware of the many specialized devices, tools, and materials now used in art classes by children with significant physical challenges. The school's special education coordinator may be able to help you in requisitioning such materials for your students:

Four-holed scissors that both student and teacher can manipulate simultaneously

Fat-handled brushes (1 or 2 inches wide) or brushes with handles wrapped with masking or surgical tape to help students get a better grip when painting

Giant color crayons, felt-nib markers (water-based); kindergarten-size pencils with soft lead

Glue sticks (which may be easier to use than squeeze bottles of white glue)

Painting stretchers assembled together and placed on desk around the perimeter of the in-process projects so students can judge their work's boundaries; other possibilities are plastic meat trays and cafeteria trays

C-clamps and duct tape or masking tape to hold artwork onto wheelchair trays; specially designed art boards for wheelchairs

Duct tape for taping brushes to hands

Forehead pointers

Mouth wands or rubber spatulas with brushes or markers taped to them

Posters and instructional signs with giant-size letters and numerals

Cameras and computers adapted for special use by those with challenges in vision, movement, and coordination

Touch table, touch box

Flannel boards and pegboards

Building blocks in assorted shapes and sizes

Magnifying glasses and colored gelatins

Wood or plastic colored beads and sticks in assorted sizes

For additional found or recycled materials useful in art classes, see Appendix A.

CHAPTER 14

Giftedness and Its Art Implications for All Students

Giftedness and Art Thinking

This chapter discusses giftedness in general, relates general-intelligence approaches to artistic giftedness, gives strategies for the teacher, and offers suggestions for outreach into the school, home, and community. Admission into school gifted programs often requires a score on the Stanford Binet Intelligence Test of 120 to 130 points, along with teacher recommendations, high grades, and acceptance by a review committee. Some experts feel that the intelligence test is overly weighted toward skills in math and reading comprehension. Too often, areas such as art ability go unmeasured.

One alternative to the IQ test is the Torrance Test of Creative Thinking, which considers four aspects of creativity: fluency, flexibility, elaboration, and originality. For all children, these desirable characteristics can be nurtured through talking with them as they create their pictures:

- Fluency: "How many can you show?"
- Flexibility: "Can you think of another way to look at it?"
- Elaboration: "Can we tell about this in more detail?"
- Originality: "Make it your *own* way, and show the special idea that you have."

Another way to look at intelligence comes from Harvard psychologist Howard Gardner, who does not believe there is one monolithic kind of intelligence. Instead, he describes seven distinct forms of intelligence or ways of "information processing" (1990):

Language
Logical and mathematical
Interpersonal (knowledge about other people)
Musical
Spatial
Bodily-kinesthetic
Intrapersonal (information about oneself)

Gardner doesn't consider artistic thinking as a separate form of intelligence. Instead, any of the seven forms can be directed to artistic ends or to nonartistic ends. For example, language ability can be used by a poet or lawyer. Kinesthetic ability can be used by a dancer or a surgeon. Spatial ability can be used by a sculptor or a sailor. You can bring this into your classroom for all students in the following ways:

Language intelligence can be related to art through discussions of art criticism, art history, and aesthetics.
Knowledge of one's own feelings (intrapersonal knowledge) can be given expression by discussing the meaning of one's own art or of masterpieces, and considering questions of aesthetics.
Knowledge of other people (interpersonal knowledge) can be shown by empathetically discussing the art of others. Students can give encouragement to peers for their art, and depict interpersonal relationships in their own art.
Mathematical intelligence can be related to art through the study of such geometric forms as icosahedra in three-dimensional constructions, fractal geometry in computer art, and linear perspective, and through the study of topologic surfaces in mapmaking and Escher prints.
Musical intelligence can be related to art through painting to music, through creating music to accompany a certain painting, for example, Moussorgsky's "Paintings at an Exhibition," and through studying how various cultures have expressed themselves through music and art.
Spatial intelligence is the area most closely related to visual art. It can be cultivated by ways of creating and analyzing space in art, especially in architecture and sculpture but also in all art media dealing with space, for example, perspective in painting and drawing.

126

A handsomely designed watercolor interpretation of boats in a harbor by a middle-grade student, Japan. Japanese schoolchildren from kindergarten up are provided with a large assortment of colors in tubes. They learn very early how to mix a variety of tints, shades, and neutralized hues.

Characteristics of Students Gifted in Art

In the qualitative approach to art we encourage all students to develop many of the characteristics possessed by persons talented in art. They have greater persistence and are able to work longer and with greater concentration. Pleasure is sought by encountering problems, which stimulates these individuals. They can become absorbed for hours in a medium. They derive deep, personal satisfaction from their involvement in art. Some or all of the characteristics on the next page are true of people who are gifted in art. These students:

Sky and Water, woodcut, M. C. Escher, 1938, 1898–1972. National Gallery of Art, Washington, D.C., Cornelius Van S. Roosevelt Collection.

In this M. C. Escher print, the dark bird shape is transformed into water. The white fish changes into sky. Although Escher was a poor math student, his prints showing transformations from two to three dimensions have been hailed as having much significance, especially for mathematicians. Nowadays, students in math classes often create their own similar transformation designs.

First reveal their giftedness through their very early drawings and may develop a personal style of drawing or painting early in their school years.

Use a greater amount of detail, pattern, and texture in their drawings and compositions than most children—some of this elaboration observed, some imagined.

Possess a richer store of images and ideas from which to draw, heightened by their acute observation.

Often possess a photographic mind, with vivid recall of events engaged in or observed that distinguishes their efforts, characterized by a richness of details.

Master certain technical aspects of drawing—perspective, foreshortening, volume, shading, overlapping, spatial handling, and movement—much sooner than their peers.

For their art compositions, may choose subjects of fantasy, with complex themes involving intricate structures and a host of participants.

Are receptive to new media, techniques, and tools.

Show great interest in the art world and in the lives of contemporary artists and craftspeople. They often visit art museums on a regular basis and sometimes carry a sketchbook to record their impressions.

Rather than merely reacting to occurrences in the world, their creativity leads them to take a proactive stance toward the world.

Learn quickly to employ the vocabulary of art effectively and confidently and to criticize and evaluate their art production for design.

Usually prefer drawing, painting, printmaking, and collage to step-by-step craftwork.

Use color imaginatively, making up their own palette of colors by combining the hues provided to the class.

Are oblivious to distractions when engaged in their art and often resent interference.

Are generally highly self-motivated and engage in art on their own—after school, at home, and even during other class periods.

Teaching Strategies

The teacher can encourage gifted children by providing a supportive environment. Students feel this is more important than any instruction they receive. However, overpraise is to be avoided, since it can lead to peer resentment.

One good approach is the minimal one of letting the student alone to follow his or her special direction—in effect, *underteaching*. The teacher can provide challenges through multimedia techniques and subject-matter assignments that demand imaginative solutions and interpretations. For example, an assignment might be the depiction of a famous person when young experiencing the first intimations of her or his future life role. While teachers should provide challenges, on no account should the gifted child be rushed into advanced forms of expression.

Letting the child pursue his or her own endeavors may pose problems for the teacher who uses the project method in which all students in class are engaged in the same subject-matter assignment using the same technique. To allow gifted children the special privilege of working on their own subject choice at their own pace while their classmates are required to stay with the assigned project is not recommended. A wiser procedure is to challenge gifted children to stretch the possibilities of the assigned project or theme to the fullest. Remind gifted students there are many moments outside the art class

St. Joseph's Elementary School, Athens, Georgia. Reproduced by permission of Jimmy Morris, Athens, Georgia.

The delightful drawing of a rabbit in a garden is the creation of a talented first-grade child. Note how primary-grade children include the multirayed sun in their drawings.

when they can soar creatively and imaginatively in subject themes of their choosing. Encourage them to share with you some of those outside efforts.

Extending into the School, Home, and Community

The teacher can foster students' creative growth not only in the art class but also in the school at large, the home, and the community. Find ways to extend art activities out into the community and the individual's ongoing daily life. Community integration may be especially helpful to creative students because of their tendency to be more socially reserved, aloof, and distanced from society. They are more questioning, skeptical, and opinionated. People may express negative attitudes to them; peers and adults may think of some as silly and perceive them as smart alecks.

The variations in pattern and texture are exceptional. Also noteworthy is the capturing of effects of light, with one side light and the other side black. This figure study by a 13-year-old from Mexico is from a costumed model who holds cultural ceremonial artifacts.

Saga Prefecture, Kyushu Island, Japan.

These fish drawings are by primary-grade children. What imaginations these youngsters possess to invent and elaborate so skillfully!

To foster creative and social growth of talented students, consider forming a club or organization for your gifted students, who might find kindred spirits in such a group. Together they can discuss and share their artwork and go to special events such as museum openings. They can contribute artistically to the school's special functions, for example, by painting a set for an assembly program. Middle-school youths can be organized into a chapter of the National Art Education Association's National Junior Art Honor Society. Be alert to the need to provide gifted students with role models from diverse

A superb pen-and-ink drawing of lush foliage by a gifted sixth-grade Japanese girl.

cultural backgrounds and especially of both genders. Both males and females need role models with whom to identify. Don't enter elementary- and middle-school children's art in competitions, because such external competitions can undermine creative interest and performance. For the one child who is reinforced by a prize, 10 or 20 children will have their confidence in their nascent ability undermined. Especially shun coloring contests of pictures drawn by adults.

The home environment is extremely important in encouraging creativity. At a parent conference share with the child's parents your

Kagoshima, Japan.

Gifted students can stretch the possibilities of the assigned project to the ful- lest. A middle-school student did this colorful simulated mosaic employing cut and torn colored paper for the tesserae. Note the gradations of blue in the harbor's water. The subject is Sakurajima Park, with a view of an erupting volcano on a nearby island.

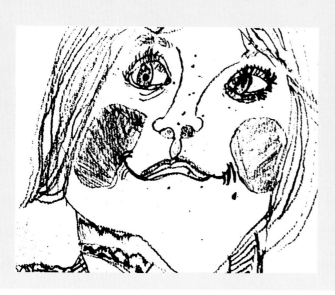

Courtesy of Baiba Kuntz, Glencoe, Illinois.

Gifted first-grade children have produced these detailed contour-line drawings. They reveal once again what youngsters are capable of achieving in drawing skills when they are encouraged to become aware. First-grade children can notice jewelry details, barrettes, freckles, eyeglass hinges, creases of skin around the eyes and at the mouth's sides, even the oval on the upper lip below the nose and the wrinkles in the lips.

notice of the child's special giftedness. Direct parents' awareness toward community children's art enrichment programs. An art specialist with hundreds of students each year might use a letter to parents to give notice of artistic giftedness and offer suggestions for how to nurture it—see the sample letter below.

To the Parents or Guardians of _____

Teaching at Anniston and Mayberry Elementary Schools for the past two years, I have had the opportunity to observe the art achievement of over a thousand students. You are probably already aware of your child's giftedness in art. However, I felt it my professional responsibility to bring to your attention my notice of and appreciation of the quality work your child does in art. As a general trait, artistic giftedness in children is shown by their being able to concentrate longer, having a lot of ideas to express, and including a lot of detail to make their drawings more elaborate. They are more self-directed, draw more realistically earlier than other children, and use art materials more creatively.

Some children talented in art have profited from several art enrichment programs in our community. Although as a school employee I cannot endorse any one program, I wanted to bring their existence to your attention if you are not already aware of them, if you wish to look into their suitability in meeting your child's needs:

Mayberry Recreation Department, Lyndon House Art Center, classes for children ages 4-12, Tuesdays and Thursdays 3:30 to 5:30, 10 sessions, cost $20 a term. The YMCA has art classes for members, Saturday 10-12. Alachua County Junior College has a gifted program on Saturday mornings which sometimes has classes focusing on the arts (546-9990). Private art teachers of whom I am aware in the community are Martha Ward, 546-7783, and James Jackson, 543-3454. In addition, there are probably more programs of which I am unaware.

Please call me at school at 543-9087 (between 2:30 and 3:30 is best) or at home at 548-4543 (between 7 and 8) if I can be of help to you about how we might work together to further your child's artistic creativity.

Art Teacher, Anniston and Mayberry Elementary Schools

The teacher of art should call parents' attention to gifted students' abilities in order that the children may receive enrichment instruction and the gift be nurtured. **Above:** *Painting of a doll by a 6-year-old from St. Petersburg, Russia, shows a brilliant use of pattern.* **Right:** *In a drawing from a costumed figure, an 8-year-old girl from Mexico shows an intuitive gift for design. Note the patterned border, the complementary colors, and the inspired white outline surrounding the face.*

Teachers who discover talented children are fortunate. They become witnesses to what children can do in art when they extend themselves to their fullest potential. Teachers can derive clues from the creative solutions which gifted children employ to help them in the motivation of other classmates. What teachers see and learn from the characteristics and working habits of the talented child is what they emphasize in a qualitative art program. They see keen, sensitive observation; rich imagination; persistence, patience, and concentration; and, above all, art that is engaged in seriously and purposefully.

PART III
Art Appreciation, Art History, Art Criticism, and Aesthetics

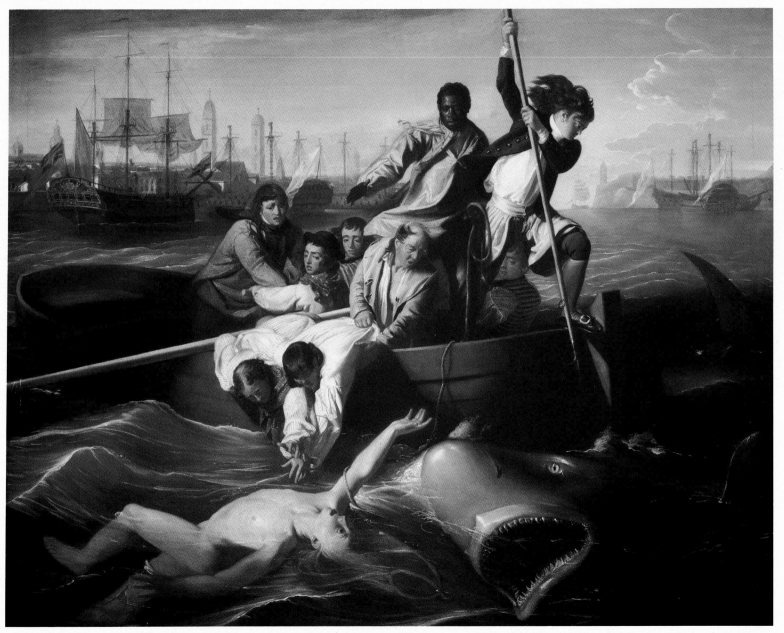

Watson and the Shark, 1778, John Singleton Copley, American, 1738–1815, oil on canvas, 72 × 90¼ inches. Gift of Mrs. George von Lengerke Meyer. Courtesy Museum of Fine Arts, Boston.

What child who has ever had an accident, or whose family member, friend, or pet has had a misfortune, would not be fascinated to speculate about this picture? As a teenager, Watson, serving as a midshipman, was swimming in Havana Harbor when he encountered a shark. The shark stripped all muscle from his leg in one first bite, and removed his foot in a second bite, before he was providently rescued. Later, Lord Mayor of London, he commissioned the artist John Singleton Copley to record the event. The painting met immediate acclaim. Observe the dramatic lighting and the zigzag and pyramidal composition the artist used, and his choice of the moment of suspense.

CHAPTER 15

New Approaches to Art Appreciation

Children today have infinitely more opportunities to see and appreciate art than ever before. Our burgeoning museums and art centers open their doors to all; mobile art exhibits tour many cities and states, and colorful murals now enliven countless urban walls. Municipal buildings, subways, and airports display a variety of commissioned art. Magazines feature articles on art. Large numbers of colorfully illustrated books on art are published, and reproductions of art are available at fairly reasonable prices. School textbooks in social studies and literature are often filled with colorful, correlative art visuals. Art councils in the 50 states promote art festivals, exhibits, and "artists-in-the-schools" programs.

Despite the presence of the opportunities to appreciate art that abound in the world about them, many school children receive minimal training in learning how to do, think about, and talk about art. They leave school programs intimidated by museums and art galleries. They feel that serious discussions about art ideas are something they have no business participating in. They think that the study of art criticism, art history, and aesthetics is something reserved for those going on for higher education. They have not grasped that art is not merely a way to respond to the world. It is a way of investigating the world and its meanings and values.

Our nation cannot afford to cut so many of our citizens off from art appreciation. *Toward Civilization,* an influential report of the National Endowment for the Arts (1988) described this situation:

> The arts are in triple jeopardy: they are not viewed as serious; knowledge . . . is not viewed as a prime objective; and those who determine school curricula do not agree on what arts education is.

Some educators believe that the activities of thinking and talking about art can give a new intellectual dimension to art appreciation, and they believe that fully implementing these activities would allow art to be accorded a higher place in the school curriculum.

Art Appreciation in the Schools: From Picture Study to Discipline-Based Art Education

The idea that students should study art masterworks and be given instruction in art appreciation is not new. In the mid-nineteenth century, the art historian Winkelman had advised artists to dip their brushes in intellect. At that time in America, a new, distinctly American art was being advocated, one which would be pure, moral, and earnest—an alliance of art, religion, and nature. Educating the child's artistic eye was considered an integral part of moral and social education. At the end of the century the "schoolroom decoration movement" worked to do this by bringing plaster casts of antique sculptures into classrooms. Sepia art reproductions with a patriotic, religious, and moralistic orientation came into the public schools through the "picture study movement." In the years from 1910 to 1920, this movement brought art prints into the schools. These pictures were filled with literary associations upon which students could speculate. Works by artists such as Rosa Bonheur, Jean-François Millet, Raphael, and Winslow Homer were deemed suitable for young, impressionable minds. Some of these prints, such as E. G. Leutze's *Washington Crossing the Delaware,* still hang in school hallways.

In the 1920s, formal design elements gained more attention, spurred by interest in art movements such as cubism, Roger Fry's writings in aesthetics, and Arthur Wesley Dow's art education writings, which focused on the elements of line, value, and color. In the mid-1950s, four-color printing of large-size art reproductions and 35-mm slides and slide projectors made it possible for masterpieces to be shown in the classroom.

Federal educational legislation helped. The U.S. Office of Education, through its Arts and Humanities Program, sponsored programs and conferences on how to improve art education. Funds from a booming "great society" economy and federal educational enrichment programs (such as the Elementary and Secondary Education Act of 1965) purchased prints and slides for school libraries, social studies classes, art classes, and elementary classrooms. Innovative librarians, teachers, and administrators seeking enrichment sources realized the educational power of such reproductions. Major art museums throughout the nation printed inexpensive reproductions, and the National Gallery of Art made available to public schools a lending program for art slides, reproductions, filmstrips, and films.

Parallel with the development of printing technology and school enrichment programs was the development in the nation's colleges and universities of the disciplines of art history, art criticism, and aesthetics. Art educators looked at their own discipline, analyzing the elements in its structure. Some argued that art history and art criticism were disciplines equally as valid as the actual creation of art. Since the 1950s, national art education conference programs have addressed the question of how to incorporate art history and art criticism into school art programs. University-level art texts made the case that the primary goal of art education is to help students to see the role of art in giving meaning to human endeavor and meeting needs in daily living. The twofold function of aesthetic education was seen. Not only should aesthetic education teach students how to experience the arts for their inherent values and delight, but it should contribute to the students' general store of perceptions and concepts that can function tacitly in a broad range of situations. The older term "art appreciation" came to be looked upon as merely implying peripheral knowledge. Newer terms, such as "art criticism," "aesthetics," and "aesthetic education," began to be used more widely.

Foundations took an interest in fostering school programs emphasizing a cognitive approach to art through art criticism, art history, and aesthetics. In 1982 the Getty Center for Education in the Arts was created to investigate the feasibility of having nonspecialist teachers and art teachers, in general classroom settings, teach students art skills in the areas of art criticism, art history, and aesthetics side by side with the teaching of art creation. The director of the Getty Center wrote: "If art education is to become a meaningful part of the curriculum, its content must be broadened and its requirements made more rigorous." In 1984 Dwaine Greer gave this movement the label *discipline-based art education (DBAE)*, by which it has come to be known. Its proponents have stressed the need for balance among the four subdisciplines: art history, art criticism, aesthetics, and art production. The

curriculum guides of several states have spelled out the content of art in a similar way.

While many art educators from the mid-1960s on agreed upon the importance of these endeavors, there was also voiced in the profession concern as to if, how, when, and to what degree such activities should supplant or supplement studio activities. Some worried that DBAE could have the effect of suffocating students' artistic creativity, since it emphasizes academic disciplines in which students might have little or no interest without a foundation of experience with art production. Others believed that DBAE does not take into account many important functions of art: for healing, celebration, social protest, personal transformation, spiritual growth, exploration of the subconscious, and sheer play. Still others objected to DBAE's tacit assumption that non-DBAE approaches are fragmented and broken.

Over the past 20 years, this textbook, *Emphasis Art*, has been a strong voice emphasizing the importance of serious, qualitative studio involvement. We believe that studio involvement, that is, thinking and problem solving in the media themselves, is primary and central. The view of children as innate artists seeking expression, communication, and self-discovery and having confidence in their creativity and inventiveness can be threatened by an overemphasis on academic study.

In the early years of this century, the "father of child art," Franz Cizek, taught that a child understands and enjoys art only to the extent that the child has acquired the understanding through personal efforts. Many art educators today believe that studio art is fundamental to the other disciplines, which are derivative. They believe that studio art production represents the idea of the artist in general education, and that it should precede academic training in disciplines such as art history and art criticism.

Thus, there continues to be a healthy professional debate on topics and emphasis in art education. This text offers the following sequential approach for aesthetic activities over the years:

In the early grades, the students should take delight in the aesthetic qualities of objects made by humans and in nature.

In grades 4 to 6, academic learning should center on the perception of artworks.

In grades 7 to 9, academic learning should center on the acquisition of a knowledge of art history.

Below ten years, production activities should always be central. This should be a time when children have hands-on involvement with the media. Especially during these early years, it is helpful to keep in mind this balance: don't give more to the mind than to the hand. When

Talking about pictures can develop thinking about art and life. The painting Road to Eternuty is by America's most famous folk artist, Reverend Howard Finster. Why do you think he painted the mountains with sad expressions? Why do you think he put pyramids in the background? Is writing all over a picture okay for an artist to do? How can we put the ideas in which we believe into our art?

students are doing perceptual, critical, and historical activities, those activities should be closely related to and whenever possible emerge from the students' artwork.

General Methods for Art Discussions

Socratic Questioning

In leading discussions about art, a preferred method is the Socratic method because it promotes the birth of ideas. The Socratic method consists of asking questions to make people think and then contesting the answers. It prompts them to give reasons for their statements, asks them to disprove alternative explanations, and encourages them to generalize about their ideas. The interpretation of an artwork or thoughts about an aesthetic concept are and always will be issues which should be contested in this way. One good way to promote discussion is by asking students "What's wrong with this picture?" The question facilitates students' putting forth their criteria, which can then be debated. Avoid questions that get one-word answers, such as, "This is an impressionistic painting, isn't it?" Instead ask open questions, such as "Why do you think this is an impressionistic painting?" Encourage the students to make inferences, to generalize, to analyze, and to synthesize. Besides Socratic questioning, some other discussion strategies are:

- Arranging the room for discussions
- Leading discussions
- Focusing discussions
- Keeping discussions concise
- Relating to the students' conceptual stage
- Choosing topics that relate to children's developmental preferences
- Promoting confidence in thinking and talking about art

Arranging the Room for Art Discussions

The environment, the climate for viewing the artwork, can help or hinder discussions. Arrange the seating, if possible, to provide each child with an up-front advantage. Rearranging the chairs into a circle or seating the children on the floor so they can see the reproduction up close, is often recommended. Invite the children to come up to the displayed art object to point out the area or detail they wish to discuss. A shy child might be asked to come up front and stand and hold the reproduction. A spotlight on the reproduction can help hold students'

attention. Avoid reproductions that are too small for class viewing purposes; these can be used instead for small group discussions.

Leading Discussions

Discussion-leading skill is essential to elicit contributions by many students. Leading discussions can be difficult, especially in large classes and classes containing students with behavioral problems. Some will want to monopolize the discussion, interrupting each other and talking over each other. Others talk so quietly that they cannot be heard and, by the softness and slowness of their speech, invite interruptions. We must keep in check those verbose, verbally domineering students who, by monopolizing a discussion, exclude the participation of other quiet, shy students. It is sometimes necessary to respond to, or even to interrupt, a monopolizer by saying, "John is saying . . . and we'll discuss this aspect of the issue later, but now I'd like to know what some of the people who haven't yet shared their ideas have been thinking about the idea of . . . [whether muscles need to be drawn in order to make a good figure drawing]." Draw in the quiet, the timid, the shy. Through both planned and extemporaneous questioning, you can make art discussions a truly exciting and rewarding time for every child in your class. Make it a time not just to contemplate, but a time to interact dynamically with classmates and with the art object.

Focusing Discussions

A discussion can go awry if it is not kept clearly focused. Most teachers are aware that the majority of children enjoy talking avidly about their experiences and their reactions. There is no difficulty getting them to express themselves vocally about the art you show them. The main problem is to keep them on the subject, "on track." If the discussion appears unfocused to the students, too wide-ranging to be helpful to their thinking and acting, they will tune it out. Use your statements to keep the discussion on one central issue. Try not to let it diverge. For example, you might say, "This is a related idea, and an important one for us to discuss another day, but for today let's see if we can focus on the question of . . . ."

Be sure, however, to be open to the idea that curricula need not be imposed from above, but can arise spontaneously from the students. Avoid overdetermining the lesson. It builds students' autonomy and their feelings of empowerment when they are allowed to take control of some situations. They can handle material which has not been predetermined and prestructured.

Keeping Discussions Concise

Another goal is to keep the discussion concise. Stimulate the raising of issues, but stop the discussion before interest dissipates. Conciseness is important because so little time is allowed for art in the school schedule. Some students in art classes think of art time as "a time when they get to make things" and resent other activities that seem tangential. Keep your art discussions from being long-winded and boring. However, there are exceptional teachers who can keep large audiences of students vitally engrossed for over an hour analyzing and talking about just one reproduction.

Relating to the Students' Conceptual Stage

In motivating artistic expression, make sure that some of the historical artworks presented are appropriate for the children's conceptual and developmental stage (see Chapters 4 to 7). This does not mean that only pictures of scribbles should be shown to scribblers. However, it does mean that artworks in a range that the child is comfortable with should be presented. In this way you do not frighten the students into feeling inadequate, raising in their minds fears that their artwork will be woefully weak. Students shouldn't feel that the teacher's expectations are at an unattainable level. Using artworks that are visually and conceptually accessible can assist the student to see alternative and attainable solutions that they can implement in their work.

Artistic activity is a universal human attribute. Nothing in our society more effectively subverts and extinguishes artistic activity than the notion that the artistic product should be a copy of reality or of someone else's version of reality. For this reason, it is often best to show historical examples as reinforcement *after* a student has reached a new conceptual and visual stage.

Choosing Topics That Relate to Children's Developmental Preferences

In choosing reproductions and slides for study and appreciation, consider the natural preferences of the children. Paintings with realistic subject matter to which students can relate are usually more popular with the upper elementary age group. Subject matter is the primary

Cat and Kittens, ca. 1872 (11¾ × 13¾), anonymous, American. National Gallery of Art, Washington, D.C. Gift of Edgar William and Bernice Chrysler Garbisch.

Consider the children's natural preferences for picture study subjects. "What's wrong with this picture? Why is one kitten mad? In how many places do you see stripes? What does this picture tell us about what life was like over a century ago?"

factor in young children's preferences, and there are strong differences between boys' and girls' preferences. Negative attitudes are expressed toward abstract works and works showing objects they do not like, such as still lifes of dead fish and birds. Young children prefer single subjects; older children can think in terms of more complex groups.

After subject matter, the next most important factor in children's preferences is color. Works that abound in color and contrast are more appealing to primary-grade children. Older children prefer more tints and shades and subtle combinations. Middle-school students will respond to more complex art themes—to moody, muted colors and to abstract, nonobjective compositions. Whereas showing just one or a few pictures is better for elementary students, a variety of examples will usually be more effective for middle-school students, since this multiple approach provides opportunity to analyze contrasting styles and imagery.

Note that purposefully choosing nonpreferred artworks can evoke strong responses, which may lead to heated and stimulating discussions.

Promoting Confidence in Thinking and Talking about Art

Students should not be put on the defensive and made to feel that their verbalizations and artistic representations are incorrect. One goal of discussion is to give those students who have not yet grasped a concept (for example, realism) the "permission" to continue in their own intuitive way of artistic conceiving. ("How would you describe this 'different' quality that Jose's drawing has and how did his sun help give that feeling?")

Art discussions should serve as a broadening, rather than a restrictive "one right way" system. Discussion should be a bridge between thinking and acting. It should help to promote in the young artist a sense of integration and a feeling of self-worth as an artist. Bounce the discussion back and forth from "what we see" to "how we can make it." In this way the discussion can reciprocally stimulate both intellectual thought and artistic creativity.

Gamelike Educational Activities

While discussion is the major way to bring about art learning, a second way is through gamelike educational activities. While research shows games to be no more or less effective than traditional methods, students enjoy educational games as changes from the usual classroom routine. The game aspect should be easy and students should do a practice round first. Games may require working together in small groups or pairs, serving as a welcome relief to the usual lecture and discussion and individual seat work routines. However, students must understand the educational purposes behind the gamelike format, lest they feel they are wasting their time or "just playing." Following up with a discussion, or "debriefing session," is critical if students are to understand the new material they have studied.

Most art games use printed reproductions. A principal source is postcards from art museums and galleries, and the sorting and matching of these can be done even on a small desktop. Also, the National Art Education Association has published a series of inexpensive art reproductions. Magazine-page-sized reproductions can be gotten from used copies of many popular magazines and art magazines such as *Artnews* and *Art in America*. Commercial firms specializing in art reproductions and the National Gallery of Art have large-size reproductions (approximately 20 × 30 inches) which may be purchased on stiff paper or stiff cardboard, or framed (see Appendix E).

Using Sets of Art Postcards to Meet Art Objectives

Art history: Two types of art history objectives are those requiring sorting and those requiring matching. Working in small groups, the students will sort the cards into chronological order or will match or group together those of one art style, such as impressionism.

Aesthetics: For an aesthetic objective, students working in small groups will decide on which one artwork they might theoretically acquire for the school. The underlying instructional objective is that the students will discuss the differences between artistic and societal values in selecting artworks. A variation for older children is to have the students role-play that they are a group of judges from different occupations, for example, a museum director, a teacher, a student, a PTO president.

Art criticism: Students will describe similarities and differences between artworks depicted. Students will describe overall concepts which a group of cards have in common. Using cards sorted into prearranged sets, the learners will describe why one of the set doesn't belong. This can lead into a discussion of categories, themes, and art elements.

Art criticism: For an art criticism objective, students will hypothesize about the artist's intent. As the students enter the room, the teacher can give each student a card with an artist's name on it. The students must then find the reproduction done by "their" artist and tell the class "why" the artist painted the picture.

Art criticism: The student will identify and describe works by master artists. Commercial sets of art reproductions are available for playing an artistic version of Old Maids, or, alternatively, sets can be made up by the teacher. The task is for the student, through playing the game, to learn about an artist's personal style. ("Find all the Hokusais, the Romare Beardens, the pre-Columbian pieces, and the Georgia O'Keeffes.") (The teacher who is alert to the importance of multicultural pluralism will make the card sets reflective of ethnic diversity and include works by both male and female artists.) A Go Fish format can also be used, in which students must remember the physical location of works that go together and try to acquire sets. An advantage of these two games is that they can be played by pairs of students. Thus they fit easily into use in self-contained classrooms as changes of activity. They promote friendships, provide activities for students who have self-directed time, and can be used in classroom learning activity centers.

Above: Courtesy of W. Robert Nix, University of Georgia, Athens, Georgia. *Left:* Museum of Primitive Art, New York City.

Pictures of a mother and child or animal with young can motivate children's creative writing about their family experiences with the birth of a sibling or a pet giving birth.

Social studies: With teams of students from diverse backgrounds, discuss how the values of other cultures are shown in the artworks. Compare these values to those of the students' own culture.

Social skills: Groups of students will arrange the cards into a bulletin board display and write captions.

Level of Objectives

In both discussions and gamelike approaches, keep in mind the level of the instructional objective. Is mere identification the goal that is desired? A higher level of objective, synthesis, can be attained by students subsequently explaining in their own words what makes up an artist's special style. Always try to set some tasks in the upper levels. The order, from lower level to upper level, is:

1. Knowledge: recall facts
2. Comprehension: participate in a discussion
3. Application: apply abstract information in practical situations
4. Analysis: separate an entity into its parts
5. Synthesis: create a new whole from many parts as in developing a complex work of art
6. Evaluation: make judgments based on criteria

In this chapter, we have given an overview of the history and issues of art appreciation, described general strategies for leading art discussions, and listed some gamelike activities that promote talking about and learning about art. We proceed in the next two chapters to think about specific ways to teach art history, art criticism, and aesthetics.

Using Sets of Art Postcards for Correlation with Other Subjects

With the students working in small groups, the postcard sets can be used for integrating art activities with other subjects.

Creative writing: Groups of students will make up a story using all the cards in one set. Individual students will tell or write the parts of the story going with each reproduction.

Math: Groups of students will describe the geometric shapes shown in the art reproductions, for example, of domed architecture, pentagon shapes in Islamic architecture, and sculptures containing icosahedra.

Science: Students will divide up the art reproductions (depicting, for example, spiders, fish, mammals, microorganisms) into the taxonomic phyla of the animal and vegetable kingdoms.

Social studies: Groups of students will sort cards into continental origin of the cultures depicted and describe an unusual custom they know about that culture.

CHAPTER 16

Teaching Art History

Conducting Art History Discussions

Art history as discussed here refers not only to the discussion of artworks by masters and ancient civilizations. It also refers broadly to objects which cultures recognize as having value, and to art expression by artists of one's time and in one's community. Some examples of instructional objectives in art history are the following:

Compare the way you have depicted something, perhaps the design of clothing or a vehicle, with the way that two other artists in art history depicted that thing. Have you used or shown something that did not appear in artworks in certain past eras?

Describe works from art history and the humanities where the portrayal of a theme has changed or remained the same. For example, tell about different versions of the Tarzan, Superman, mad scientist, werewolf, vampire, or brute theme. Find examples of how women have been shown as Eve or Cinderella, beautiful innocent maidens, or witches.

Describe how symbolism has been used. For example, why was the ruler usually shown on his horse? What ideas does the theme of the dragon express?

Describe how different artists have given different meanings to the same themes.

Discuss how representations of a group of people, such as Native Americans, have been shown in art.

Describe why you think an artwork style was replaced by a different style. Describe world events that may have contributed to such changes in artistic representation. How does the art of an age say something about its character?

Describe changing and constant elements in an artist's work and relate this to changing and constant elements in your own art style.

When children talk about art, they grow not only in vocabulary describing visual phenomena but also in verbal sophistication. Stu-

dents are weaned away from relying solely on their ordinary speech and are helped to form a new art language. Verbal instruction using art exemplars helps students to categorize artworks. New words and phrases such as those in the following list become part of their expanding vocabulary.

Action painting	Dadaism	Magic realism
African classical art	Earthworks	Mobile
Art nouveau	Encaustic	Naive art
Assemblage	Feminist art movement	Op art
Bauhaus	Folk art	Painter's style
Caricature	Gallery installation	Painterly
Critic	Genre	Patron
Critique	Happening	Pop art
Cubism	Impressionism	Postmodern art

Art History Teaching Methods

Perhaps you just visited a museum or watched a television program about an artist and want to share your excitement with your students. This is the simplest way to make art history material interesting and relevant to your students—to be interested in the material yourself. For then your interest will be infectious. There are certain other specific strategies teachers have found useful for adding interest.

Presentations on an Artist's Life

One method, especially suitable for middle-school students who are beginning to look for adult role models, is to have students select an artist to research and role-play. Pretending to be the artist, (perhaps even dressing up like the artist), the student tells the class the artist's

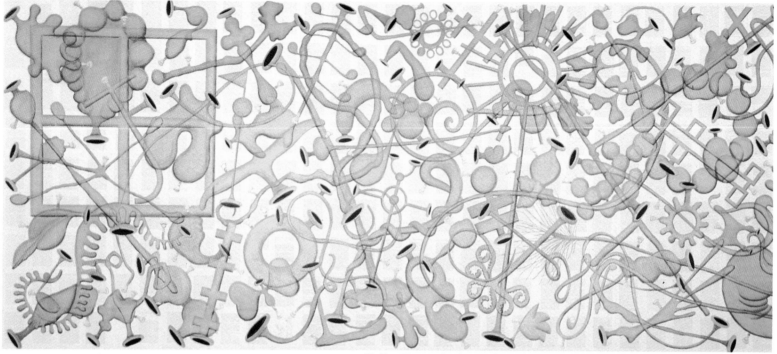

Hirshhorn Museum and Sculpture Garden, Smithsonian Institution, Museum Purchase, 1991. Photographer: Lee Stallworth.

Tim Rollins and K.O.S. (Kids of Survival). Amerika, Land of the Free. *A former public school art teacher, Rollins has created a student art workshop in one of New York City's roughest neighborhoods. The collaborative artworks he and his students create grace major museums throughout the world. A beauti-ful overall pattern is created by the mysterious abstract forms. They remind one of boxing gloves, trumpets, gears, and windows. What do the forms suggest to you?*

life story. Then the class asks the actor questions about what the artist did. What was the artist's personality like? What was the culture like? Where did the artist live? What tools did the artist use? How did people of the time treat the artist? What was the artist's intention in making the art? A related activity is to do an artwork in the style of the selected artist. The presentations can be videotaped and shared with other classes or at a PTO open house. Another situation can be an interview show of a small group of these artist-actors at a supposed exhibition opening or a panel discussion between the artists. One student acts as the emcee and interviews the participants; other students role-play critics and critique the pictures.

Correlating Art History and Studio Projects

Art making and art criticism, art history, and aesthetics are most successful and most meaningful when they complement each other in an orchestrated, coordinated endeavor. Children's intense, purposeful studio involvement should be related to richly planned art motivations that include art history examples. Then their critical faculties in appreciating and in creating art are mutually enhanced.

Teachers have added to children's insights regarding African and Native American art motifs through studio projects in mask making. Others have coordinated the study of Egyptian tomb friezes with the making of group murals. Others have introduced students to artists' diverse painting styles during studio work in figure and portrait painting. Every phase of world art through the centuries can be given immediacy in an art-studio environment. It can be the mosaics of Ravenna in Italy, the T'ang ceramics of China, the illuminated manuscripts of medieval Europe, the Benin bronzes from Africa, the marble sculptures from Greece, the ukiyo-e woodblock prints of Japan, or the mobiles of Alexander Calder. Many teachers of art have imaginatively combined studio and art history to provide the child with a growing treasury of knowledge about art, artists, art styles, and the permeating influence of art in our everyday lives.

To ensure success in this venture, the teacher should have access to color reproductions, filmstrips, and color slides. If that is not possible, most public libraries have folio-size "coffee table" art books containing pictures large enough to show to groups. Sets of large reproductions can be ordered by the school librarian for use by the entire faculty. Some commercial sources of art visual aids are listed in Appendix E. Resourceful teachers have collected and organized their own extensive picture and color-slide files. The following table lists some familiar art education studio projects along with the names of a few artists whose works might serve as exemplars.

Suggested Art Project	Correlative Art Appreciation
Drawing-painting: Helping at home or school	Genre paintings of Jan Vermeer, Winslow Homer, Andrew Wyeth, Jean Chardin, Susanne Valadon, Grandma Moses, Benny Andrews, Grant Wood, Thomas Hart Benton, Laura Wheeler Waring, Lily Martin Spencer, Norman Rockwell, Jacob Lawrence, Horace Pippin
Drawing-painting: Portraits and self-portraits	Portraits by Hans Holbein, Domenico Ghirlandaio, Leonardo da Vinci, Elizabeth Vigee-Lebrun, Mary Cassatt, Andrew Wyeth, Andy Warhol, Chuck Close, Alice Neel; self-portraits by Vincent Van Gogh, Rembrandt van Rijn, Paul Gauguin, Max Beckman
Drawing-painting: Objects on a table, chair, or bench	Still lifes by Paul Cézanne, Clara Peeters, Margaret Angelica Peale, Odilon Redon, Georges Braque, Pablo Picasso, Jean Chardin, Juan Gris, William Harnett, Bernard Buffet, Janet Fish, Audrey Flack
Drawing-painting: The landscape or cityscape	Maurice Utrillo, John Constable, Paul Gauguin, Vincent Van Gogh, Raoul Dufy, Dong Kingman, Edward Hopper, Gabrielle Münter, Grant Wood, Georgia O'Keeffe, George Inness, Paul Cézanne, John Marin, Richard Estes, Robert Duncanson, Mattie Lou O'Kelley

Suggested Art Project	Correlative Art Appreciation
Drawing-painting: Fauna	Cave paintings at Lascaux and Altamira; Leonardo da Vinci, Jean Louis Gericault, Rembrandt van Rijn, Albrecht Dürer, Henri Rousseau, John James Audubon; Indian Moghul, American Indian, Chinese, and Japanese animal drawings
Drawing-painting: Flora	Georgia O'Keeffe, Maria Sibylle Merian, Lowell Nesbit
Drawing-painting: Figure composition	Pieter Brueghel, Edgar Degas, Käthe Kollwitz, Paul Gauguin, Henri Matisse, Mary Cassatt, Marie Laurencin, Pablo Picasso, Francisco Goya, Diego Velasquez, Rembrandt van Rijn, Angelica Kauffman, Paula Modersohn-Becker, Henry Tanner, Ben Shahn, Robert Gwathmey, Joseph Hirsch, George Bellows, Alice Neal, Jacob Lawrence, Clementine Hunter, Keith Haring
Drawing-painting: The abstract, the nonobjective, the surreal, op, pop, and fantasy	Piet Mondrian, Salvador Dali, Joan Miró, Joseph Albers, Victor Vasarely, Paul Jenkins, Mark Rothko, Georgia O'Keeffe, Ad Reinhart, Sonia Terk-Delaunay, Wassily Kandinsky, Mark Tobey, Arthur G. Dove, M. C. Escher, Frieda Kahlo, Sophie Taueber-Arp, Rene Magritte, Bridget Riley, Jackson Pollock, Frank Stella, Helen Frankenthaler, Tim Rollins and Kids of Survival
Printmaking: Collograph, plastic meat-tray print, linoleum block, glue-line-relief print, monoprint	Albrecht Dürer, Rembrandt van Rijn, Leonard Baskin, Mauricio Lasansky, Warren Colescott, William Hayter, Gabor Peterdi, Japanese ukiyo-e artists, Ando Hiroshige, Katsushika Hokusai, Kitagawa Utamaro
Mask design and construction	African ritual masks; masks of North Pacific Indians; masks from Melanesia, Malaysia, Mexico, Indonesia; Japanese Noh play and Bugaku masks; Chinese opera, Greek drama, and Mardi Gras masks
Photographs	Matthew Brady, Ansel Adams, Edward Weston, Gordon Parks, Margaret Bourke White, Dorothea Lange, Cindy Sherman, Sherry Levine

Suggested Art Project	Correlative Art Appreciation
Three-dimensional construction (and use of found materials)	Alexander Calder, David Smith, Lee Bontecou, Louise Nevelson, Pablo Picasso, Marisol Escobar, Edward Kienholz, Judy Chicago, Judy Pfaff
Sculpture in plaster block, soapstone, firebrick, balsa wood	Jean Arp, Henry Moore, Barbara Hepworth, Isamu Noguchi; Easter Island sculpture, North Pacific Indian totem poles
Collage: Varied subject matter	Georges Braque, Kurt Schwitters, Henri Matisse, Romare Bearden, Alexis Smith, Robert Raushenberg
Clay pots and containers	Korean Koryo period, ancient Greek vases and jars, Chinese Ming and pre-Columbian pottery, Japanese Jomon ceramics; Thai Sukothai period; Indian pueblo pottery; Peter Voulkos; Shoji Hamada
Clay figure modeling	Clay figures of Greek Tanagra style; Japanese Haniwa period; Mexican, Peruvian, and Guatemalan pre-Columbian ceramic sculpture

Cast bronze plaque, 1550–1650 A.D., Kingdom of Benin, Nigeria. The University Museum, University of Pennsylvania, Photo Malcolm Varon, NYC. © 1989, Malcolm Varon, 1989.

The artistic power of this African chief sculpture is magnified by the surrounding figures and their objects. Seen are his two lieutenants, his secretary, assistant with the spiral cone, his children, and the maces, shields, clothing, and headdresses of authority. Further power and richness are produced by symmetry and repetition. Patterns of dots, zig zags, circles, and interlocked forms add beauty.

CHAPTER 17

Teaching Art Criticism and Aesthetics

Conducting Art Criticism Discussions

Two other ways of building students' artistic awareness are through discussions in art criticism and aesthetics. In art criticism, a major goal is the ability to point to evidence in the work to support the students' interpretations. In the primary grades, encourage the children to ask questions about visual phenomena, to list special eye-catching items in the picture, and to decide what they like. In the upper grades, have students discuss criteria for judgment (realism and accepted methods for representation) and determine categories of works. Have them hypothesize about how else a picture might have been made or what alternate messages it might have conveyed. Encourage them to bring out questions about social significance.

A highly condensed summary of sequence of children's development from grades 1 to 8 is:

Personal preference → Realism → Expressive aspects

While visits to art galleries and museums are ideal, it is often more practical to bring art to the students. Use original art, if possible; if not, then use colorful reproductions, color slides, and book illustrations.

The purpose of art criticism in the schools is to develop appreciation and understanding. This purpose should not be confused with art criticism as it might take place in a college studio art course where the professor's objective is to judge and improve the students' artwork. Another helpful distinction for students to be aware of is the difference between portrayal criticism and persuasive criticism. Portrayal criticism helps the viewer to slow down and see what the work includes. It suggests there is no one "right way" to see an artwork, but instead several. In contrast, persuasive criticism (like some newspaper reviews) is judgmental and argues the worth of the work.

Three different approaches to art criticism and aesthetics used in schools are (1) art elements, (2) themes, and (3) cultures. The teacher's willingness to help students to look at their own and each other's culture is very important; some exemplars should reflect the community and cultural background of the class. Local artists and craftspeople can be invited to visit classes, demonstrate skills, and discuss what it is like to be an artist. Acknowledge the neglect which non-Western cultures have received. Cultures such as the African, Asian, and Native American have different ways of responding to art that are nonacademic and not part of the European tradition. People who have different cultural backgrounds can share their approaches with the class.

A Sequential Approach to Art Criticism

In schools, art criticism is usually done by having students study the features of an artwork in a sequential way, answering specific questions in order. The steps and questions listed below are often used. The teacher and students may not know precise answers, but what is important is that they go about searching for answers in a scholarly way, through inquiry. Even if the teacher knows little about a work—its medium, who made it, or when or where it was made—learning can take place as long as an attitude of inquiry prevails. When the minds of the students and teacher are applied as if in solving a mystery, successful analysis will occur.

Cirque, plate II, *Jazz*, 1947 (color stencil in gouache), Henri Matisse, 1864–1954. National Gallery of Art, Washington, D.C. Gift of Mr. and Mrs. Andrew S. Keck.

Wheelchair-bound for the last 13 years of his life, the French artist Henri Matisse was unable to paint and was prepared for death. Instead, he returned to making paper cutouts, a technique he had used decades earlier for stage decorations, and created some of the world's most life-affirming artwork. What do you see in this picture? How did the artist arrange colors and shapes to make a beautiful design?

Bicentennial School, Nashua, New Hampshire. Courtesy of Mary E. Swanson, Nashua, New Hampshire.

Athens, Georgia.

Having studied Matisse's cutouts, students can use cutouts in collage to gain an awareness of the power of positive and negative shape. **Left:** *Figures drawn in contour line and cutout depict a street fight at night. The abstractness of the collage medium makes it an excellent choice for such emotional themes.* **Right:**

Fifth-grade classmates modeled for these contour-drawn and cutout figures of individuals in athletic poses. Wallpaper was also introduced for pattern. Details such as hats, numerals, letters, and sports equipment were added last.

A Sequence for Art Criticism

1. Identifying the content or subject matter of the art	What things do you see in this picture?
2. Recognizing the technique or art medium	What art materials did the artist use and how were they used?
3. Identifying the compositional or design factors in the art and recognizing their importance	How did the artist tie the picture together?
4. Recognizing the unique, individual style of the artist	Why do we think this other picture might be made by the same artist?
5. Searching for the meaning of the art and inquiring into the artist's intent	What does the picture say to you?
6. Identifying the context	What do you think might have been going on in the world at this time?

Identifying the Content

Category 1, *identifying the content or subject matter of the art*, sets the stage for understanding a work of art. What does the viewer see: woman, child, dog, house, tree, vase of flowers? What event is being depicted: wedding, riot, sports event, fair, family reunion, rite of passage? Enthusiastic student participation usually develops when the subject matter is real or recognizable. Try to complete the inventory of what is perceived before going on to interpretation.

Identifying the Medium

Category 2, *recognizing the technique or art medium*, often proves challenging. There are so many new directions in contemporary visual expression other than painting per se. These include collage, montage, assemblage, etching, lithograph, collograph, mobile, light sculpture, site sculpture, or earthwork. Actual studio involvement by the children with the media, the techniques, and the artist's materials helps them to appreciate the artist's solutions.

Identifying Design Features

Category 3, *identifying the compositional or design factors in the art and recognizing their importance*, is one of the most enlightening tasks in the whole process. Detect the basic line structure, the main thrusts, the avenues into the composition, and the dominating and subordinating themes. Find the rhythms, balances, and contrasts of line, shape, value, color, pattern, and texture, and pinpoint those which unify the picture. All this can develop into a fascinating game of search and self-discovery, an art adventure wherein both students and teacher learn that the whole is indeed greater than the sum of its parts.

Identifying the Artist's Style

Category 4, *recognizing the unique, individual style of the artist*, is another intriguing and rewarding aspect of learning through art appreciation. When students, guided by a knowledgeable and imaginative teacher, achieve the critical and perceptual skills to identify the work of Michelangelo, Rembrandt van Rijn, Pablo Picasso, Louise Nevelson, Jacob Lawrence, and Joseph Beuys by recognizing their individual styles, they are on their way to a richer understanding and enjoyment of art's world of treasures.

Interpreting Intent

Category 5, *the search for the meaning of the art and thinking about the artist's intent*, is no doubt the most subjective phase of the cycle. There are many opportunities to influence and/or convince the students with the teacher's own judgments and prejudices about the meaning. If students merely parrot the teacher's views of art, children may not be able to relate the artwork to the aesthetic dimensions of their own lives. Avoid telling the students what *you* see in the art, what *you* feel about it, until they have had a chance to tell you what *they* see, what *they* feel. Children can spontaneously come up with ways to

---

A good way to begin thinking about a picture is to have students first describe what is seen. Seated on a tiny white-faced horse is a large human figure. Its hands are anxiously cupped together, its eyes are open very wide, and its lips are tightly drawn. It wears an unusual white costume. Also seen is an adjacent figure in a skirt and with a scarf on head, probably a woman, with head in hands, perhaps weeping. At their feet is a 1-year-old baby, with two upraised hands, and lying on the ground.

Espana, 1959 (color intaglio), Mauricio Lasansky (32 × 21 inches). Collection of the author.

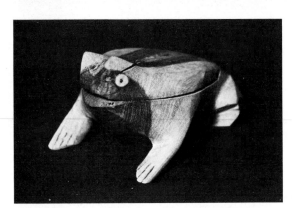

Photos courtesy of W. Robert Nix, University of Georgia, Athens, Georgia.

explain what they think paintings mean. You may not always agree with their analysis and judgment. However, don't force your opinions on them. The meaning the student finds may not be the artist's intent, but that does not invalidate the student's interpretive process.

As in the inductive method of science, let the students form hypotheses based upon the evidence they assemble. Allow the artists, the craftspeople, the architects, to speak for themselves through their art and their journals. For example, in a critique of the work of Vincent Van Gogh, introduce to them the letters the artist wrote to his brother Theo. Help the students gain a deeper understanding of how Van Gogh's painting related to his creative highs and his frustrating, disappointing lows. The general classroom teacher, who is charged with teaching interpretive writing, creative writing, and expressive writing, is in an even better position than the art specialist to have students write about artworks using metaphoric, expressive writing. What could be a better subject for such correlative writing than the most interesting visual objects on earth—artworks?

Understanding the Context

Along with the personal interpretation, examine the *context* (category 6) in which the work was made: What did the artist do to make a living? Where were power and domination coming from in the world at that time? What was the social, religious, and economic nature of the artist's world? The teacher can supply significant information, or, at this point, the students might use materials in an art learning center or in the library. In recent years a new emphasis on cultural relevance and an openness to many different interpretations has come about in part through developments in feminist art criticism and contemporary theories of art.

Discussing how the art medium is used is one way of understanding art. Students can compare how the theme of an animal is carried out in a variety of subtractive sculpture media. Clockwise, from top right, are a wood-pod monkey from Malaya; a cryptomeria rooster from Japan; an ivory elephant from India; a boxwood bird from Indonesia; a wood elephant from Africa; an ivory horse from China; and, in the center, a wooden frog from Mexico. Discuss how the carver achieved form. Did the medium present limitations, perhaps in the grain? How much detail is desirable or possible? Describe the main form from which the piece was carved ("like a barrel, like a rectangle with extra ears attached"). Also discuss how shapes are repeated and varied to present a unified and charming representation. Discuss, as well, its context, where was it made, and what that animal might mean in that society.

Conducting Discussions of Aesthetics

Discussing aesthetics is the third way of learning about art in discipline-based art education. As teachers, we want our students to think about what makes objects and phenomena artistic; this is what constitutes aesthetics. Children love to ask "why" questions. The questions "Why?" and "How do you know that?" are central to aesthetics. The most important teaching strategy in leading discussions of aesthetics is to encourage questioning. Essential to success is the ability to admit there are things we do not know. Most importantly, teachers must believe that students can gain something through being encouraged to question and to wonder about art ideas. Thomas Ewens (1990) said:

> Wonder is something which comes upon us, overwhelms us and suggests a kind of transcendence, out of the ordinary, the wonder-full, the extra-ordinary. It is a combination of the intellectual, the emotional, and the sensuous. It is the not-taken-for-granted. Our task is to protect the wonder of the young. The disciplines of thinking and artmaking grow out of and are nourished by this soil. Their roots are in wonder.

Some goals which many teachers want their students to achieve are the ability to:

- Speculate
- See implications
- Handle abstract ideas
- Use language for clear thinking about art
- Raise questions and make statements about aesthetics
- Present reasons in support of their positions and thus justify their judgments
- Listen to others' points of view and ask questions about the other students' ideas

Furthermore, aesthetics is not just about knowledge, it is also about feelings. Instructional objectives in the arena of feelings, or affect, are that the students will be able to tolerate uncertainty, to value questioning, to be curious, and to respect thoughtful disagreement.

Because aesthetics is so much a part of ordinary conversation, it can easily go unnoticed. Listen for such questions and comments as, "Why is that weird thing supposed to be art?" and "Ugh, gross." Naturally occurring instances of art criticism need to be allowed, so they can be transformed into significant discussions of aesthetics. On hearing students ask such questions and make such responses, we must learn to bite our tongues. We must not immediately answer, "Because

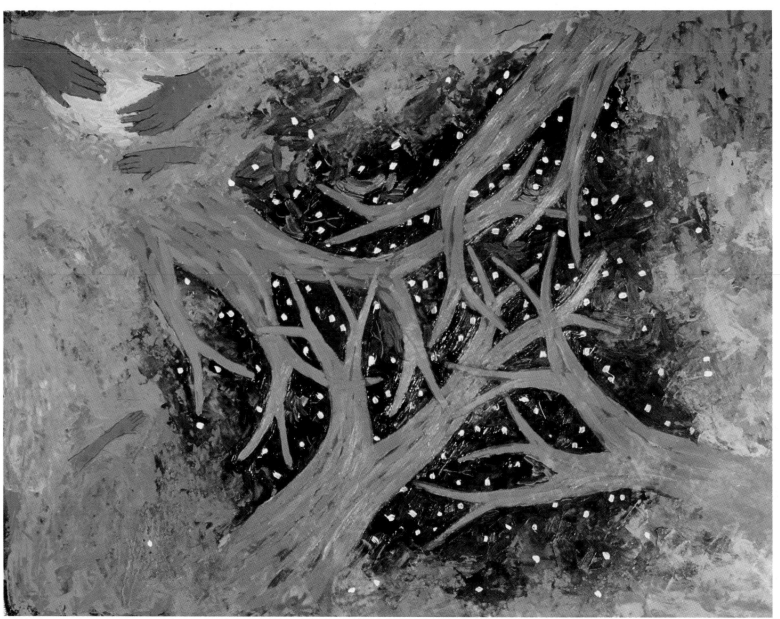

Untitled (36 × 24 inches). Private collection.

Wonder comes into one's mind contemplating the tornado-tossed trees against a starry night. Also, what could be the meaning of the red hands against a sun? This painting is by New York neo-expressionist painter Louisa Chase.

the paint is so wonderfully thick, because it shows deep emotion, because it's in the museum." Instead, ask questions back to the students, using the new questions as ways by which the students themselves can learn to come up with answers.

Say to them, "What makes you say that?" "Does everyone agree?" Model for the students the use of strategies in good reasoning. Help them to learn how to think logically about their statements. Logical extension is one way: "If that is true, then how can [cave art] be explained?" Another way is through counterargument: "Is this always the case? Can anyone think of an instance when this isn't true?" The teacher's role is not to indoctrinate students with one "right" view, or to inundate our students with information. This would defeat the purpose of aesthetic inquiry, its concern with contested issues. Our challenge is to promote critical thinking.

Social studies can be combined with aesthetics. Aesthetic questioning can be used as a vehicle for social inquiry. Students can conduct interviews investigating issues of art in their neighborhoods. For example, if a new civic building is built or a public sculpture is placed in town, students can poll family and neighbors concerning its aesthetic merits.

A project which combines aesthetics, language arts, and social studies is to have the students write an oral history of a family member, relative, or neighbor who does arts or crafts. The class as a group can then discuss the meaning which the art making and art objects have for the creator and for the community. Because children often can't figure out why people go to the trouble to make artworks, this investigation helps them realize how important art is in peoples' lives.

Aesthetics and art criticism tend to blend together; however, a helpful distinction to keep in mind is that aesthetics focuses on the ideas behind the artwork, not on the artwork itself (which is the subject of art criticism). However, for starting aesthetic discussions, it is useful to have around the room or on display above the chalkboard some art reproductions which can be used as references. Ask the students if any one of the pictures has raised any questions in their minds. The most obvious beginning is the open question, "What do you think about this picture?" Another good way to begin a discussion of aesthetics is by asking, "What's wrong with this picture?" since this presumes ideas about right and wrong. Still another way of generating discussion is for students to select shocking art or ugly art—anything out of the ordinary—and then to defend their selections. Topics and questions such as those in the table on pages 156 and 157 can be brought up matter-of-factly when they arise as a part of an ongoing classroom discussion.

Private collection.

Questions can be raised as to whether, in showing the figure, correct proportions and shading should be used to depict muscles. The direct expression of the African-American folk artist Mose Tolliver is shown here. His painting Black Jesus (20 × 12 inches) defies certain "expected" artistic conventions. Is realism always better? Is a balance between naiveté and realism desirable?

Topic	Aesthetic Question
Accident in design	Can a picture that looks like the artist just threw paint around be called good art?
Advertising art	Should art be used to make people want to buy things they don't really need?
Anatomical accuracy	Is art better when figures depict muscles rather than sausage-looking arms? Are cave paintings with stick figures any good?
Art's role in life	Is art work or play?
Artist's intention	If someone gets a different idea or meaning from your picture, does that mean that your art isn't as good? Is it better if the person knows exactly what you wanted to say?
Artist's involvement	Can art be made by just calling up a factory and saying "make me a red metal cube 6 feet square?" Does the artist need to be directly involved in actually making it?
Art critics	If experts say something is good or bad, should we believe them?
Art institutions	Does putting something into a museum make it art? If an artwork isn't in a museum, does that mean it isn't art?
Art support by government	Should the government give money for art that some people think is bad?
Clarity and metaphor	When you see an artwork and you can't put into words exactly what the artist was saying, does that make it better or worse?
Commercial design	Can objects like bicycles and T-shirts and fancy dress gowns be called art?
Disabilities	What if a person is color-blind and uses colors nonrealistically and makes a good piece of art, can it still be called art even though the person couldn't see it right?
Economic validity	Because someone spends a lot of money for a piece of art does that mean it is always good art? If no one spends any money for a piece of art, does that mean it is not art?
Education	Are artists born or made? Does art that looks like little kids made it mean that it isn't good art? Do people who go to school a long time usually make better art than people who don't go to school much?

Discussions of aesthetics might concern whether the medium that is used should look like itself or whether it should look like things. Can beauty in painting be created by using tools other than paint brushes? Is beauty always desired? What is beauty? If realism isn't most important, what is? Here, James Herbert, a professor of painting at the University of Georgia, employs rubber-gloved-encased hands to apply paint to his mural-sized canvas.

Topic	Aesthetic Question
Function	What good is art, after all? If art is used for bad purposes, is it still good art?
Gender	Why aren't there more famous women artists? Why are women usually represented as helpers and as just waiting around?
Human art	Can monkeys make art?

Topic	Aesthetic Question
Human endeavor	Why do people bother to make art when they could just relax and enjoy life instead of working so hard to make something people probably aren't going to like much anyway?
Individual authorship	Is it really art if several people make it instead of just one person?
Judgment	Does an artwork mean just whatever anyone says it means or are there right and wrong answers?
Mental and emotional functioning	Can people who have mental or emotional problems make good art even if it shows an upset world? Do people have to be sort of crazy to make art that has a special weird quality?
Quality and intent	Can you name some things that are bad art? What is the difference between things that are bad art and things that aren't supposed to be art?
Realism	Can a piece of art still be called good art even if the objects in it aren't drawn so they look like they are in realistic three dimensions?
Realistic depiction of nature	Can a picture be good if the sky doesn't touch the ground?
Scale	Are buildings or pictures that are big usually better art than those that are little?
Source and object	Are real rainbows art? Are wasps' nests art?
Spontaneity	Are pictures that took a long time to make usually better than pictures that were done very fast?
Technology	Can art made with machines be called art? If a camera or computer makes an artwork, can it be called art?
Text	Can art be just some words on a piece of paper or canvas or a light-emitting screen? Why or why not?
Time and effort	Can junky, carelessly made stuff that looks like someone just brought in a bunch of junk be called art?
Ugliness	Is art supposed to be only about beauty? Can it also be about ugliness?

Remember that discussions of aesthetics can use the students' everyday language. The students need not use special terminology. Discussion of aesthetics is not something foreign to art teaching but rather central to it. Good teachers of art have always have done it.

Art Criticism at Home

Parents may be at a loss concerning what to do with their child's artwork when it is brought home. Some parents feel compelled to criticize their child's art: "You're just like me–can't even draw a straight line." Of course, negative assessment is not the kind of art criticism we wish to promote. A brief letter to parents sent home along with the first artworks of the year can suggest ways for talking with their child about the works. It can describe what will be taught in art history, art criticism, and aesthetics. This is a good way to connect the student's art production and art criticism abilities. Suggest ways to build confidence through displaying the works. Suggest ways that the child's art can serve as a vehicle for generating family dinner table discussions, and ways that the child's opinions about issues of aesthetics can lead to the family's discussing such ideas. Let the parents know what your art program goals are so they can help build their child's interest in art. Here is a sample letter:

Dear Parents and Guardians:

This letter is being sent home, along with one of your child's first art pieces done this year, to tell you something about our art program.

This year we will be discussing what makes a good picture. We will talk about whether looking real is the only thing that makes a picture good, and how friends and neighbors make art. We will be studying art history masterpieces, especially Egyptian art. A major way you can help foster your child's interest is through visits to museums and through helping your child to participate in enrichment classes. Weekend art museum hours at the Quinlan Art Center (548-2314) are Saturdays 9-3 and Sundays 1-5, and it has Family Art Days four times a year. The Recreation Department at Lyndon House Art Center (546-9968) has children's art classes on weekdays 3:30 to 5:00.

Research has shown that it is helpful for the child to have a place for art materials at home and a quiet place in which to make art. Collections, artwork, and posters artistically arranged in a child's bedroom stimulates interest in art. When adults have their own artistic and cultural hobbies, involving the child spurs the child's interest.

During the course of the year, we will be sending home with your child about eight art projects, including a still life, a group of figures in motion, a portrait of a classmate, an oil pastel of a farm scene, a computer art design, and a clay castle.

If you want to talk with me about your child's growth in art, or if you have access to human resources or art materials which could be used in our school art program, please call me at 546-9987 between 2 and 4 or at home, 543-7654. I hope that I will meet you soon at a PTO meeting (the last Wednesday of each month, 7 to 8 p.m.) where you will have the chance to see more of our class's artwork.

Students might sort art reproductions into chronological order or match those of similar cultures and describe similarities and differences among them. **Top:** *Ashura, Buddhist deity, eighth century, dry lacquer, Kofukuji Temple, Nara, Japan.* **Bottom:** *The Calfbearer, ca. 560 B.C., Greek, stone.*

Photo A courtesy of David Hodge, Oshkosh, Wisconsin. Photos B, C, E, and G courtesy of Mary Sayer Hammond, Fairfax, Virginia.

CHAPTER 18

Drawing

Overview of Art Production

Mounting evidence, exemplified and corroborated by contemporary child art creations such as illustrated herein, suggests that we have been underestimating children's capabilities. In many instances, we have not even begun to tap their true potential for "thinking" and "problem solving" through art media. A host of art projects and techniques in both two and three dimensions recommended for a qualitative art program in elementary and middle schools is described in the ensuing pages.

These chapters should prove most helpful to those classroom teachers who themselves may be untaught in the basic art disciplines of drawing, painting, printmaking, collage, and sculpture. The lessons described will also help art specialists who are searching for new dimensions and challenges in school art programming. The projects and their documentation are the result of many years of in-depth teaching by dedicated and knowledgeable instructors of both elementary and middle-school art. This has entailed continuing motivational experimentation, media exploration, process and product evaluation, and continuing research in qualitative art practices in schools around the world.

The art program at all levels should be planned for in-depth involvement and sequential growth. An in-depth method may not be as popular as a smorgasbord of quick, unrelated projects, but it will in the long run produce greater gains as students come up with their own ideas and create art of the highest quality.

The following descriptions of art projects include motivational possibilities, clarify complex art techniques, offer solutions for organizational and supply problems, and suggest evaluational criteria. In no instance is the implication intended, nor is the reader to assume, that the projects and processes described herein are the only possible choices. For, of course, the best lessons are those which come from the teacher's heart and soul. This deep belief, informed by the needs of the class and in combination with recommended art education practices, results in the best lessons. However, the projects described in the following chapters have been tried and found highly successful in situations typical of today's elementary and middle schools—in classrooms filled with eager, bright, boisterous, fidgety, dreamy, energetic, inquisitive, and, sometimes, apathetic students.

Three Kinds of Drawing

Elementary-school children should be drawing every day. A drawing curriculum should address not just one way of drawing, but all three families of the world of visual art objects: depictions, patterns, maps. This chapter will mainly address the first, realistic depictions that are usually thought of as "children's art,"—the creation of drawings and paintings from nature and life.

The second family, patterns and design, consists of creative play with shapes and spacing. This is usually thought of as design rather than drawing. Design receives more emphasis in later sections of this book, those about architecture, mosaics, printmaking, clay, and sculpture. However, designing and creating patterns are also important in making drawings and paintings. The doodles one makes while on the telephone represent this kind of play with shapes and spacing. A design approach using shapes, lines, and blocks was central in the Froebel kindergarten method, which influenced Frank Lloyd Wright's architecture so profoundly. It was also central in the teaching at a famous German design school, the Bauhaus. Because design is based

Courtesy of David Hodge, Oshkosh, Wisconsin.

The contour-line technique is perhaps the most viable and successful drawing method for upper-elementary-grade and middle-school youngsters. Suggest that the students draw in a soft-lead pencil slowly and deliberately. Urge them to look intently at the object they are drawing. The figure above is by a middle-school student.

on intuitive balance and measure, it lends itself well to correlational activities with mathematics, architecture, and engineering.

The third family of the world of visual objects consists of maps, which are visual representations of what one knows rather than what one sees. Conception, not perception, is here the focus. The problem of communicating an idea through a map is not governed by criteria of photographic realism. Assignments can be to map the events of one's daily life, how a pumpkin grows, how one's insides function, where the food we eat comes from. Children can make a map of their neighborhood, or show the cycle of evaporation and rain. Mapping helps students conceptualize the relationships among the ideas they have in their minds. ("Using the international travel signs and symbols, show how you get home from school.") The student uses graphic equivalents to represent objects and functions. Mapping lends itself to correlation with science. This type of "visual thinking" is embodied in such conceptual artworks as Alice Aycock's piece on cloud dispersion and Maria Merz's artwork based on Fibonacci series. Some other drawing activities which promote flexible visual thinking are drawing something from a nonhuman point of view, such as an ant's-eye or a bird's-eye view.

When children of preschool age draw their families, their drawings are like maps in that they draw what they know, not what they see. Similar visual representation of knowledge is found in works by folk artists and native artists, who do not feel so constrained by demands for realism. Yet this kind of drawing is unfortunately too often discouraged by some teachers who set up perceptual realism as a standard for artistic excellence. An example of a young child's "thought representation" not meeting a teacher's criteria for perceptual realism occurred when the sculptor Henry Moore was in primary school. He felt crushed when his teacher criticized him for drawing feet pointing downward, rather than realistically pointing sideways. The solution is not for teachers to be laissez-faire, but instead for teachers, especially of young children, to foster both ways of representation, perceptual and conceptual. For, in a class, some will draw what they know, others will draw what they see, and most will use a combination.

Figure Drawing

What skills and techniques in figure drawing should be introduced and developed in elementary- and middle-school art programs? What should teachers say to the child regarding the delineation of the fig-

ure? When, if ever, should the relative proportions of the human figure be identified and emphasized? The strategy most often proposed, unfortunately, is a laissez-faire placebo, "Let the children alone. They will find their own solutions." This injunction admittedly provides the teacher with a face-saving excuse if the results are less than satisfactory. However, it is hardly the kind of advice given to teachers of subject areas such as math, reading, and language. Through lack of guidance, students fail to meet their potential in drawing and painting the human figure. Instant art and gimmicky shortcuts, like cutting and pasting photographs, keep students from developing basic skills of creative self-expression.

If teachers want the students to grow in their representation of the figure, they must provide learning experiences and practice sessions for such growth. Direct the students' attention to details. Extend the child's frame of reference, with statements, for example, such as, "Show us how your face looked when you were in the dentist's chair." Children want to be able to draw well. Students of all ages feel that the level of realistic representation is the most important criterion in determining the quality of each other's artworks.

Fortunately, there are some avenues a teacher can pursue to help children develop confidence in life drawing. Teachers can ensure more intense awareness of the human figure and its characteristics by using posed models at every grade level. The delineation of the figure in even the youngest child's drawings does not spring forth from a vacuum. It is the result of the varied encounters the learner has had in perceiving and conceptualizing the human figure, both in and out of school, through books, comics, television, and peers' art. Sadly, the drawings of most nonartistic and artistically untaught adults are no better than those of preadolescents. They first draw a large head, then ill-defined facial features. Hands and feet are often not visible, the body is segmented, and the picture shows an overall lack of organization. Too many students graduate from school with a sense of inferiority about how they draw. Teachers can help them to acquire or maintain confidence in their ability to draw.

Before the students actually begin the drawing, a warmup session is recommended. Motivating, leading questions should be proposed. What action is the model performing? What is the model wear-

One art project enthusiastically undertaken by schoolchildren around the world is the radiation design illustrated on this page. Inspired by radial wonders in nature—star, sun, flower, and snowflake—youngsters create their own radiating compositions. No two designs will be alike.

Courtesy of Jimmy Morris, Athens, Georgia, and Mary Sayer Hammond, Fairfax, Virginia.

Most children delight in creating nonobjective, abstract, free-form designs. The teacher can facilitate their involvement by suggesting imaginative painting themes such as "explosion in a paint factory," "war of the planets," and "fourth of July fireworks." This intermediate-elementary-grade child's work shows the advantages of tempera. More than any other art medium, tempera painting provides youngsters with the opportunity to use color boldly, expressively, and imaginatively.

ing? What portion of the model do you see from your drawing station? How large is the model's head in comparison to the body? How big are the hands? Ask students to place one hand over their own faces to realize its size. How large are the feet? They must be big enough to keep the model balanced. Where is the model's arm the biggest—at the shoulders, elbows, or wrists? Where is the model's leg the biggest—at the ankle, knee, or hips? Where does the body, neck, leg, and arm bend? How wide can the feet stretch apart? How high can the arms reach above the head? How far can the body turn around while standing in one position? How far does the arm reach when held at the side?

As the students draw, encourage them to look at the model constantly, carefully, intently—tell them to get their eyes full! Caution them against rushing through their drawing, scribbling, or making hasty, random, meaningless lines. Remind them always to look first and then draw. Encourage making the figure large, filling the page with it. Then there will be space to enrich it with many details, many individual characteristics. See, for example, the illustrated full-figure

self-portraits. In general, it is helpful for children to begin their drawing of a figure with the head at the top of the page.

In drawing figures, the size of the head generally determines the size of the figure. If the students draw the head too small, the body won't fill the page. If they draw the head too large, they will not be able to fit the whole body on the page. Children in the primary grades often draw a three-heads-high figure, like the *Peanuts* cartoon character Charlie Brown, and minimize the rest of the body to fit it on the page. Others will draw tiny heads and stretch the legs to reach the bottom of the page. In both cases, the results should not be discouraged, for the drawings capture the child's development at a moment of special charm.

Because many teachers believe they lack the expertise to guide children in figure-drawing techniques, they settle for what the students can accomplish on their own. The children should get help, but the wrong kind of direction is not the answer either. Formulas such as stick or sausage figures and face proportions measured by rulers can create a stultifying dependence on stereotypes. The best instruction emphasizes heightened observation.

Adult artists pay careful attention to contours and how planes are implied, and as you teach your class, you can point out these

Encourage both ways of representation, what is conceived in the mind and how it appears. This beautifully detailed drawing of a tree was created by a second-grade youngster from Saga Prefecture, Japan.

Courtesy of David Hodge, Oshkosh, Wisconsin.

A middle-school life drawing class in action. Notice that the tables were arranged to make a unified drawing area where the model can be viewed easily by all the students. Paper size for sketching was 18 × 24 inches. Tools for drawing included sharpened dowel sticks and twigs dipped in India ink containers. If several drawings are planned, the class model, as well as the position of the model, should be changed so students sketching are afforded a variety of views.

Danielsville, Georgia. Courtesy of Mary Sayer Hammond, Fairfax, Virginia.

features to your students. As children learn to draw, first they use outlines that do not suggest form. This is followed by strong interior contour lines overlapping each other. Later there is some implying of form through planes, and still later, children begin to join interior lines with outlines. In older grades, teach contour line drawing by discussing how the line of an interior edge becomes visible and then joins the exterior silhouette. As it rounds the form, it becomes hidden. In the upper grades, talk about planes—the plane of the front of the body, the plane of the head, or the plane of the box. Show how the plane is revealed by its edges. You will be pleased at some of your students' ability to suggest planes in space.

Figure drawing, like all drawing from life, teaches the child to be observant in many ways. Very quickly the perceptually aware students notice and draw embellishing details, such as belts, ribbons, shoelaces, buttons, necklaces, earrings, bracelets, wristwatches, pockets, collars, cuffs, wrinkles, zippers, pleats, eyeglasses, teeth braces, hair combs, and clothing patterns such as stripes, checks, florals, and plaids.

An alternative approach to figure drawing does not use a model but instead relies upon the representational devices of comics and TV cartoons. Some young people's interest in drawing is triggered by comic book illustration techniques: a series of scenes, thought balloons, speed lines, star-and-lightning-bolt symbols of violence, and strongly contrasting effects of light on muscles.

When children draw their classmates, be prepared for the occasional self-conscious titter or embarrassed laughter. Emphasize how we are all learning to see. Show examples such as Jean Dubuffet's *art brut* drawings to show that realism is not the sole criterion of art. Be understanding when a student does not want to model for the class (due perhaps to embarrassment about appearance or clothing), for there are always other volunteers.

Students, especially in upper grades, can later use their linear figure drawings in a painting, collage, print, or mural. However, the line drawings themselves often have a validity, presence, and charm of their own. Subject-matter themes such as playing ball, riding a bike, flying a kite, brushing teeth, holding a pet, playing a musical instrument, holding a bouquet, cheerleading, skipping rope, ballet dancing,

The vibrant colors of oil pastel were skillfully employed to enhance the composition. A real motorcycle was brought to the middle school art room to make the drawing more true to life.

Courtesy of Baiba Kuntz, Glencoe, Illinois.

Left: How marvelously observed are the details, such as eyelets and wrist-bands and folds in clothing and cheekbones. See how the pattern changes in the falling socks. A first-grade child did this! Have high expectations and your students will rise to meet those expectations. ***Above:*** *Many students are highly impressed by the ability of cartoon superhero artists to depict an exaggerated play of light and dark on exaggerated muscles. Some students, like this eighth grader, seek to emulate this "chiaroscuro" style and foreshortening. Use a spotlight or place the costumed model close by the window to encourage seeing shadows.*

Courtesy of David Hodge, Oshkosh, Wisconsin.

Rich visual stimulation is extremely important for students to create quality artwork. Many teachers build an ever-changing still-life environment in their classrooms as a challenging and continuing motivational resource. Here a young adolescent is attired in goggles, snowflake patterned sweater, striped pants, and high boots. He models against intriguing antique Americana artifacts.

playing football, basketball, tennis, on the swing, setting the table, twirling a Hula Hoop, and lifting barbells lend themselves to space-filling compositions. Some other figure-drawing strategies are:

Pose a student in a colorful costume (clown, cowboy, dancer) or sports uniform. So everyone has a clear view of the model, pose the model on a table or counter top.

Pose the model in the center of a circle of sketching classmates affording each child a different view. For an overlapping, multifigure composition, change both the action and the direction of the model on later poses.

Introduce new drawing and sketching tools. Try free-flowing felt-tip markers, small watercolor brushes, Q-Tips, eyedroppers, turkey feathers, twigs and balsa woodsticks sharpened at one end as ink applicators, as well as charcoal and conté crayon.

Pose the student model against a sheet of cardboard, plywood, or Masonite approximately 4 by 8 feet—in any case slightly larger than the model. This will help the students relate the posed figure to the boundaries of their paper. For additional interest, decorate the board with drapery, fishnet, or colorful posters.

Consider having the model wear items of ethnic costume and using similar ethnic designs of patterned cloths in the background, thus opening up opportunities for social studies correlation.

Demonstrate new techniques and directions in drawing the figure: contour, gesture, scribble, and mass methods. Following Henri Matisse's example in his famous paper cutouts, have students try cutting the figure out of construction paper without first making a preliminary drawing.

Use a pose with more than one student taking part. The figures might be socially interacting, such as one handing something to the other, or one helping another put on a coat. Stage the models with a related still-life arrangement in the background.

Challenge the students to use their imaginations. Let the action or stance of the model trigger a fantastic or legendary figure they can capture in line. Fill in the background with ideas from the imagination and re-membered experiences.

Assign different class members to take 5- or 10-minute turns posing in various sports actions. Suggest that the students overlap the figures as they draw them on their paper.

Vary the size of the paper the students use for drawing or sketching. Try a 9- × 18-inch or 12- × 24-inch sheet for a standing figure, or use a long, wide paper for a group of figures. Challenge them to fill the page.

If there is sufficient space in your room, have the students use large 24- × 36-inch paper with wide felt-nib markers, giant chunk crayons, or big brushes.

Introduce a variety of papers: plain newsprint, cream or gray manila, recycled papers, assorted-color construction paper, computer printout pages, classified ad sheets from newspapers. Newspapers may donate the ends of newspaper rolls, and these are useful for large drawings.

Older students might benefit from using resources such as a real skeleton, a department-store mannequin, or a life-size medical chart of the body muscle structure.

For action or gesture drawing that requires a loose and free approach, the students should hold the crayon, pen, pencil, charcoal, or chalk horizontally as they sketch, rather than in the tight, upright manner used in writing.

Inexpensive, lightweight drawing boards, excellent for field trips, can be constructed out of heavyweight chipboard, hardboard, or Masonite, about 18 × 24 inches, with the edges protected with masking tape. During the drawing sessions, these boards can be propped against a table or desk, and they give the students a better working position from which to capture details.

Portrait and Self-Portrait Drawings

The self-portrait or portrait of a classmate should be on the agenda of every school art program. What more effective and immediate subjects for expressive drawings in all grades than the children themselves? Children of all school ages like to draw the figure. Only a few 6-year-olds can draw reasonably correct proportions, but this increases to over half by 14 years of age. A small number of 12-year-olds can draw true to appearance.

If possible, discourage the students from doing the typical portrait stereotype: the symmetrical frontal pose with arms stiffly at the side. Instead, suggest using the arms and hands to create contrasting directions in the composition. Add interest and relevance with uniforms, costumes, and a variety of headware and assorted objects to hold. Encourage three-quarter or full-profile views. Some suggested poses are:

- Arms folded above the head or akimbo
- Straddling a chair with head resting on folded arms
- Holding a musical instrument, sports equipment, an open umbrella, a bouquet of flowers, or a pet
- Putting on a hat, combing or brushing hair, applying makeup, or using a hand mirror

---

Top: *In the center of the room, a standing girl and seated boy pose on a table. The table contains objects to break up space.* **Middle:** *On a table, three girls pose as if holding kites. (Notice also the beautifully organized, stimulating classroom environment!)* **Bottom:** *With stiff boards to back the drawing paper, peers draw each other in small groups.*

The background adds immeasurably to the composition: a foliage arrangement, a multipaned window, a giant travel poster, a folding screen. The teacher might encourage the students to add features to the background drawn from memory and imagination, for example, "my interests" or "something I care about."

Stereotyped portraiture is usually the result of hasty, superficial observation. Urge the students to look intently at the model, whether it be their own image in a mirror or classmates posing for them, and to pay close attention to unique characteristics. To encourage self-acceptance in self-portraiture, show portraits of famous women and men and discuss their widely dissimilar, far-from-perfect features. Discuss different shapes of the head. Call attention to the hairline, how the hair follows the contour of the head. No scribbles allowed! Discuss the shape of the ears (tell them to feel their ears) and their junction to the head. Discuss ways of delineating the nose; show drawings by Pablo Picasso and Ben Shahn. Use a rich motivation of color slides or reproductions showing different portraiture styles from a variety of times and cultures. Show how to draw the lips as two subtly differing forms, and the eyelids so important as complementary features to the eyes. Bring out the astonishing fact that no two people, no two faces, are alike. Furthermore, explain that even the two sides of the same person's face are not alike.

For upper-elementary- and middle-school students, blind contour drawing is a good way to get students to try to capture the spirit or character of the subject rather than strive for absolute realism. In *blind contour drawing*, the students look intently at the subject but not at their paper as they draw. If the students become concerned that their drawing does not look like the posed model, tell them that the aim of expressive portraiture is not to achieve a photographic likeness. Remind them that the same model drawn by various artists will look different in each rendition.

Although many of the suggestions on portraiture offered here are more applicable to upper-elementary-school or middle-school students, wise teachers will be able to adapt the recommendations to benefit younger children as well.

Drawing the Landscape or Cityscape

Although very young children in the primary grades enjoy drawing simple themes and single objects such as a butterfly, bird, pet, themselves, a classmate, or a house, maturing students will respond to the challenge of the complex composition: the still life, the landscape, and

Courtesy International Children's Art Collection, Illinois State University, Normal, Illinois.

The most important and architecturally distinguished building in the town makes a good subject. It is of value both for the study of drawing and of architecture, as in this Colombian 13-year-old's drawing.

the cityscape. In the upper elementary grades and middle school they are interested in outdoor sketching and the excitement of field trips. The busy and infinitely varied world beckons and unfolds at their doorsteps. They are fascinated by:

Nearby building construction
The colorful and crowded street of shops
The county fair or park bandstand
The boat marina or harbor with its ships
The highway interchange
The factories and foundries
The bus, train, and airport terminals
The challenging perspective down an alleyway
The giant city skyscrapers
The cluster of farm buildings on a country road
The community's elaborate architecture
The view from a bedroom or classroom window
The amusement parks
The gas station

These sites, as well as imagined cities of the future, can become the inspiration for their sketches, compositions, paintings, prints, and collages. A variety of media can be used for field-trip sketching. These

How sensitively observed, drawn, and delineated is this charmingly complex neighborhood scene viewed from a school window. Notice how the free-form preliminary washes tie the composition together and how the overlapping trees create a subtle depth in space. Notice, too, the variety employed in the lines, shapes, and positions of the buildings, the windows, and the roofs. Observe how the houses and trees terminating at the paper's edge create avenues leading the viewer into the composition. Brush, ink, and watercolors on white drawing paper, actual size. Grade 9, Dubuque, Iowa.*

include pencil, chalk (school chalk is recommended for sketches and preliminary drawings on colored construction-paper backgrounds), charcoal, crayon, felt-nib or nylon-tip marker, conté crayon, even a stick dipped in ink (depending on the maturity of the students).

A majority of children on a field trip draw with enthusiasm and confidence. However, some will besiege the teacher with perplexing questions such as: "What should I draw first?" "Where should I start on the paper?" "Must I put everything in my picture?" Sometimes the complex view overwhelms them. Often the spatial and perspective problems confuse them. Remind the students that they will be creating an entirely new aesthetic unity out of the vast conglomeration of visual stimuli. One recommendation for successful landscape and cityscape drawing is to use a light pencil or chalk sketch to establish the basic shapes and general outline. Values and details can be added later.

Another strategy, especially recommended when the view is complex, is to have the students begin by drawing the shape in the center of the site (a doorway, window, telephone pole, tree) as completely as they can. Then have them proceed to draw the shape to the right and left of it, above and below it, and so on, until they fill their paper to the border. They will find and discover that incomplete shapes touching the paper's edge will create line avenues leading into their compositions. Encourage them to enrich their drawings, adding details, patterns, and textural effects.

Problems that students have defining distance in space can often be clarified by an understanding and use of the following guidelines. Objects or shapes in the foreground plane, those closer to the observer, are usually drawn larger, lower on the page, and in more detail. Objects farther away from the viewer, in the background plane, are usually drawn smaller, higher on the page, and with less observable detail. Effective space is subtly created by overlapping shapes and elements in the composition, such as a fence, tree, or telephone pole against a building.

Drawing landscapes or cityscapes directly at the site is recommended for upper elementary grades and middle school. However, sometimes conditions make it inadvisable, and the center and bottom illustrations show what can be accomplished when youngsters draw from a sequence of projected color slides. First, slides of towers, steeples, and chimneys were drawn high on the page. Then storefront facades and signs were projected for the middle plane. Finally, street furniture, lamps, telephone poles, hydrants, traffic lights and signs, parked cars, motorcycles, and trucks were projected to complete the foreground.

Simple perspective principles based on the employment of the horizon line, vanishing points, and converging lines should be introduced when the students indicate a need for them. Some students in grades 7 and 8 in the middle school will want to take up this challenge. Simple exercises in perspective may appeal to them, but remind them that mastery of perspective rules does not ensure that they will achieve compositional success.

Sketching field trips should be undertaken only with adequate preparation on the part of both teacher and students. Exciting subject matter should be scouted by the teacher beforehand. Avoid the barren view or monotonous vista that provides little opportunity for a varied breakup of compositional space. Permission to be away from school must be cleared with the principal's office, and, when necessary, signed permission slips should be obtained from the parents. Arrangements for using the school bus should be made well in advance.

A class discussion before the field trip should emphasize specific challenges. Tell the students to look for the architecturally significant character of the buildings, to see the value contrasts of windows in daylight, the foreground space allowed for steps and porches, and the receding of roads, sidewalks, and fences. Bring in aesthetic concepts. ("Will we see and depict nature as it is dominated and controlled by humans, or nature in the wild?")

On the day of the field trip the teacher should review rules of behavior and caution students to respect private property in the sketching vicinity. Directions for proceeding to and returning from the sketching site should be made clear, especially if it is within walking distance from the school. Keep the class in a line or group, bringing up stragglers when necessary. If roads are to be crossed, stop signs to be held by teacher or monitors to warn and halt traffic are recommended.

In most instances materials or supplies for drawing or sketching should be distributed to the students before leaving the classroom. In some cases the teacher may want to carry the drawing tools until the site is reached. At the close of the field trip, gather them up again. If students walk to the site, they can carry their own drawing boards. If a bus is used, class monitors can bring the materials, drawing tools, sketchboards, extra paper, and thumbtacks, which can be distributed on arrival.

At the sketching site, discourage students from sitting too closely together. Many a field trip can end up as a time-wasting social hour.

Remind the students that in drawing, they may use the artist's prerogatives of changing, adding, deleting, or simplifying what they see at the sketch site. Explain that the criterion is not necessarily

Still-life arrangements need not be limited to the usual floral arrangements. They are all around us. Consider the motorcycle parked behind the school, the open car trunk, the tool shed, cupboard, or closet. How about the piled-up desk, the cluttered kitchen sink, the box of playground equipment, and the table set for dinner?

Photos of still life courtesy of W. Robert Nix, Athens, Georgia.

photographic reality or rigidly measured perspective. If the students desire, they may add more trees, fences, telephone poles, fire escapes, air vents, chimneys, or windows. They may change a roof line or the cast of a shadow. They may delete a parked car, or a trash dumpster. In the sky, they may add helicopters, birds, clouds, and fantasy creations. Each decision they make, though, should embody the dynamic rules of art: variety, unity, balance, emphasis, contrast, and repetition.

The most important responsibility of the teacher at the sketching site is to guide the students in a self-evaluation of their drawings, employing the perennial principals of composition and design. In the final analysis, if all the teachers have done is to bring the students to see something they have not really seen before, to notice something they have never noticed until that moment—perhaps the molding or cornice on a door or window frame, the shadow of a tree against a wall, the overlapping of shingles, the variety in tree bark, or the texture of a brick wall—they have succeeded in enriching the lives of their students a thousandfold. The teacher may have started them on an exciting quest for shapes, patterns, textures, and color—on an endless journey of discovery.

Drawing the Still Life

Whether as inspiration for drawing, painting, print, or collage, the still-life arrangement fosters an appreciation of commonly observed everyday objects. It encourages keen observation and sensitivity to shapes, contours, and overlapping. From the third grade on, children can be guided to see the limitless design possibilities in still-life compositions. In acquiring objects for still lifes, scavenge for old and new objects in secondhand stores, flea markets, attics, basements, and at garage sales. Avoid trite objects such as miniature figurines or bud vases. Plant life is popular and can trigger nature discussions of why plant leaves have developed in shape and texture the way they have. Also popular is clothing such as ballroom gowns, costumes borrowed from theater programs, athletic uniforms, and military uniforms and apparatus from army surplus stores. Objects from outdoor life and camping, taxidermic specimens, and targets and bull's-eyes from shooting ranges will interest some students. Large art reproductions, posters from athletic wear stores about athletes and sport shoes, and posters about new cars, jeeps, motorcycles, and trucks from car dealerships make interesting backgrounds.

The placement of the various objects is critical to the success of the composition or design. Have the students participate. Make the

Facing page: Do you know someone who would be willing to loan your class interesting taxidermic specimens or large unusual cultural artifacts to draw? **Top right on facing page:** *A combined collage and oil-pastel work made from a still life. Preliminary drawings for collage projects in primary grades are not required. However, the separate parts of the composition may be drawn before being cut out.* **Above:** *Floral arrangements can be executed in an unusual material such as patterned wallpaper.*

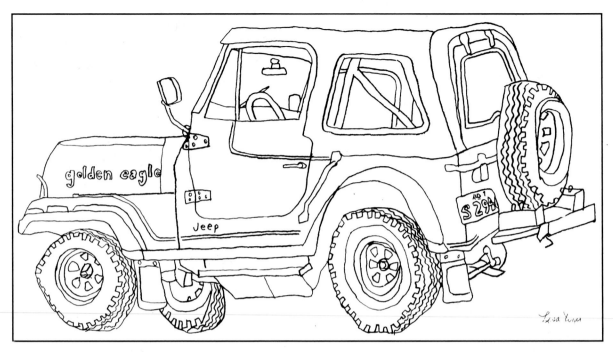

Top: Courtesy of Michael F. O'Brien, American Military Dependents School, Seoul, Korea. Bottom: Courtesy of David Hodge, Oshkosh, Wisconsin.

construction of the still life a motivating, adventurous part of the lesson. For example, arrange the objects on an antique table, old sewing machine, rocker, stepladder, window ledge, desk top, or table in the middle of the room so the students can be seated in a circle around the still life as they draw. Employ a variety of heights and levels (use cardboard cartons as well as plastic or wooden crates or storage units as supports). Create space through placing some objects behind others. Work for an informal rather than formal balance in the arrangement. Use assorted fabrics, colorful beach towels, flags, banners, fishnet, bedspreads, quilts, or tablecloths to unify the separate elements and to create visual movement.

In most cases the more objects used in the still-life group, the more opportunities the students have for selection and rejection. Indeed, the more objects the students include in their compositions, the more likely they are to achieve success in design.

There are several ways to begin drawing. One successful strategy is to have the students begin by drawing the central object in the still life, seen from their point of view, in the middle of their paper. They continue by drawing the objects next to it, left and right, above and below, until they have either filled the page or completed the still-life arrangement. Thus, the more varied and abundant the still life is, the more the students' compositions will have the space filled.

Another tactic is to have students select items from a general store of still-life material, choosing one object at a time to sketch at their desks or tables. They will build their compositions gradually, employing the principles of variety in size and shape of objects; overlapping; repetition; avenues into the composition; and informal balance. Talk with the children about how shapes are described by their edges and how an object's interior lines and outlines join together.

Some teachers suggest to their students that they make a light, tentative sketch in pencil, charcoal, or chalk to indicate the general, overall arrangement. This preliminary drawing is then developed, stage by stage, employing value (light and dark) and texture effects, pattern, shading, detail, and linear emphasis.

Drawing Animals

Most children respond enthusiastically to drawing pets and other animals. Students at the upper-elementary-school and middle-school lev-

Facing page: Vehicles such as Jeeps, campers, and station wagons afford excellent possibilities for contour-line drawing.

Drawing of rabbits by a first-grade child, Japan.

els are often especially interested in drawing horses. However, if the drawing of animals is to become a significant experience for the students, whenever possible have them observe live animals at zoos, aquariums, natural history museums, pet shops, farms, parks and animal shelters. Pets brought to class provide a stimulating and immediate source of drawing inspiration.

Skill in drawing realistic animals develops slowly. Nearly all first graders draw "just an animal"; by sixth grade a third of students still do so. "Horselike" animals are drawn by 20 percent of second graders and perhaps 50 percent of sixth graders. Even by seventh grade, only 5 percent of students are able to make drawings classified as "true to appearance."

Before an animal drawing field trip, let the students look at celebrated animal drawings. Include Rembrandt van Rijn's lion and elephant; Rosa Bonheur's horses and those by Chinese Han- and Sung-period artists; Albrecht Dürer's hare, squirrel, and rhinoceros; and Andrew Wyeth's birds. Discuss the animals' special characteristics: the textural pattern of the rhino's skin; the repeated yet ever varied spots of the leopard; the rhythmic rings of the armadillo's protective shell; the beautiful op-art variations of the zebra's stripes; the gracefully curved horns of the antelope, and the wrinkled, leathery face of the orangutan.

Discuss the animals' sociological and cultural significance, for example, sacred tigers and cows, imperial dogs, and royal lions, their strength symbolically representing the emperor. Encourage the students to think of the similarities between people and animals in resting, eating, running, bathing, grooming, and caring for their young.

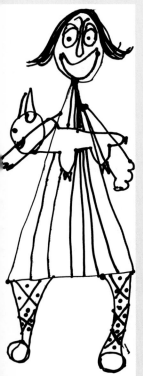
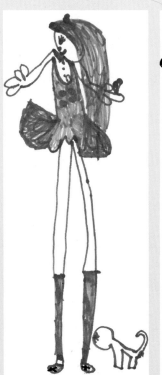

For, as John Dewey wrote, "The roots of art and beauty are in the basic vital functions, the biological commonplaces man shares with birds and beasts." (Dewey, 1934).

To stimulate kinesthetic awareness, students can dramatically reenact with their bodies the animals' poses and actions. Older students can be challenged to capture the animal's peculiar stance, the swinging rhythm of the chimpanzee, the arching stretch of the giraffe, or the sway of the elephant's trunk.

Careful observation and sensitive variation of line are required in drawing animals. As the students draw, remind them to fill the page. The larger the drawing, the more opportunities the child will have to define special details, patterns, and textures. Pencils, sticks cut to a point and dipped in ink, and felt-nib or nylon-tipped pens are good for small sketches. Charcoal, conté crayon, chalk, crayon, oil pastel, Q-Tips, eyedroppers filled with ink, and large-size blunt or square-tipped ink markers can be used for large works.

Limit the drawing activity to a single animal, developed in depth, rather than cursory attempts to draw several. Students might also be encouraged to draw detailed studies of an animal's eye, ear, snout, or horns. Since textural nuances can be added later when the students return to class, on-the-site drawings might be limited to capturing significant form. It might be a sketch showing the animal's spirit, rather than an attempt to make a completed, detailed study.

Sketching from the live animal or taxidermic specimen is best. When this cannot be done, color slides, films, filmstrips, and opaque projections of illustrations can provide supplemental motivation. In the primary grades the visual material might be discussed and then posted on the bulletin board for further reference. Photos and slides fulfill a definite need, but they should serve for inspirational and informational reference only and are not to be traced or rigidly copied.

Remind the students to consider the entire composition. In too many instances the animal is isolated in the middle of the paper, floating in space without a hint of complementary foreground or background atmosphere. Discuss the drawing of the surrounding space.

Facing page: Children holding animals make superb subjects for drawings of high interest both to the children who make them and to those who appreciate them. **Right, top and middle:** *The animal world has always interested child artists. Rembrandt's use of wrinkle lines in the elephant's baggy skin indicate form and can give children ideas for their drawings.* **Bottom:** *A sixth-grade Iowa City youngster used oil pastel for this ant-eating aardvark at a natural history museum.*

Bottom: Courtesy of Baiba Kuntz, Glencoe, Illinois.

Blue Mule (12 × 18 inches). Private collection.

Above: *African-American folk artist Nellie Mae Rowe's family plowed many hours with a mule. She brought this knowledge to her rich colored-pencil drawing. In the background, imaginative patterns of checkerboards and circular, floral, and overlapping scallop designs create a thrilling feast for the eyes.*
Right: *A fourth-grade child created this outstanding painting of an iguana. Observe its excellent space-filled composition and color. The coloring is dominantly variations of red-orange, along with accents of the other triadic colors, yellow-green and blue-violet. Of the three main colors, one color is bright, one color (light-blue-violet) is light, and one color is dark (black). This "light, bright, dark" scheme for the main colors helps vary the values and promotes color success.*

Add compositional elements such as trees, shrubs, grasses, rocks, bushes, vines, hills, cliffs, clouds, and companion animals in the foreground or background. Follow the example of Henri Rousseau who used his house plants as models to create his jungles. Use plants, dried foliage, roots, rocks, and twigs from the immediate school vicinity drawn giant size to become ledges, mountains, and jungle trees for the animals' imagined habitats. Students should be provided with continuing opportunities to become aware of nature as an endless source of design inspiration.

Courtesy of Shirley Lucas, Oshkosh, Wisconsin.

CHAPTER 19

Crayon and Oil Pastels

Crayon

At the turn of the century crayons began to be manufactured for American elementary schools. Artists such as Henri de Toulouse-Lautrec, Georges Seurat, Henri Matisse, and Käthe Kollwitz have used them. Today they are available in as many as sixty-four colors. More recently, resourceful teachers have combined crayon with other media to provide renewed interest in its exciting potential. Some of these innovative techniques, including crayon resist, crayon encaustic, crayon engraving, and multicrayon engraving, are described in the following pages.

Unfortunately, the rich possibilities of the wax crayon with its own singular merits as an expressive coloring agent have not always been fully investigated in the schools. The typical classroom projects in crayon are usually weak in color intensity, value contrast, and texture quality. In most instances, crayon is employed as a pallid, sketchy coloring agent instead of the glowing, vibrant, and excitingly expressive medium it can and should be. If children are expected to grow in crayoning skills, the crayon's rich possibilities must be explored from the first grade on.

Wherever possible, request that the students or the school supply agent obtain the large 48- or 64-color crayon boxes, with their beautiful range of color tints and shades and their wide selection of neutralized hues. To bring out the deepest, richest color, prompt the students to apply the crayon with heavy pressure. ("Who can make the color sing?" "Who can make it shout?" as opposed to "Who is making it mumble?") Remind children to use a lot of newspaper padding under the paper to be crayoned. Point out the effects of using contrasting colors, of juxtaposing dark next to light colors, neutral next to high-intensity colors. Challenge the students to create patterns of stripes, checks, plaids, diamonds, stars, spirals, and dots. Use paintings

by artists such as Vuillard, Bonnard, Ida Kohlmyer, Mariam Shapiro, Van Gogh, and Gauguin as exemplars of vibrant color, and show them Picasso's crayon drawings.

The entire mood of crayon work changes when the crayon is applied to varicolored or varitextured surfaces. Work on backgrounds other than the commonly used cream manila or white drawing paper. Pleasing results come about when crayon is employed richly on pink, red, orange, purple, blue, green, and even black construction paper. Tell the students to allow some of the background to show between objects, so the background paper color will unify their compositions. Color changes its appearance on different color papers. Yellow changes to dull green on black construction paper. All of the warm colors are slightly neutralized when applied to green paper but shimmer vibrantly when applied to red, pink, and orange surfaces.

Preliminary sketches for crayon pictures on colored papers may be made with school chalk or a light-colored crayon. Do not let them use a pencil, since students become frustrated when they try to manipulate a blunt crayon to color in a pencil sketch's tiny details. Encourage bold use of the crayon. Urge color repetition throughout the composition to achieve unity. Completed crayon pictures may be given a sheen by rubbing them with a facial tissue or folded paper towel.

Some issues of aesthetics to discuss include: What does color add to a picture? Why should colors be intense? Should all colors be intense? Why should we push a medium to its limit?

One vexing problem the teacher of art faces is that of children who rush through their crayoning, who quickly color in a few shapes and claim they are finished. Some suggestions are given in Chapter 10, "Motivation," and Chapter 11, "Evaluation." As always, the most successful strategies involve a teacher's well-planned, resourceful motivation, which taps students' concerns. This leads to a richly detailed drawing, which sets the stage for the crayon's expressive coloring.

Reproduced by permission of Jimmy Morris, Athens, Georgia.

Crayon alone was used to create the glowing rich colors in the artworks on these two pages. Here, a cat and kittens were brought to class for motivation. The preliminary composition on 12- × 18-inch paper was drawn in line with a white crayon on yellow construction paper. Patterns of stripes were carefully observed on each animal. The background shows superb intuitive color wisdom in the use of both related and contrasting colors. Three 50-minute class sessions were required, and no rushing.

Crayon Resist

For students of all ages, an exciting, creative art experience is the combination of vibrant, glowing wax crayon with translucent, flowing watercolors. For this technique, subjects that are rich in pattern and allover design, such as fish, birds, reptiles, insects, and butterflies, are recommended. Students are genuinely excited by the variety of insects found in their environment, and the teacher can stimulate further interest by having them collect specimens to share with classmates. Illustrated books, wildlife periodicals, color slides, and films will broaden the students' awareness of nature's adaptational variety. Studying the design of insects' bodies increases general knowledge of design. For example, help them examine and capture the filigree pattern in insects' wings, the rhythmlike segments of a grasshopper's abdomen, the symmetrical balance of a ladybug's body, and the grace of a praying mantis's legs.

Wax-crayon still lifes created by university students. College students will hopefully discover in their teacher training classes the luminous beauty inherent in the common everyday wax crayon. Then they will be more motivated and qualified to help children in their classes bring forth the rich potential of the crayon medium used by itself.

The pattern, details, and designs of the subject are of utmost importance in the crayon-resist technique, adding as they do to the sparkling effect of the finished painting. Whatever the theme, the more detail incorporated and the more overlapping of shapes, the richer the design becomes. When the design is rich and complex, the negative areas created evolve into varied shapes as well. Background embellishment—adding flowers, weeds, trees, vines, webs, rock and cloud formations—will tie the composition together.

A successful crayon resist requires the following:

The crayon must be applied with a heavy pressure. This is necessary so it will resist the watercolor (or water-diluted tempera) in the final stage. A teacher demonstration of the results of light and heavy crayoning should show students how hard they must press.

Putting several layers of newspaper padding under the paper facilitates heavy crayoning.

Leave some of the paper uncrayoned, for example, between two solid shapes, between two colors, and between object and background color.

Negative space can be enriched with a pattern of radiating lines. These might include effects like those formed around a pebble dropped in water, together with dots, spirals, circles, hatching, and crosshatching.

Encourage the students to be imaginative in their choice of color. Reliance on natural or realistic colors should be minimized.

Show the paintings of Raoul Dufy as examples of fantasy choices and use of washes. White crayon can be especially effective in this technique, providing a happy, magical surprise when the paint is applied. If a final black tempera wash is not planned, black crayon provides strong contrast.

When the crayoning is completed and the child is given the teacher's go-ahead, two techniques of resist may be employed—the wet- or dry-paper process. In the dry-paper method, students paint directly on their completed crayon work using watercolors or tempera. If tempera is being used, it is highly recommended that the teacher first test the tempera's viscosity on a sample. Students may limit themselves to one color in painting the background. They may also employ a variety of watercolors, as exemplified in the multileaf composition illustrated in this section. If the crayon has been applied heavily, paint can be applied directly over the crayoned area, which provides an attractive texture.

In the wet-paper method the desks or tables should first be covered with newspapers. If there is a sink, the students should put their piece on a solid surface such as a Masonite board and immerse both in water until soaked. The paper is fragile when wet, and must be handled carefully. The students then transport their pieces to the painting station, still on the board, and lift them off carefully. Students

A summer flower garden comes to life in this enchanting crayon-resist paint-ing by a second-grade child. To be successful in this technique the children must be encouraged and guided to apply the crayons with a strong pressure.

This is so the wax will resist the subsequent watercolor. White paper is recom-mended for the background. A preliminary drawing in a light-colored crayon rather than pencil is suggested.

should then load their brushes with watercolor or diluted tempera and drop or float the paint onto the uncrayoned areas. They may also direct the paint-laden brush around the edges of the crayoned shapes and let the color flow freely. They may use one watercolor wash (blue or blue-green is a favorite) or a variety of hues. However, they must be careful that several bright colors do not flow together to make a dull,

neutralized color. The wet resist method is especially suited for under-sea, aviary, and flying-insect themes. To add to the picture's charm, leave some white areas of the paper unpainted. For a large class the teacher might prepare in advance several containers of water-diluted tempera. A large table or counter space near the sink can be desig-nated as a painting area. Students can take turns applying the wash

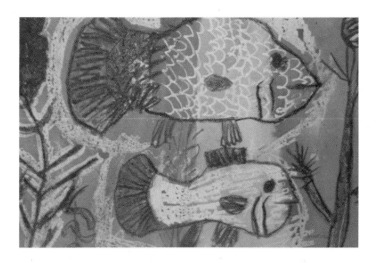

Above: Underwater themes are particularly good for crayon-resist paintings. The predominant use of a blue wash has one area of highly effective contrast. The child chose a contrasting and off-center vertical band of pink water-diluted tempera going across both fish and background. *Right:* Steps in a crayon-resist painting. Ordinarily, the preliminary crayoning in contour line takes one class session. The crayon patterns, background details, and selected solid crayon areas occupy a second class period. The watercoloring requires a final art class. Remind students to keep the watercolors transparent by adding sufficient water so the paint does not obliterate the crayon design.

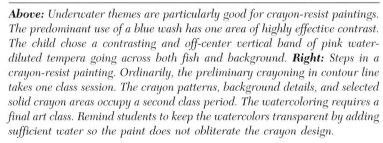

over their crayon composition while the rest of the class is still crayoning or otherwise engaged.

In addition to subject ideas mentioned earlier, the following themes are recommended for crayon-resist projects: a flower garden, fireworks display, the circus, the fair, umbrellas in the rain, halloween parade, falling autumn leaves, kites in the sky, in the swimming pool, underwater explorers, and jungle birds of plumage.

Crayon Engraving

Crayon engraving, sometimes referred to as "crayon etching," is a fascinating technique involving the use of sturdy, white drawing paper or manila file folders, wax crayons, black tempera paint, soap, brush, and engraving tools. It is a standard and popular school project, although its many possibilities are seldom carried to maximum expres-

Crayon engraving is used boldly and directly to make a statement about flowers and insects. Children express their ideas in direct, inimitable ways. In the foreground butterfly and in the huge right-hand flower, the child's intuitive use of positive and negative pattern is brilliant. What youngsters depict so honestly and naively can be awe-inspiring.

Courtesy of Mary Sayer Hammond, Fairfax, Virginia.

A youngster applies a heavy crayon undercoat for his crayon engraving.

siveness. If teachers allow students to be satisfied with quick, superficial scribble designs and later with random scratches, the students will never discover the new worlds of pattern and color overlay, or the rich enhancement that results when crayon engraving is combined with other media, such as oil pastel.

Crayon engraving uses a linear approach. Therefore, materials rich in line, pattern, detail, and texture are ideal subject matter, and the natural sciences are a rich source. Some examples are animals such as the porcupine, anteater, armadillo, zebra, leopard, tiger, and rhino. Birds are good subjects, especially those of exotic plumage, as are reptiles such as turtles, iguanas, and horned toads, and insects such as dragonflies, praying mantises, butterflies, grasshoppers, and beetles. Also of interest are crustaceans, such as crabs and crayfish; fish, shells, and coral of many species; and all varieties of plant life.

The preliminary drawing for a crayon engraving should be made in pencil on a separate piece of newsprint or manila paper that is the same size as the study paper that will be used for the final work. Keeping sizes constant will prove beneficial if students retrace their drawings with dressmaker's white transfer paper.

The first step in a crayon engraving is to apply varied colors of crayon solidly to the sturdy paper's surface. The crayon should be applied evenly with a strong pressure so that no part of the paper background is revealed. Sometimes coloring in two overlapping directions will ensure a rich coat of crayon. Newspaper padding under the paper to be crayoned will also promote rich coloring. Since this can be a tiring process, a small size paper may be desirable for those with limited stamina. The children may begin the crayoning phase by first making scribble designs in a light-colored crayon all over the paper and then filling in the resulting shapes solidly with a variety of bright colors. As an alternate method, they may apply swatches or patches of color or have their crayoned areas coincide with their compositions. Avoid black and metallic crayons. Use the most brilliant colors.

After the crayoning has been completed, the surface crayon flecks should be brushed off with a cloth or paper towel. *Caution:* Be sure the students put their names on the backs of their crayoned sheets before the paint is applied. The black tempera paint should be about the consistency of thin cream. To make it adhere to the waxy, crayoned surface, in most cases it must have liquid soap or detergent added. Approximately 1 tablespoon per pint of tempera is needed. Alternatively, the brush filled with tempera can be rubbed over a bar of soap before it is applied to the crayoned surface. The teacher should make a test swatch and, when it is dry, determine its engravability. If the paint is too thick, it chips off during the engraving.

When the paint is thoroughly dry (overnight or longer), transfer the preliminary line drawing as follows:

Coat the reverse side with white crayon or chalk, or use dressmaker's white transfer paper.

Paper-clip the drawing (crayon surface down) to the black tempera-coated side of the sturdy paper, and with a pencil or ballpoint tip make the transfer.

Engrave the lines through the tempera coating down to the crayon surface, using a nail, scissors point, compass, or similar tool. (*Note:* Newspapers on the working surface are required because the engraving phase can be messy.)

After the lines are engraved, add textures, patterns, and details with nut picks, forks, and pieces of old combs.

High contrast can be achieved by scraping away some solid shape areas down to the crayon surface using a plastic, picnic-type disposable knife. A recommended tool, if the school budget will allow it, is the Sloyd or Hyde knife. This sturdy, short-bladed knife can engrave a fine line with its point or scrape away a whole surface with its edge.

After completing the engraving, students may enrich their compositions by applying oil pastel colors back over some of the black tempera surfaces. Finally, the composition may be further enhanced by engraving details and texture through the oil-pasteled areas.

Crayon engraving is a challenging mixed-media technique. It opens up new avenues of discovery in line, color, contrast, pattern, and texture, especially for students at the upper elementary level and above. (See pages 188 and 189 and also pages 40, 94, and 101.)

Three stages in a crayon engraving by a third-grade child. **Left:** *The initial line engraving was done with a nail through the black tempera coating to the crayoned surface underneath. Also seen are characteristic details and some textural effects.* **Middle:** *The scraping away of black to produce some solid crayon shapes, as well as the introduction of oil-pastel areas.* **Right:** *The completion of the oil-pastel embellishment. Notice the beautiful effect created by saving the important black linear borders along with some undisturbed black areas.*

Crayon Encaustic

Crayon encaustic is a challenging painting medium to add to the upper-elementary-grade and middle-school art repertoire. Many museums contain ancient Egyptian Fayumic mummy portraits which still glow with the inner light of wax. The Greeks used encaustic on marble, and early Christians mixed into it little glass pieces called tesserae. The encaustic process is the kind of creative adventure which is reserved for those teachers who are brave in spirit, eager to try something new, and persevering enough to collect a year's supply of broken crayons. Some teachers make encaustic painting an annual late-spring event, which the students eagerly anticipate. One teacher times the activity with the blossoming of colorful anemones, which become the visual motivation for the project.

The steps are as follows: Remove paper wrappings from the crayons, break the crayons into small pieces, and put them in glass babyfood jars or similar containers (not plastic or paper) or metal muffin tins. Each jar or compartment should contain a different color. If a muffin tin is used, make sure it fits into a deeper and slightly larger baking tin. To prevent fires, a double boiler arrangement is required.

Facing page: *In these three crayon engravings, students wisely preserved certain dark areas intact to contrast with the light-colored areas from which they scraped away the crayon. Approximately half of the areas are light and half of the areas are dark. The dark areas are either plain black or remain dark even after having been gone over with crayon.* **Top:** *Fish by middle-school students.* **Bottom:** *Insects by a third-grade student.*

Top right: Courtesy of David Hodge, Oshkosh, Wisconsin. Bottom: Courtesy of Mary Sayer Hammond, Fairfax, Virginia.

Courtesy of Mary McCutheon, Athens, Georgia.

These charming paintings were created by employing the melted crayon or encaustic method. The size of the cardboard is approximately 8 × 12 inches. Color reproductions of flower paintings by artists such as Odilon Redon, Vincent Van Gogh, Paul Cézanne, and Paul Gauguin were displayed and discussed during the project. A bouquet of freshly picked, multihued anemones provided the immediate visual motivation. Grade 3, Athens Academy.

The jars or muffin tin must be placed into a slightly larger cake tin containing water. Because of space limitations, the number of colors may need to be limited to the primary and secondary colors plus white, black, and a few tints.

The most functional working station for encaustic painting is a large, sturdy, newspaper-covered table. Place one end of the table against a wall near an electrical outlet. Place one or two electric hot plates in the middle of the table. Put the crayon-filled containers or muffin tins in a 2- or 3-inch-deep metal baking pan. Fill the pan two-thirds full of water and place it on the hot plate. When the crayons have melted, reduce the heat and place one or more Q-Tips or watercolor brushes into each crayon container. These brushes should be old, reserved for this encaustic project only. Keep the water at the temperature of the melted crayon, to maintain a consistent flow of crayon.

Note the floral fine art reproductions displayed, the live anemone bouquet, the newspaper-covered table, and the jars of melted crayon in the double boiler-type pan within a pan, over a hot plate.

White or colored cardboard approximately 9 by 12 or 12 by 12 inches is recommended for the painting surface. Scrap mat board, chipboard, gift-box covers, and grocery carton cardboard coated with latex are some possibilities.

A preliminary sketch for a crayon-encaustic painting is recommended unless the theme is purely nonobjective in the manner of Jackson Pollock, Helen Frankenthaler, and Hans Hoffman. Subject-matter possibilities include a flower bouquet, butterflies, an exotic bird in foliage, a fantastic fish among shells and seaweed, an imaginary monster, and a clown.

The teacher must supervise encaustic painting carefully. Never crowd the working station. The group must be limited to four to six students, depending on the size of the table. To prevent wax fires, the water must not be permitted to boil out of the pan. The electric current may need to be regulated from time to time so the melted crayon does not cool off. Additional pieces of crayon will have to be placed in the containers. Remind students that brushes or crayon applicators should *not* be switched from container to container. Students must be patient and learn to wait their turn for a color. *Caution:* the crayon containers are filled with molten wax, and must not be taken out of the heated pan during the painting.

This project cannot be rushed. Sometimes the beauty of encaustic does not materialize until several layers of melted crayon have been applied. If layers are built up, the finished work will take on an exciting, thick impasto quality. When one color is applied over another, there is the possibility of further embellishment. This can be done by incising lines with a nail through the top coat to reveal the crayon color underneath. To solve the problem of insufficient old crayons when a large area has to be covered, powdered tempera can be mixed with melted paraffin. Crayon encaustic produces paintings with color richness and glow that are unsurpassed. (See also page 81.)

Oil Pastel

The introduction of oil pastels in their rich and exciting array of hues has opened a whole new world of color exploration and expression in both elementary and middle schools. These glowing oil pastels are generally within the budget range of most schools. (The only caution is that because of their oil content, they may stain clothing.)

The most attractive feature of oil pastels is the ease with which students can apply them to obtain shimmering, vivid, painterly color compositions. Thus, students can produce rich results without the

Animals in the Jungle. *Oil pastel on pink construction paper. Color slides of jungle animals were projected on a screen. The children made their preliminary drawings in school chalk. After animals were drawn, slides of trees, bushes, and birds were projected to provide further motivational and compositional ideas. Grade 3. Other examples of oil pastels appear on pages 10, 20, 25, 52, 64, 78, 80, and 103.*

pressure required with regular crayons. Oil pastels work especially well on deep-colored construction paper in which the colored background serves as a unifying or complementary factor. Young students should be encouraged in their first efforts to apply the pastels boldly in solid color areas, pressing hard to achieve a glowing surface, and to use color contrasts. Because the intensity of the pastel hues is affected by the paper color, it is suggested that students note the effects of experimenting on the reverse side of their paper with small color swatches. Recommendations for oil-pastel projects, especially when colored construction paper is used for the background, are:

Make the preliminary drawing or sketch with white or light school chalk or crayon. Chalk is excellent, because it is easily erased (use paper towel or facial tissue if the students want to make changes).

Press for richest effects. One suggestion for coloring in small or complex shapes is to apply the pastel in a line close to the chalk outline and then fill in the shape. Discourage haphazard, scribbled coloring.

Remind students that colors have many tints and shades, which are especially important for capturing leaves and grassy fields, with their nuances of light and shade.

Black, white, and grey add to any color scheme.

Colors, both tints and shades, bright and dull, including the blacks and whites, should be repeated in different parts of the composition to create unity. This color repetition should employ differences of size, shape, and intensity. A hue repeated for unity should be differentiated in value so the echo of the color is there without the monotony of pure repetition. This is especially true when the student is making a pattern such as bricks on a wall, tiles on a roof, or stones in a walk, where the repetition of the same color becomes static and lifeless unless it is sensitively varied.

Remember that contrasting values are stronger than contrasting hues.

When the colored paper background should show through in a complementing way, apply the pastel impressionistically in strokes, lines, or dots.

New colors can be created by applying pastel over pastel. However, a very light color cannot be totally darkened unless the light is first scraped off. A dark color can be lightened somewhat by the application of white, and colors can be dulled through applying their complements: red over green, orange over blue. To alter a color, first use soft pressure with varidirectional strokes and then increase pressure.

Top: A collection of butterflies, as well as color photographs of butterflies in a garden, provided motivation. They inspired this oil pastel by an upper-elementary-grade youngster. Notice how large and small butterflies in different shapes create variety and beauty. A host of patterns was used for the background: circles, dots, and wiggly and rippling lines. **Middle:** *Oil pastel on black paper of birds in trees.* **Bottom:** *Astronauts in their spaceship was the theme for this third-grade oil pastel.*

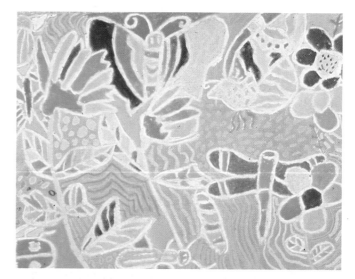

Courtesy of Mary Sayer Hammond, Fairfax, Virginia.

Oil-pastel resist takes oil pastel a step further. The resist color of wash goes into the lines left empty to create a stained-glass effect and also adds texture on the plain areas. Here, many shapes of different sizes and types help create beauty.

Oil-Pastel Resist

Oil pastels alone can be beautifully employed as a final step in many techniques: tempera paintings, crayon engravings, and vegetable or found-object prints. However, they can also be used in the oil-pastel-resist process for stunning results.

Teachers and students familiar with the crayon-resist technique will welcome oil pastel as another resist medium. It does not require the time or the intense exertion on the part of the students demanded by crayon.

The same steps as outlined for the crayon-resist technique should be followed:

• Make a preliminary drawing in chalk.
• Vary the width of the chalk line and emphasize thicker lines.
• Apply the oil pastel heavily so that it will resist the final coat of black paint.
• Leave the chalk lines uncovered.
• Use the brightest, most intense pastel hues.
• Avoid black.

Before applying paint, evaluate the final oil-pastel composition for a variety of repeated colors. Also look for a variety of patterns: dots, circles, overlapping wiggly lines, radiating lines in circles or rays, ripple-in-a-stream lines, hatch and crosshatch lines, stars, asterisks, diamonds, and spirals.

Before applying paint, gently brush off the chalk lines. Place the composition on a newspaper-protected surface and apply a coat of black tempera paint. The paint must be of exactly the right consistency—not too thin, not too thick. Since paint formulas change, always do a test first (some tempera paints now contain an adhesive and can't be used). The brush should have soft bristles that will float over the pastel, not scratch through it. If the paint covers the oil pastel areas, it is too thick. The resisting oil in the oil pastels will dry out soon after it is applied to the paper, so don't wait too long to apply the black paint. Oil-pastel-resist compositions may be given a protective coat of gloss polymer medium to enhance their beauty.

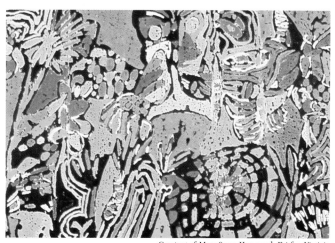

Steps in the process of oil-pastel resist. **Top:** *Preliminary drawing in school chalk on colored construction paper.* **Middle:** *Oil pastel applied in solids and patterns up to but not covering the chalk lines.* **Bottom:** *Slightly water-diluted black tempera applied lightly with a soft-bristle brush.*

Courtesy of Mary Sayer Hammond, Fairfax, Virginia.

CHAPTER 20

Painting

Painting with Watercolors

While tempera is the most common and most popular painting medium in elementary- and middle-school art programs, in many instances teachers use transparent watercolors. These come in semimoist cakes or tiny tubes packaged in metal or plastic containers, and are available in primary and secondary colors plus black. Transparent watercolor painting demands special technical skills, and mature painters devote countless hours to its mastery. They employ a wide range of beautiful colors available in tube form and costly sablehair brushes.

The watercolor paintings on page 198 are by Japanese elementary-school children. They are provided with a spectrum of watercolors in tubes and painting palettes from the first grade on. The majority of their watercolor paintings begin with a preliminary sketch in pencil or pen. In some cases the children moisten the paper before beginning the coloring. As these paintings reveal, many persevere to produce rich, space-filled compositions that exhibit the characteristic spontaneity of transparent watercolors.

Teachers often employ the semimoist watercolors to teach about the color properties of hue, value, and intensity. Mixing of primary colors will produce secondary colors, and mixing secondary colors will produce tertiary colors. Diluting a color with water in gradual stages can produce a color-value chart. Color can be neutralized through mixing with complementary hues. Creating watercolor washes on moist paper achieves dark-to-light sky and water effects.

The following recommendations constitute a kind of "primer" for watercolor projects.

White watercolor or construction paper is recommended.

Newspapers under paintings help speed cleanup and also provide a practice surface.

Round, pointed, soft-bristle, camel-hair brushes are recommended. They should always be rinsed clean at the end of the period and stored bristle-side-up or flat in a container.

Watercolor boxes containing the semimoist cakes of paint should be rinsed and wiped clean at the close of the art period and then allowed to dry open.

Water containers should be changed when the water in them becomes muddy. Paper towels are handy for spills and for blotting up excess paint on works in progress.

Preliminary sketches in pencil or felt-nib or nylon-tipped pen, or light watercolor applied with a small brush, are recommended.

Areas to appear white or light in the final painting can be masked with masking tape before the paper is moistened or the painting begun. When the painting is completed and dry, the mask may be removed and a final touch-up made.

Watercolor washes of the same color in the same value applied over one another will darken the color. It is recommended that students begin a painting with light colors or values of colors and build to darker colors for detail.

When painting is done on a wet surface, the paper may have to be remoistened by lightly sprinkling the surface with water from time to time.

Paintings appear vibrant and contrasting when moist but unfortunately lose their brilliance when dry. A second application of watercolor paint over a dried color may help.

While wet or moist, paintings should not be stored on top of one another. If no drying rack or counters are available, store the paintings on the floor around the perimeter of the room.

Exhibited at the School Art Symposium, sponsored by the Art Department of the University of Georgia, Athens, Georgia.

Some very successful watercolor projects are those in which watercolor is combined with colored crayons or oil pastels in a resist method (see Chapter 19, the sections on crayon resist and oil-pastel resist).

Study art history exemplars: watercolors by Winslow Homer and John Singer Sargent, and brush paintings from China and Japan.

An issue to be considered in aesthetics is the importance in art (and in life) of spontaneity, verve, and assuredness—vibrant, fresh appearance versus a labored, overworked, fussy, muddled appearance.

The boldly direct and colorful painting of a watercolor box in use is by a talented teenager. Notice the use of thin and thick lines and the overall spontaneity, particularly desired in watercolors.

Reproduced by permission of Jimmy Morris, Athens, Georgia.

This delightfully entrancing watercolor, My Friend and Me, *is the work of a first-grade child in Japan. Notice the variety of lines in the hairy, toothy main figure. Opposite colors, yellow and purple, along with mixtures of each color give the work power. (See also pages 112 and 127.)*

The watercolor painting of a still-life bouquet of flowers was created by an artistically gifted sixth-grade Japanese girl. Patterns are found in the lilacs, dahlias, lilies, and background tablecloth. Note that the objects are carefully observed, yet drawn with freedom and spontaneity. A pattern of white shapes is left uncolored in the dominantly blue painting.

Painting with Tempera

All children should have the opportunity to express their ideas in brush and paint. The best quality tempera paints, whether in powder or liquid form, are rich in color and have excellent covering properties. Children who paint with tempera can apply color over color freely to achieve jewellike effects or repaint areas with which they are not pleased.

Although teachers are aware of the possibilities for colorful art expressions offered by tempera, they sometimes do not include it in their art programs because of its cost and the housekeeping chores involved. It is true that tempera projects require more materials preparation, more careful storage, and more controlled cleanup procedures than watercolor or crayon projects. These factors, however, should not prevent teachers from discovering how tempera painting can enrich children's art repertoire. Even when classes are large and facilities limited, there are expeditious, time-saving methods of incorporating tempera into the art program.

Cardboard soda-bottle containers and discarded glass-tumbler carryalls can be used as carrying cases. Discarded baby-food jars and half-pint milk cartons can be used as containers. To prevent the paint from drying out between classes, the milk cartons can be resealed with spring clothespins.

Students can both perform a service and gain color knowledge by helping to prepare the tempera paint. They can mix various hues, tints, shades, and neutralized colors. For extra beauty in the paintings, consider restricting the color choices to, for example, all triadic colors or all analogous colors or all very light colors. For a class of 30 children, about 60 containers of varying colors should be prepared, with an additional 6 white containers and 4 black ones. Containers should be filled to one-half capacity.

If class time is limited, the teacher may need to prepare the color assortment in advance. Those who object to this procedure on the grounds that this does not give the students the opportunity to learn about mixing colors should be reminded that professional artists usually have at their disposal a wealth of colors, tints, shades, and neutrals to create their paintings. The children deserve the same advantage. When the class is limited to a few basic colors because there is not enough time to mix a variety, the expressive output of the children suffers and the joy diminishes.

Individual containers of paint should be placed on a table or rolling cart accessible from all sides. It should be low enough so the various colors are visible. If possible, a brush for every container

Painting with tempera on large paper surfaces gives the children a real opportunity to express their ideas in paint. This bold portrait by a primary-grade student is on 24- × 36-inch paper. Newspapers covered the floor and the child painted freely.

A primary-grade child used tempera paint very expressively and in a wide range of hues to make this delightful painting on 12- × 18-inch colored construction paper, The Bunnies' Easter Egg Hunt Party.

should be available. This procedure saves time, paint, and squabbles over brushes. The children take turns choosing a container of color, and when they have finished with it, they return it with its brush inside to the supply station. To keep paint from covering the brush's metal ferrule and the students' fingers, fill containers only partly.

It is recommended that children use one color at a time and use it thoroughly throughout the painting. To achieve unity and balance in their paintings, encourage them to repeat colors around the picture. This injunction, while primarily aesthetic, has the practical advantage of minimizing traffic around the supply station.

Adequate time should be allotted for cleanup. Because brushes left standing for long periods of time in paint lose their elasticity, they should be taken out of the paint containers and the excess paint remaining in the brush squeezed back into the container. Then they should be placed in a large basin of soapy water to soak overnight. The next morning they can be rinsed in clear water and stored bristle-side-up or flat in a box. Brushes with wood handles must be washed and stored to dry immediately after the class; otherwise the wood handle will shrivel. Unless the paint in the baby-food jars can be covered, store the jars in an airtight cupboard or drawer or put the containers on a tray and seal the tray in a giant plastic bag. To prevent the lips and edges of containers from sticking, they should occasionally be wiped clean or waxed.

Some teachers of art use plastic egg cartons or ice-cube trays as tempera paint containers. In this method each student has a brush, and the brush is washed clean each time another color is chosen. Preventing drying of leftover paint is more difficult with this method, but the cartons or trays can be sealed in plastic bags. To help prevent the unpleasant odor of aging tempera, a drop of wintergreen can be added to the big jars of tempera.

Semimoist cakes of opaque paint are now available in tubs or tins. Some teachers claim that they save time in cleanup and storage procedures. Others who have tried them say that they inhibit the free-flowing style that liquid tempera encourages in children.

In the primary grades tempera painting is a natural for children. The very young child especially enjoys making bold, splashy designs in paint and needs only the materials and an invitation to get started. Themes such as explosion in a paint factory, fourth of July fireworks, butterflies in a flower garden, bunny rabbit's Easter party, a kite fight, and planets in outer space fire the imaginations. Colored construction paper, including black, provides an excellent surface because the color of the paper can unify the composition. Consider adventurous choices like wallpaper samples and newspaper classified pages.

The following strategies have proved helpful in tempera painting projects.

Students should be encouraged to make preliminary sketches on their paper in chalk or using a brush and light-colored paint.

Minimize cleanup by using protective newspapers on paint supply stations and on individual painting areas. Have moist towels available for accidental paint spills. Use protective plastic on the carpet.

Develop preventive strategies for those likely to spill: for example, a minimal amount of paint in the containers, or special holders and containers.

Encourage children to wear protective clothing; an old shirt as a painting smock is suggested.

Remind students to wipe the excess paint from their brushes back into the containers.

Lest the colors run together, caution children about painting next to a wet paint area.

When making a color change, suggest that the children wait until a color is completely dry before painting over it.

If brushes must be cleaned during the painting session, tell students to squeeze out the excess water thoroughly before using the brush to paint again. If not, the paint in the individual containers will become water-diluted and less intense.

In the upper-elementary grades and middle school, students can design with paint on moist, colored construction paper. They can use the dry-brush or pointillistic approach to achieve texture. They can explore mixed-media techniques, combining tempera and crayon, tempera and pastel, and tempera and India ink in a semibatik process. Encourage older students to mix a greater variety of tints, shades, and neutralized hues to achieve a more individual and personal style. They can use discarded pie tins, TV dinner trays, and plastic cafeteria trays for their palettes. They must be cautioned, however, to be economical and not mix more paint than they need. For tints, they should add the hue a little at a time to the white paint rather than vice versa. Paint tins should always be rinsed out at the end of painting class.

Students cannot rush through a tempera painting project any more than they can hurry through any qualitative creative endeavor. Therefore, sufficient time must be allotted for all phases of the undertaking. First comes the motivational time; then the preliminary sketching session. These are followed by the studio work, which involves choices of colors, then achievement of contrast, pattern, and detail. Throughout the studio activity, there should be evaluation of the work in its several stages. Finally, the completed paintings are exhibited. Tempera painting should be included in every school art program!

Courtesy of David Hodge, Oshkosh, Wisconsin, and Mary Sayer Hammond, Fairfax, Virginia.

Tempera-resist paintings by middle-school students. Note how beautifully they fill the picture plane.

Tempera Resist

For middle-school students who have had many elementary-school experiences painting with tempera per se, try tempera resist. Tempera resist, which employs both a liquid tempera underpainting followed by a final coating of India ink, is a challenging new technique replete with hidden surprises. Although highly recommended as an exciting project in painting, it presents some materials problems, among them the high cost of India ink.

The tempera paint employed should be a good quality liquid tempera. Powdered tempera is not recommended, although some art teachers claim that the powdered tempera works when it is mixed with a small amount of liquid glue. Liquid or powder, the paint must be of a thick, creamy consistency, not watery. Watery paint will absorb the final ink coating rather than resist it.

Bright, intense hues of tempera should be employed for the highest contrast of black ink against color. Discourage the use of dark blue, dark purple, and brown, which will not show up. Subtle, lightly grayed hues such as sienna, ochre, light umber, and light gray are effective. White may be employed with discrimination but generally should be repeated, since a solitary white area often detracts from the rest of the composition. Recommended papers are construction paper in white or light colors and cardboard from store cartons.

Considerable time is needed for the various steps in the process: the preliminary drawing, the tempera painting, the inking, the rinsing, and the optional coating with gloss polymer.

The sketch or preliminary drawing should be made in chalk. Encourage the students to vary the pressure of the chalk lines, making lines from thick to thin. The importance of this will be revealed in the second phase when the ink is applied and soaks into the space left by the chalked lines. A relevant aesthetic consideration for this project is that the more the students break up large shapes into small shapes, the more beautiful the finished result will be. As students paint with the tempera, suggest that they paint up to, but not over, the chalked lines, leaving a gap from one-sixteenth to three-sixteenths of an inch in width. The more varied the chalk lines, or the paper surface remaining between painted areas, the more successfully contrasting the composition will be. Remind the students not to paint the shapes, areas, and details they want to appear black in the completed painting.

Caution the students that a tempera color painted over another dry tempera area will wash off in the final rinse. Therefore they must plan their color scheme in advance. However, patterns painted into wet tempera areas can be effective. Encourage students to be expressive in their color usage, for example, to employ many kinds of green for grass and trees, many values and intensities of blue for skies. After all of the desired colored areas are painted, the work should be stored to dry completely.

For the inking phase cover a working surface with newspapers. Wipe off the chalk remaining in the lines with a tissue. Place the painting on newspapers and paint with the India ink in random, circular strokes. Cover the painting completely and store overnight to dry completely.

Wet paintings tear easily. For the final rinsing phase, put the painting onto a protective backing, such as a Masonite board or an old

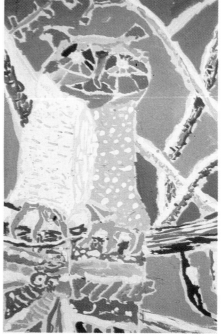

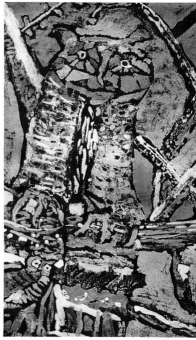

Courtesy of David Hodge, Oshkosh, Wisconsin.

Left: *Steps in creating a tempera–India ink resist. The preliminary drawing is made in school chalk on white or light-colored construction paper. Paint is applied up to the chalk outline but not covering it, and allowed to dry completely. Then undiluted India ink is applied generously over the tempera surface, allowed to dry thoroughly, and rinsed off at the sink.* **Above:** *Before-and-after results in a tempera and India ink resist project by a middle-school youngster. For successful results, be sure that the tempera paint is a quality brand liquid type and the India ink is used undiluted.*

cafeteria tray, and then put them into the sink and rinse with cold water or take them outdoors and rinse with a hose. Begin the rinsing in the center of the work and move outward. Do not direct the water to the same area too long, or too much paint will wash off, or, even worse, the paper will disintegrate. A moist sponge or finger run may bring out the color where the ink stubbornly sticks. After rinsing, lift the painting very carefully onto a counter or the floor, and blot it with paper towels. When the tempera-resist painting is completely dry, give it a protective and enhancing coat of liquid wax or glossy polymer medium.

An upper-elementary-grade youngster retouches the lines on the painted rhinoceros he contributed to a jungle theme group mural. The preliminary drawings were first made with school chalk on large cardboard sheets salvaged from mattress boxes. Then chalk lines were gone over with brush and black tempera to provide unity of line quality throughout the mural. The children then colored up to but did not cover the black outlines. Finally, the murals were taken into the community to enliven a children's ward in a local hospital. (See also pages 7, 9, 15, and 282.)

Mural Making

Mural projects help students to acquire not only art knowledge, but also possibly an even more important kind of knowledge, what it means to plan and carry out a project through working together. Collaborative art builds self-esteem and diminishes alienation. Memorable experiences are achieved through group involvement in projects of large scale and scope, for example, decorating the classroom for a celebration or presenting a series of works on a central theme. With the teacher acting as facilitator, the students as a group can generate ideas. Educational goals can be organized according to objectives, and strategies for assessing the project's effectiveness in solving problems in social settings can be developed.

Some subjects have almost universal appeal to particular age groups, and certain themes are especially appropriate. For very young children, suggested topics are a butterfly dance, land of make believe, fish in the sea, Noah's ark, and a flower garden. Intermediate- and elementary-school children respond to on the farm, birds in a tree, animals at the zoo or animals in the jungle, fun on the playground, when dragons roamed the world, and fun at the beach. Upper-elementary-grade and middle-school students react positively to astronauts in space, a kite-flying contest, aquanauts exploring the sea, the rodeo, rock festival, block party, state fair, three-ring circus, winter carnival, world of the future, and where and how young people in our community play and relax.

Before the class begins a mural, the teacher interested in correlating social studies with the project can ask: "What is the purpose of a mural?" "Who painted the first murals?" Show cave paintings from Altamira and Fonte de Gaume. Are there any murals in your community's buildings, post offices, schools? What was their original social, political, or educational intent? Art history knowledge can be developed through discussion of the artist who made the mural. Using art criticism methods, debate the relative merits of each mural. Discuss the aesthetic issues of realism and abstraction, of colors muddied by aging.

The great Mexican murals were made to promote both social consciousness and aesthetic awareness, and older students can be involved in decisions about how to include real community concerns and goals in the mural. When murals are painted out in the community, a rich social setting comes into play and enriches the process. In mural-making projects, when aesthetic interests go along with other interests, such as civic, commercial, health, or moral issues, the combination can make the experience doubly important to the students.

Iowa City, Iowa.

The group mural Fun at the Park *was painted by elementary-school children on a 10- × 200-foot plywood construction barrier. The preliminary sketch on the previously primed barrier fence was made in chalk and then reinforced with black enamel applied with ½-inch- and 1-inch-wide utility brushes. Parents donated leftover paints in a variety of colors for the project.*

Having settled upon a theme, other questions follow: What medium or technique should be employed? How large should our mural be? Where can we work on it? Where will it be displayed when completed? How shall each student's contribution to the mural be decided?

If, for example, a collage-type pinup mural is agreed upon, the following procedure is recommended: When all students have completed their individual contributions to the total mural, the teacher and students should devote at least one art session to composing the mural. Discuss the merits of the placement and design. Here the

See Virginia S. Robinson and Robert Clements, "Mosaic Panels," *Arts and Activities*, May 1982.
Photo courtesy of Virginia S. Robinson.

Hundreds of clay balls were flattened and stamped with designs. Some were stained. Then they were arranged by middle-school students into a mural of lasting beauty.

teacher's tact and gentle persuasion play an important role. Bring to the children's attention that a mural in one sense is like a giant painting and requires the same compositional treatment. Urge the students to strive for varied sizes of objects or figures, varied heights, and varied breakup of space in foreground and background. Encourage overlapping of shapes, grouping of objects to achieve unity, and quiet areas to balance busy or detailed ones. Have them use larger shapes or figures at the bottom and smaller ones at the top to create an illusion of distance.

Children who complete their assigned main segments early can enhance the compositions with space-filling elements such as rainbows, clouds, and pets. Put in recreational and transportation equipment: balls, kites, cars, trucks, bicycles, motorcycles, frisbees, planes. Some can make street furniture: telephone poles, mailboxes, signs, fences, benches, and landscape elements of trees, bushes, rocks.

When the separate segments are finally arranged in a composition that is pictorially unified, they are stapled or glued. If the mural is attached to a separate piece of plywood or heavy carton cardboard, display it in the school's entrance foyer, hallway, or lunchroom for

Courtesy of Mary Sayer Hammond, Fairfax, Virginia.

A collage-type pinup mural was created from fourth graders' oil pastel drawings of astronauts and spaceships. Students then cut them out and transformed them into an exciting group mural project.

everyone to enjoy, exhibit it in a building out in the community, or exhibit it first in the school and then in the community.

Take, for example, Fun on the Playground as the theme for a mural employing collage (cut and paste) as the medium. Ask the following questions: How many different kinds of games or sports should be included? (List them on the chalkboard.) How shall we decide which activity each student will select to portray? How many different areas of the playground will be included? What types of playground equipment will be included? Why shouldn't all children be the same size? Will they all be dressed alike? Make a list on the chalkboard of the different kinds of clothing and uniforms they might wear. What patterns might be shown on their clothes? (wallpaper samples or fabric remnants may be used). What else can be included? (Make a list on the chalkboard: trees, fences, airplanes, signs, etc.)

Some other mural techniques and media are the following. For freestyle, expressive murals that are painted directly on surfaces such as oaktag, cardboard, poster board, and hardboard, use tempera paint, enamels, or latex paint. Use a preliminary outline in black paint to give unity and to spark the composition. From designs made by individuals or small groups, one may be chosen, or several effective designs may be incorporated into one design, that will be painted by small groups taking turns painting.

For a detailed description of this unusual project by Diane Turner, see the February 1983 issue of *School Arts* magazine. Illustration courtesy of Davis Publications, Worcester, Massachusetts.

Billboard mural, 10 × 25 feet, designed and created by second-grade children in Laurens, South Carolina. The medium is wax crayons on billboard paper. The children made small sketches of dragons from which a selection for the billboard was made. Several youngsters worked in tandem on each dragon, so that every child could contribute. Two donated billboards were on display in the community during the March Youth Art Month Celebration.

CHAPTER 21

Paper Projects in Two Dimensions

Collage

A popular form of visual expression in elementary and middle schools today is collage with its related family of montage, decoupage, mosaic, collograph, and assemblage. Over a half-century ago, shocked dismay greeted the initial collages of Pablo Picasso, Georges Braque, Carlo Carra, and Kurt Schwitters, in which the artists dared to include cardboard and printed words. Today their creations in paper, cardboard scraps, and paste (the word *collage* derives from the French *coller* "to glue") appear relatively tame. The wellsprings from which contemporary artists, such as Robert Rauschenberg and Alexis Smith, now draw their materials are so bountiful that the technique is limitless in its possibilities.

The collage technique promotes design using overlapping of shapes and colors, positive and negative shapes, value contrast, pattern, and texture. Students have the unique opportunity of rearranging the elements in their work until they achieve a satisfying composition. Approaches to collage range from simple cutting, tearing, and pasting of paper to complex sewing, shearing, and gluing of fabric, plastics, posters, plywood, cardboard, Day-Glo paper, wallpaper and rug samples, paint chips, colored tissue paper, and colored magazine pages. The artist Jean Dubuffet even used coffee grounds and butterfly wings!

A preliminary sketch is recommended when the subject matter is the landscape, figure composition, or still-life arrangement. For themes from the imagination, for fantasy, or for purely nonobjective designs, direct cutting, tearing, and pasting are acceptable. However, in both processes the permanent adherence of the separate parts should be postponed until both student and teacher critique the work's strengths and weaknesses. Some other suggestions are:

Cut and arrange the large shapes or motifs first. If employing a colored background, include it in your design by allowing some of the background to show and unify the composition.

Small details and patterns can be pasted on the large shapes before they in turn are glued to the background surface. Overlapping of shapes is a major feature of collage making.

Eye-catching materials such as aluminum foil, synthetic silver and gold foils, shiny plastic, and cellophane fascinate children, who may use them indiscriminantly. Guide the students so they use such materials as points of emphasis only. Remove them if they detract from the whole.

Repetition of a color, shape, value, pattern, or texture adds unity to a collage; however, instead of repeating the element, color, or shape exactly, vary it somehow.

Recommend using an uneven rather than even repetition of elements. For example, repeat a certain shape or color three times rather than twice.

Encourage the use of informal (asymmetrical) rather than formal (symmetrical) balance.

Avoid a lot of "sticky" problems by using discarded magazines as paste applying surfaces. When a clean pasting area is needed, turn to another page.

Ambitious teachers may want to enlist parents and children in making cloth banners from the students' paper designs. Army units in ancient Rome each had their own decorated standard. Cloth banners were first used in the middle ages during the Crusades, when each force had its own insignia. Artists such as Miriam Shapiro, Jim Dine, Henri Matisse, and Richard Lindner have had banners made of their collage designs.

First a large drawing which bumps the edges is made with chalk on a piece of 12- × 18-inch colored paper. Then the child cuts cloth scraps to fit the areas. Yarn, buttons, rickrack, and colored paper scraps can also be used. Here, oil pastels were added on the face and hands.

Recycle scraps of colored construction paper into collage projects such as these. Primary-grade youngsters arranged paper scraps in assorted sizes, shapes, and colors for their compositions. Supplemental details, patterns, and motifs were added with crayons, oil pastels, markers, paper punches, brush and paint.

What could have more power and charm than the collagelike quilts made by African-American Harriet Powers (1837–1911), a former slave from Athens, Georgia? Her artworks now hang in our nation's most important museums. You can give your artwork strength by using her ideas. A large checkerboard pattern gives unity. Color is restrained to mostly white and very dark. Tints and shades of essentially only two complementary colors, orange and blue, are used. The almost abstract figures create bold positive and negative shapes.

Most important, the artwork is about deeply felt Biblical stories and combined with personal anecdotes in her own words, such as, for the lower left square, "Cold Thursday, 10 of Feb. 1895. A woman frozen while at prayer. A woman frozen at a gateway. A man with a sack of meal frozen. Isicles formed from the breath of a mule. All blue birds killed . . . ." Can you find the dead blue birds, woman praying, man with sack, and the mule with icicles?

Tissue-Paper Collage

On the first day of a tissue-paper-collage project, the teacher can surprise the class by unfolding a package of tissue papers of assorted colors. Excitement grows as one color tissue overlaps another on a white paper background or against the window. The students can tell the teacher which colors to overlap, and then they can invent a name for the resulting hue.

To encourage color awareness and color exploration, a free-design, nonobjective, colored-tissue collage is recommended for children from the third grade up. Using a sheet of oaktag, white drawing paper, or construction paper approximately 12 × 18 inches as a back-

The colored-tissue compositions illustrated above began as free-form collages. The youngsters cut or tore the tissue and applied it on white construction paper in overlapping stages with liquid laundry starch. When it was dry, they used black and colored felt-nib markers to search for and outline recognizable shapes. Some children used crayons, others paint and brush. Suggest that the students begin pasting light values of tissue first and progress to darker values. This is because a dark-color tissue area is difficult to change to a light value. One solution is to paste a sheet of white paper over the area and start again.

Courtesy of David Hodge, Oshkosh, Wisconsin.

The beautifully composed colored-tissue-paper collage illustrated above is by a talented middle-school student from Athens, Georgia. Photographs and color slides of matadors, toreadors, and "brave bulls" provided the visual stimulation. The preliminary drawing was made with a felt-nib pen (permanent black-ink type) on white construction paper. Before the application of the colored tissue, the student chose certain shapes—matador's trousers, jacket, and so on—for a patterned embellishment and pasted colored sections from magazines on those parts. The tissue was applied by coating an area first with liquid laundry starch and placing the tissue over it. Then the area was coated again with the starch, making sure all edges were smoothly secured. Light-colored tissue was applied first, progressing to the darker colors. Caution was employed in the final stages so dark-value tissue did not obliterate the important form-defining ink lines.

ground surface, cut or tear different sizes and shapes of tissue. Adhere them to the background using undiluted liquid laundry starch as the adhesive, and overlap the various shapes. A 1/2-inch utility brush or a large watercolor brush makes an excellent starch applicator. Begin with the lighter-colored tissues first and proceed to darker values, since it is most difficult to change the value of a dark tissue by overlapping. Reserve the darker colors for the second phase of pasting.

First apply a coating of starch to the area to be covered with tissue. Then the tissue should be placed down carefully over the wet area and another coat of starch applied over it. If brushes pick up some of the color from the moistened tissue, rinse them. Be sure that all loose edges of tissue are glued down well. Discarded half-pint milk cartons are economical and practical starch containers. Since tissue is expensive, and wrinkles and crumples very easily, it is recommended that storage boxes be used to store the tissue, one box for each hue.

Although the abstract composition has an aesthetic validity of its own, it can be augmented as follows: After the students have filled up their composition to the borders of the paper, challenge them to look for hidden shapes. These might be suggestive of animals, birds, insects, fish, or fantasy creatures. Once a form emerges, the students can glue on additional torn pieces or strips of tissue in deeper colors to represent appendages which give it character and individuality. Avoid outlining the revealed figure so boldly that it is isolated from the rest of the composition. Employ a variety of dark-color tissues for this step rather than a single hue. Black tissue can be used but only in a most restrained way. Similarly, if students outline only one figure with a black felt-nib marker, that one figure will be isolated. But if all emerging figures are outlined in black, a unity will be achieved.

In addition to black markers, students can use crayons, colored markers, and tempera paint in white, gray, or black to delineate desired shapes, such as bark on a tree, scales on a fish, feathers on a bird, and veins in a wing or leaf. Wait until the tissue surface is dry, especially if using water-soluble markers.

The free-design approach with colored tissue described above is only one of many avenues for creating with colored tissue. Another technique uses a preliminary drawing made with black or dark-color

A drawing with permanent marker of a seated boy with bird and bicycle wheel was made on 18- × 24-inch white paper. Then a tissue shape was cut or torn and an area selected for it. Next, laundry starch was applied to that area and the shape firmly pasted down. For extra interest, tissue shapes do not follow the figure's form.

Courtesy of David Hodge, Oshkosh, Wisconsin.

crayons on light-colored, heavy paper. After the drawing is completed, the cut or torn tissue paper is applied; as in the previous method, begin with the lighter hues. Cut or tear the tissue sheet slightly larger than the shapes drawn. The drawn lines are sometimes obscured by dark tissue overlays, but when the tissue layer is dry, the lines may be redrawn for emphasis. Using lettering from printed publications in conjunction with colored tissue adds a new dimension to the tissue collage. Further, this is one way to incorporate text concerning social issues into the artwork, an important consideration in contemporary art expression.

Mosaics

The multifaceted technique of mosaic art, with its colored pieces called tesserae, is a welcome, albeit challenging, technique for children's art expression. It requires a generous time allotment, supplemental storage, and, above all, students with patience and persistence. Standard art materials such as colored construction paper, paste, and scissors are used in this project. Creating mosaics, a pleasantly repetitive and creative project, calls for much small-muscle, tactile activity. It teaches that wholes are made up of parts, an important concept in mathematics, science, and social studies.

Motivation for the project might include visits to mosaics in the community. If available, show color films and slides of mosaic art, past and present. This can include San Vitale in Rome, Gaudi's Cathedral in Barcelona, Simon Rodia's Watts Towers in Los Angeles, and the mosaic-paved avenues of Rio de Janeiro. Subject matter for paper mosaics that is manageable yet exciting includes birds, fish, and animals in their habitats; flower bouquets; butterflies in a garden; dragons; and clowns.

In mosaic design, as in most two-dimensional art expression, an important initial step is the preliminary sketch. Make it from life and nature, from visits to museums, or from references to photographs and color slides. The preliminary sketches are then developed into a satisfactory linear composition the size of the actual mosaic desired.

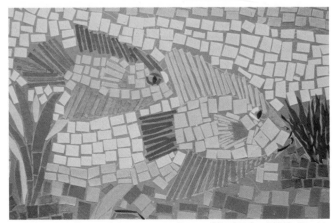

Courtesy of David Hodge, Oshkosh, Wisconsin.

Underwater themes are especially effective for mosaics because of the variety of shapes, details, and patterns found in fish, shells, coral, and seaweed. These beautifully space-filled compositions are by upper-elementary-grade youngsters who used a variety of sizes and shapes of the tesserae.

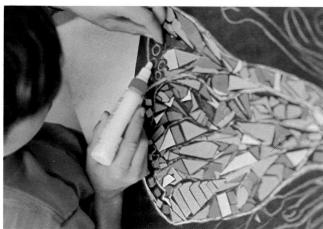

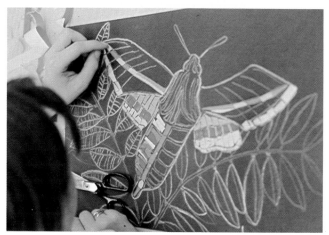

Courtesy of Mary Sayer Hammond, Fairfax, Virginia.

The background surface may be colored construction paper, chipboard, or salvaged gift-box container.

Critical to the project's success is an adequate supply of tesserae. Cut narrow strips of colored construction paper, not necessarily the same width, and store them according to color in shoe boxes. Students then cut these strips as needed into individual tesserae. They need not cut all the strips into perfect squares. Some can be rectangular or

A group mural in which each student's mosaic insect on black paper was cut out, with border preserved, and then mounted onto a large piece of brown cardboard.

Campus Elementary School, University of Iowa, Iowa City.

Above: *Recommended background surfaces for paper mosaic projects include construction paper in assorted colors, railroad board, chip board, oaktag, or discarded gift-box covers. Suggested adhesives include school paste, white glue, or glue sticks. The bird mosaic employed vinyl and linoleum tesserae glued to Masonite board with color-tinted grout as a filler. Grade 6.* **Above, right:** *An attractive colored-construction-paper mosaic of an angelfish and seaweed by an upper-elementary-grade student.*

triangular. Some adventurous teachers have used vinyl, tile scraps, linoleum, and even colored glass (with caution) instead of construction paper.

During a mosaic project, students should take turns selecting the desired color strips or tesserae from the supply-table boxes. Apply school paste or white glue to the background paper and press the tesserae firmly into the adhesive. Usually, it is best to begin on the outer edge of a shape and work inward toward the center of the shape. To achieve the mosaic effect, tesserae should not touch or overlap each other. The students should be reminded that in professional mosaic work, a grout is mortared between tesserae. Avoid a rigid, bricklaying technique—the minute, open spaces between tesserae should vary somewhat for best effects.

Students may create excitement with their mosaic compositions through a contrast of colors in specified areas. They have contrasted the wing of a bird against the body, the stamen against a flower petal, an insect against a leaf. An important strategy in achieving expressive mosaic quality is to employ several values of a color in the larger areas: For example, use two or three values of blue in the sky and two or three values of green in the grass and leaves. Use several kinds of brown ochre, umber, and sienna colors for earth and tree trunks. The brightest, most intense colors may be reserved for sharp contrast or emphasis—on the beak or claws of a bird, the eyes of a tiger, the stamen of a lily, or the horns of a bull.

CHAPTER 22

Printmaking

Printmaking with Found Objects

Printmaking projects should range from simple processes in the primary grades to complex techniques in the upper elementary grades and middle school. Some of the most colorful and successful prints can be made by very young children employing vegetables and fruit. Found objects such as buttons, flat or round wooden clothespins, wooden spools, bottle caps, mailing tubes, corks, sponges, and erasers can also be used. Cord can be glued to the smooth metal top of a condiment container in a free design to produce a printing stamp.

A science-correlated study of nature's form and function can use assorted vegetables (okra, cabbage, mushrooms, peppers, carrots, artichokes) that are cut in half or in pieces, painted, and printed. The excitement quickens when the students gain awareness of the hidden design in these natural forms. The halved or quartered vegetables are painted on the cut side with colored tempera of a creamy consistency or pressed on a tempera-coated, folded paper towel. Water-soluble printing ink can also be used. They are then printed repeatedly on a sheet of colored construction paper or tissue paper to form an allover or repeat design.

For best results the vegetables must be fresh, crisp, and solid. They should be kept refrigerated between printmaking sessions. The most popular vegetable for the project is the potato. It is cut in half with a paring knife, and the flat, open surface is incised to create a relief. Children must be reminded to exercise caution when using vegetable-cutting tools. Recommended tools include small scissors, fingernail files, nut picks, dental tools, and assorted nails. Melon-ball scoops are excellent for creating circular designs. In the upper elementary grades and middle school, paring knives, Sloyd knives, or Hyde knives may be employed if used with extreme care.

Students should strive for a simple, bold breakup of space in their cutout or incised designs. Suggest the use of crosscuts; wedges as in a pie; assorted-sized holes; and star, asterisk, cogwheel, sunburst, and spiderweb effects. Students can use large potatoes to print monogram motifs, but letters must be reversed to print correctly. Students should make a preliminary drawing on paper the shape of the cut potato to guide them in their cutting. It is possible to reverse the drawing at the window and then copy it onto the potato surface.

Construction paper in assorted colors is perhaps the most popular and most serviceable surface for vegetable printing, although colored tissue, wallpaper, and fabrics have been used. Generous newspaper padding should be placed under the paper to be printed to ensure a good impression. Standing up helps students to exert firm pressure. Wedges cut out of the holding end of the potato can improve the grasp.

A few practice applications of the vegetable stamp on scrap sheets of paper are recommended. Students might be encouraged to develop a repeat pattern in several places on their paper (this does not have to be a measured, mathematical repeat), allowing some prints to go off the page to create an allover effect. In other instances the design can be left to the child's own inventiveness. However, discourage rushing to finish, which often results in sloppy printing. Often the imperfection of a child's effort lends a fresh, spontaneous quality to the product. By sharing their stamps children can produce exciting variations.

For a project correlated with writing, have the students use vegetable and found-object prints as covers for their creative writing notebooks. The prints can also be used for pencil containers (glue the printed paper to a discarded box or can). In both cases, students can coat the surface with gloss polymer medium.

217

Left: Vegetable prints are enhanced by the application of oil pastels. **Top left:** A youngster applies the pastel colors between the printed motifs, allowing some of the background paper to show. Notice in the bottom example how the light blue pastel complements the yellow-orange paper color. **Above:** Vegetable-print, allover repeat designs make excellent covers for notebooks, pencil holders (recycle a soup or coffee can), and household dispensers. To protect the surface and make it shine, apply a coat of gloss polymer medium.

Vegetable and found-object prints have artistic potential in their simplest, unadorned form. They can also be embellished with other art media for added richness. One or more crayon or oil-pastel colors can be added in the negative spaces between the printed shapes. Unity can be achieved by allowing some of the background surface between the pasteled or crayoned areas and the printed motifs to remain uncolored.

Glue-Line-Relief Prints

A printmaking process that is remarkably successful with students in all grades is the glue-line-on-cardboard print. It is a relatively simple technique but requires at least two class sessions. Time is needed both because the glue must dry overnight before printing and because students must take turns at the inking stations.

In addition to pencils, other materials required are:

Printing plates—use a smooth-surfaced cardboard (discarded, glossy-surfaced gift-box covers are excellent) or tagboard; plate sizes recommended are 9 × 9, 9 × 12, 12 × 12, or 12 × 18 inches
White liquid glue in the small, plastic containers with nozzle
Water-soluble printing ink (black is recommended)
A soft rubber brayer or roller for inking
An inking surface, such as a discarded cafeteria tray or metal cookie sheet
Protective newspapers
Newsprint, tissue paper, or newspaper classified pages on which to print

Appealing subject-matter choices for young children are butterflies, birds, fish, flowers, and animals. Students in the upper elementary grades and middle school may choose more complex themes: historical legends, space and science explorations, still life, cityscape compositions, portraits, and figure studies.

A preliminary drawing is definitely recommended. The students should keep the basic drawing bold and simple; intricate details blend

Vegetable-stamp printmaking appeals to youngsters, but caution must be exercised in cutting the designs. Use nails, plastic knives, and melon scoops for this process. In the printing phase do not insist on a measured, rigidly controlled design. Vegetable prints may be embellished by an application of oil pastels between printed motifs. Allow some background paper to show, unifying the composition.

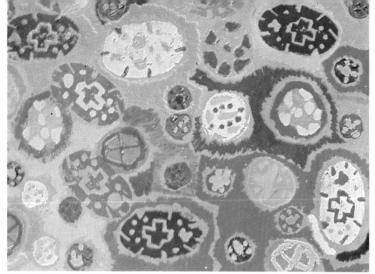

Courtesy of Mary Sayer Hammond, Fairfax, Virginia.

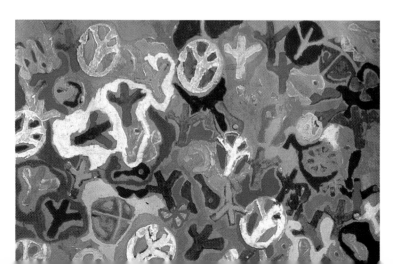

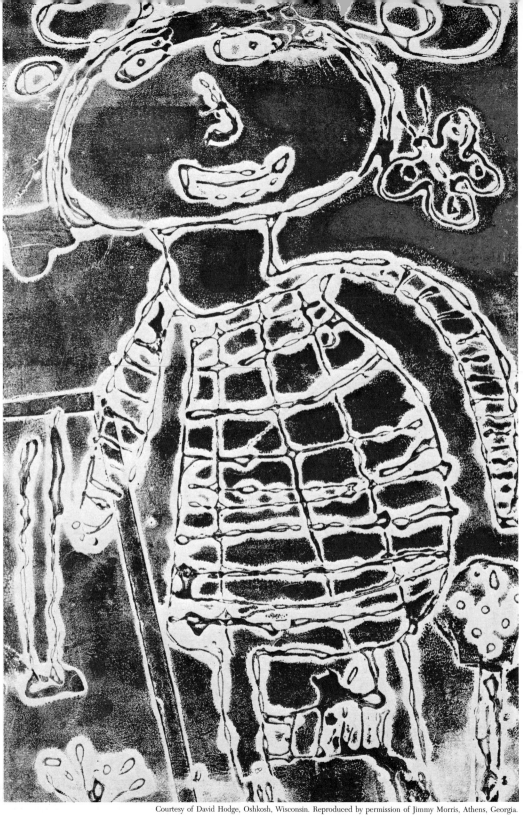

Courtesy of David Hodge, Oshkosh, Wisconsin. Reproduced by permission of Jimmy Morris, Athens, Georgia.

together in the glue line and are lost. It is best to limit the composition to one large motif (bird, insect, fish, animal), with its complementary foliage or seaweed, rather than use several smaller motifs. With only one large figure, there will be room to clearly delineate details, such as eye, beak, whiskers, antenna, claw, feather, and fish scales. Evaluate the compositions with the student for space-filling design, shape variation, and pattern.

The cardboard plate with its linear composition is now ready for the glue application. Gently squeeze the container, trailing the glue over the drawn line. A linear variety is achieved naturally, because it is difficult to manage an even, steady flow of glue. Dots of glue will produce sunburst effects in the final printing. The glue must be allowed to dry thoroughly overnight before inking. When completely dry, the glue will look transparent and free of white ridges and welts.

Designate both an inking and a printing station, protected by newspapers. To save time spent giving individual instructions, demonstrate the glue application, the inking, the printing, and the wet-print storage procedures for the entire class. At the inking station, squeeze out a brayer-width ribbon of water-soluble black printing ink onto the inking surface. Roll out the ink with the brayer. Keep rolling until the ink is tacky—you'll hear a snapping sound—and then apply the ink to the cardboard plate with a strong pressure. It is recommended that students stand during this procedure. Roll the ink on the plate with the rubber brayer in several directions—up and down and across—to be sure all parts of the plate, especially the edges and corners, are inked thoroughly. Then lift the inked plate carefully and carry it to the printing station. Since water-soluble ink dries quickly, print it immediately. Place a sheet of newsprint or tissue paper (cut slightly larger than the cardboard plate) over the plate and apply pressure with the palm of the hand. Begin in the center and smooth out to the edges, being careful that the paper does not shift. Some teachers recommend

*On facing page: Glue-line-relief print, 12 × 18 inches. This self-portrait is by a first-grade child. The checkerboard pattern on the body gives the design strength and the figure's jaunty angle gives it verve. **At right, top:** On sturdy cardboard, the initial drawing is made, preferably having one large form. Avoid small details which get lost in the glue application and instead try to find bold patterns. **Middle:** The white glue is applied over the pencil lines. **Bottom:** After the glue is transparent and thoroughly dry, the plate is inked. Use a soft rubber brayer, water-base printing ink, and heavy pressure until the entire surface is inked. See pages 227 and 228 for later stages.*

Courtesy of Jimmy Morris, Athens, Georgia, and Mary Sayer Hammond, Fairfax, Virginia.

Courtesy of David Hodge, Oshkosh, Wisconsin.

Glue-line-relief print by a sixth-grade student based upon a drawing from a posed model. Because of the pressure applied by the soft-rubber brayer, the printing ink covers parts of the background as well as the glue lines.

that students tap the paper down all over with the palms of their hands before smoothing it down.

The most successful prints are those which capture both the raised glue lines as well as the inked areas of the background. This will require pressure with palm and fingers into the smaller background areas. Uninked areas between glue lines and background provide the necessary light and dark contrast. For the demonstration, the teacher might use white tissue so the students can actually see the ink absorb-

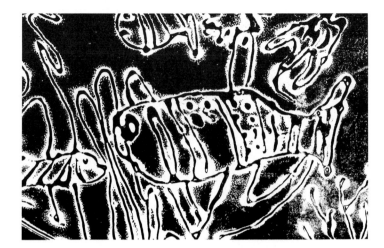

Above: *Beauty is achieved through the flowing parallel lines and clarity of forms.* **On facing page:** *In this collograph, each sixth-grade child cut out one or more figures and one or more bulildings to illustrate the story of the Pied Piper. The pieces were then combined in this group project from Japan. Houses on opposite sides of the street are upside down or shown as if folded back from the street's center line. This charming and powerful way of representing objects is called "folding over." Alas, children give up this graphically interesting method as they mature.*

ing into the paper and detect areas requiring more pressure. Several prints may be made from the same plate. Trim borders, if necessary, and mount the print on colored construction paper for an exciting display.

Collographs

Students in the intermediate and upper elementary grades as well as middle school are interested in and challenged by more complex approaches to printmaking. Cardboard prints are sometimes referred to as *collographs* (a word combination of *collage* and *graph*). Collographs can be created with commonly available materials and nonhazardous tools, yet the final results are often comparable to those of woodblocks and lino prints. An especially welcome advantage of this technique is the flexibility it allows in rearranging or deleting compositional elements before the final gluing.

The following tools and materials are required: a sheet of sturdy cardboard, such as the lid or bottom of a gift box), chipboard, dis-

The Jungle, *18 × 36 inches. Group project collograph by intermediate-elementary-grade children. A paper punch created pattern in the leopard and on the bushes. Pinking shears were used to cut the palm tree leaves. Additional* cut-out holes and little squares and triangles of paper were also pasted down onto the cardboard plate. See especially the gorilla's exciting background at left. The plate was then printed.

carded scraps of illustration board (tagboard is not recommended), glue, scissors, assorted-weight papers (smooth or textured), assorted-size paper punches, soft rubber brayer, water-soluble printing ink in black or dark colors, newsprint, gloss polymer medium, a utility brush, and lots of protective newspapers.

The animal world is a favorite theme for collographs. A strong, lively design is desired. Especially important is using a variety of cut-out shapes to fill the space. While helpful, an overall preliminary drawing is not a requisite. Separate motifs or shapes may be drawn first before cutting. Large printing plates may create a management problem in crowded classrooms. Therefore, a recommended plate size for students in the intermediate and upper elementary grades is a sheet 9 × 9, 9 × 12, or 12 × 12 inches.

Students draw and cut out the separate, individual shapes from tagboard (oaktag), construction paper, brown wrapping tape, and other assorted-weight papers. They then create open patterns in some of these shapes, employing paper punches and utility knives, and arrange these elements on the background cardboard until a satisfactory composition is achieved. Some shapes may overlap for unity, spatial effects, and interest. Students can add a variety of found materials to create diverse textural qualities, using masking tape, gummed reinforcements, textured wallpaper samples, fabric, string, yarn, confetti, liquid glue, and flat found objects. However, if the relief is too high, the print will not be successful, and students should avoid thick cord, bottle caps, buttons, and similar items. When the students, with the teacher's guidance, achieve a satisfying, space-filling design, they care-

Bottom: Lily Hill Middle School, Manila, Phillipines.

Steps in making a collograph print. **Top left:** *Gluing down the paper-punched birds. Caution: If water-based printing ink is employed, the teacher must give the plate a protective, water-resistant coating.* **Left middle:** *Inking the collograph.* **Bottom left:** *The finished print.* **Top right:** *A middle-school student peels back the print from the plate while checking that areas have been sufficiently inked and pressed.* **Bottom right:** *The finished print with very attractive tree shapes.*

fully glue down the pieces. Use a discarded magazine as a gluing surface and turn to a clean page for each application. All edges must be glued down securely.

The whole composition is then sealed with a coat of polymer medium to further prevent the separate pieces from coming loose during the printing and cleaning phases. A separate table or counter protected by newspapers should be designated as the sealing area, and the plates allowed to dry overnight before inking.

The inking and printing are very exciting, but without careful planning this stage can develop into a chaotic bedlam. Have on hand several inking surfaces; soft rubber brayers that are 3 or more inches wide (do not use the gelatin type); black water-soluble ink; and newsprint or light-colored tissue paper. The inking and printing tables should be covered with newspapers and positioned so that several students can stand and work comfortably. After squeezing and rolling out ink on the inking surface until it feels tacky, apply it to the plate in both directions. Use an even, strong pressure, inking every part of the plate, especially the edges and corners. Quickly take the inked plate to the printing table and set it down, inked-side up. Carefully place a sheet of newsprint paper (slightly larger in size than the plate itself) over the inked surface and pat it down with the palm of hand. Pat gently at first, then apply more pressure and, using the heel of the hand, bear down in circular motions over the whole plate from the center toward the edges. A rubber brayer may also be used. Using fingers, press down on edges, corners, and between pasted shapes. Where the print is to be darker, press harder. *Caution:* Do not wait too long to remove the newsprint from the plate. The water-soluble inks dry quickly, and the paper may stick to the plate. Lift it off very carefully and store the wet prints on counters or on the floor, or spring-clip them with clothespins to a line.

The process of inking and pulling a print should be demonstrated step by step for the whole class. So all students can get a turn to print, the number of initial prints a student pulls must be limited. Additional prints can be made later. Plates need not be washed between printing sessions.

Finished prints can be attractively mounted for display. Students may want to exchange prints. The plate itself can be painted and mounted. It can also be covered with heavy-duty aluminum foil and further embellished, as described in the following section on aluminum-foil relief.

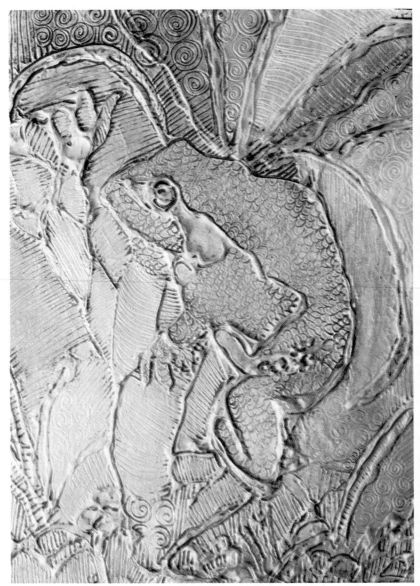

Courtesy of Mary Sayer Hammond, Fairfax, Virginia.

The aluminum-foil relief is an exciting adventure in bas relief and embossing that has untold possibilities for exploration in the art program. The glowing finished product makes a gift which is often preserved by families for decades.

Aluminum-Foil Reliefs

The aluminum-foil relief over collograph plate, collage, or glue-line-relief plate is an exciting and novel technique to which students in the upper elementary grades and middle school will respond. The process is not technically a printmaking process, but rather a later process following the making of a glue line or collograph print.

Materials needed include heavy-duty aluminum foil, blunt-point pencils, soft rubber brayer or inking roller, white glue (check for consistency—should not be watery), gold patina, masking tape, water-soluble printing ink (black or dark hue), and protective newspapers.

If students have been pulling prints from a collograph or glue-line plate, they can reink the plate and, while the ink is still sticky, cover it with a sheet of foil slightly larger than the printing plate with the shiny side up. Then, stretching the foil with heel of hand toward the edges of the plate, overlap the foil on the back of the plate. Secure the excess foil on the other side with masking tape. Fold the foil at the corners to keep it as flat as possible.

On an uninked collage, be sure the pieces of the collage are secured. With glue-line prints, be sure the glue relief lines are thoroughly dry. Then give the plate a coat of white glue and apply the foil while the glue is wet.

Next, using a blunt-pointed pencil, press into the foil along both edges of the glue lines and along edges of collage shapes to emphasize the relief. Avoid puncturing the foil. Teacher and student should both check to see that all relief edges have been sufficiently emphasized. Next, enrich the relief by indenting the foil with the pencil point to create additional details, patterns, and textures. These can be leaves on a bush, veins in the leaves, grass, feathers on a bird, scales on a fish, bark on a tree, and ripples in a stream. Incorporate a variety of invented patterns, such as hatching, and crosshatching; dots, circles, dots within circles; triangular and diamond shapes; wiggly, jigsaw, and radiating lines; asterisks; stars; and spirals. The more detail, pattern, and texture employed, the more effective the result will be.

At right, top: The glue-line print from page 221. **Center:** *Aluminum foil is dropped over the still wet inked plate. It is then pressed down with hand and brayer, and the excess foil secured to the back of the plate. Details and patterns are indented into the foil with a blunt pencil.* **Bottom:** *Coat with India ink or shoe polish. Wipe off with paper towel or fine steel wool.*

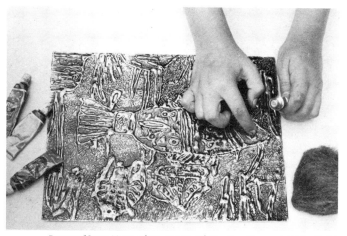

Courtesy of Jimmy Morris, Athens, Georgia, and Mary Sayer Hammond, Fairfax, Virginia.

Courtesy of Jimmy Morris, Athens, Georgia, and Mary Sayer Hammond, Fairfax, Virginia.

The aluminum-foil relief begun on page 221 and completed on page 227 is shown here in its final richness. A positive feature of this project is that it uses readily available materials. These include household heavy-duty foil instead of expensive copper sheeting, cardboard, white glue, blunt pencils, and water-based printing ink. The project also affords an ideal medium for learning about ways to create texture and pattern.

To print, apply water-soluble black printing ink to the surface with a soft rubber brayer so the whole plate is covered except the deep pencil indentations. Some teachers recommend applying the ink with a dauber to be sure it gets to all crevices. You can make a serviceable dauber by rolling several paper towels into a tight cylinder and taping it together. To apply strong pressure, students should stand during the inking.

Take the inked plate to a clean area protected by newspapers. Place a sheet of newsprint or tissue paper (slightly larger than the plate itself) over the inked foil plate. Tap it gently with palm and heel of hand to make it adhere. Then, using stronger pressure, use palm and heel of hand, fingers, or a soft rubber brayer to ensure a good print, being especially careful to print the borders. Water-base printing ink dries rapidly, so peel the paper off the plate quickly and gently. Lift it half off to check the impression and, if not satisfied, press down again.

While the ink is still moist on the plate, use newspapers to remove the excess. Press one sheet at a time over the moist plate with hand or brayer. When no impression is visible, take a moistened paper towel, folded flat (never bunched or crushed), and wipe the plate gently to remove excess ink from all areas except the indented ones. When one side of the towel gets inky, unfold and fold it again to a clean surface. When the moist towel no longer shows an ink residue, use folded, dry paper towels to burnish the plate, but allow ink to remain in the indented lines. This can be the final stage of the project, or you can enrich the raised surfaces of the plate by the slightest application of gold patina (see page 228). Aluminum-foil reliefs can be attractively mounted and displayed, and they make excellent gifts.

Linoleum Prints

A technically demanding form of expression recommended for students in the upper elementary grades and middle school is linoleum ("lino") block printing. Students are challenged by using diverse tools and by manipulating, if available, a heavy roller press. Because of these built-in attractions, teachers will have little trouble introducing lino prints into the art program.

Unmounted, grey, pliable linoleum suggested for this project may be obtained from art-supply companies. It may also be obtained from furniture, floor covering, and department stores, but be sure it is the pliable type and not the brittle, hard-surfaced plastic kind. Cut linoleum plates large enough to give the students ample opportunity for a rich composition. A minimum size of 9×9, 9×12, or 12×12 inches is recommended. The basic materials and tools needed include sets of lino-cutting gouges for the students to share, rubber brayers, inking surfaces of cookie tins or old cafeteria trays, and water-soluble printing ink. Papers to print on can be newsprint, brown wrapping paper, colored construction paper, colored tissue paper, wallpaper samples, fabric remnants, classified newspaper pages, and colored pages from magazines.

Subject-matter themes for lino prints are almost unlimited, but the most effective promise a strong light- and dark-value composition with a variety of shapes, pattern, and detail. Some possibilities are birds, jungle animals and their young, insects, fish, shells, old houses, legendary or mythological figures, portraits, and still-life arrangements composed of musical instruments, antiques, plants, household utensils, and sports equipment. A field trip to a natural history museum will provide a wealth of motivational material.

A preliminary drawing on paper with black crayon, felt-nib pen, brush and ink, or white crayon on black paper is an important requisite for a successful lino-print project. It usually determines the final composition, and establishes the dark and light pattern, variety of textural exploitation, points of emphasis, and lines of motion. Letters and numerals must be reversed in the sketch.

After preliminary drawings have been made and evaluated for design potential, the students may use them as a reference for their drawing on the lino plate. Another way is to transfer them to the lino plate with carbon paper or dressmaker's white transfer paper. If the lino surface is dark and no white transfer paper is available, paint the block with white tempera paint first. To reverse a sketch before transferring it to the block, hold it against the window and trace lines on the back of the sheet. Another solution is to transfer the design by placing the drawing pencil-side down onto the block, taping it down to secure it, and rubbing over it with a metal spoon.

Before the cutting begins, check to see that there are enough sharpened gouges in various sizes for the entire class. Students should be introduced to the potential of the many gouges through a teacher demonstration emphasizing the correct way to hold and manipulate the gouge. Never put a supporting hand in front of a cutting tool. Some schools have acquired equipment to make lino cutting less hazardous, such as a wood bench hook. This device is anchored against desk or table edge and provides a supportive ridge for the block. Each lino gouge makes its own particular cut, and although gouges are not as easily controlled as pencils or pens, they produce lines that are

Iowa City, Iowa.

often more dynamic. The richest print effects are achieved using a range of gouges, from veiners to scoops and shovels. Number 1 and #2 veiners or V-shaped gouges are suggested for making the initial outlines. Another approach is to use the scoop or shovel gouges, working from inside the shapes and thus minimizing tightly outlined compositions.

Students can prevent mistakes in cutting by marking an "X" on those areas of the lino surface that are to be gouged out. Use directional gouge cuts to follow the object's contours, like ripples around a pebble tossed into a stream. The students should be instructed not to make their cuts too deep into the lino, because the low ridges remaining will produce an attractive texture. If the students have difficulty cutting because the linoleum is too hard, heat it on a cookie tin over an electric hot plate turned to a low setting.

Proofs of the work in progress may be made by placing paper over the cutout block. Then, using the side of a black crayon or oil pastel, rub over the paper with a steady and even pressure. The resulting proof will reveal to the students how the print is progressing.

As in all printmaking activities, paper-protected areas for inking, printing, and print storage should be designated. Printing papers include newsprint, brown wrapping paper, construction paper and tissue paper in assorted colors, wallpaper samples, and colored pages from magazines. Squeeze out the water-soluble ink onto the cookie tin and roll it out with a rubber brayer until tacky. Apply it to the lino block (which has been cleaned with a moist towel and allowed to dry) with pressure in two directions so the whole block, including border and corners, is completely inked.

On page 230, top: *Two examples of linoleum blocks printed over colored-tissue collages. At left, white printing ink was employed over a dark tissue design. At right, black printing ink was used over a lighter-valued tissue underlay. Which of these middle-school designs do you like better? Be sure the tissue is glued down firmly and smoothly and is thoroughly dry before pulling the print.* ***On page 230, bottom:*** *Linoleum prints with bold designs by fourth- and fifth-grade children. The left picture of monkeys uses a series of monkeys—big, small, and smallest—to set up a rhythm. The right-hand kangaroo picture has an interesting feature, a positive and negative cactus.* ***At right:*** *These woodblock prints of a bird and its hungry babies, cows at milking time, and three hens are by Japanese children, grades 4 and 5. Notice how much was observed and recorded in these space-filled compositions. Printmaking incorporating woodblock cutting tools is introduced in the third grade in Japanese schools. Note in the top design the skillfully cut pattern of positive and negative shapes in the leaves and branches.*

After quickly carrying the inked block to the printing station or individual desk, place the paper (cut slightly larger than the block) carefully on the inked lino plate and tap it down gently with heel of hand. Then, exerting stronger pressure with rubber brayer, heel of hand, jar cover, spoon, or commercially available baren, go over the entire surface, especially the borders and corners. The ink dries quickly and may cause stickiness, so pull the paper off the block carefully. To check the impression, the student can lift the paper partially off the block from various sides and if not satisfied apply more pressure. Wood scraps are an alternative to using linoleum. Wood scraps can often be secured from building sites or lumber yards. Especially with small blocks, the use of a bench hook is required for safety. Seal the wood's porous surface with a coat of dilute white glue.

Actual size woodblock print. This seventh-grade student found and created strong patterns in the tree branches and feathers. The block was painted with colored tempera and printed in several stages to achieve the color overlays.

A woodblock print by Käthe Kollwitz (1867–1945) was the motivation for the three self-portrait prints by upper-grade Japanese youngsters.

Courtesy of David Hodge, Oshkosh, Wisconsin.

Busy upper-elementary-grade youngsters at work on a group project, a reduction linoleum print. **Step One:** *In this variation of the regular lino print process, the students first cut away selected areas of the linoleum and pulled several prints using red printing ink.* **Step Two:** *While the prints were drying, the youngsters gouged out additional sections of the block.* **Step Three:** *The cleaned plate was inked again in green and printed over the first red edition, with care being taken to "register" or match the second printing over the first.* **Step Four:** *While the two-color prints dried, the students cut away the final selected areas. They then used black ink for the third and last impression. The completed print is shown above.*

CHAPTER 23

Computer Art, Photography, and Video

Computer Art

There are a number of advantages to including computer art activities in the overall art program:

Computers have an already established importance as central elements in education. Thus the use of computers in the art program can lend prestige to the program as a whole. In addition, art students and teachers can help the school use their desktop publishing programs to create school publications with top-quality design and graphics.

It is sometimes possible to obtain computer resources on a scale unheard of with traditional art teaching materials.

Computer equipment is now available in a growing number of elementary and middle schools. However, teachers of traditional academic subjects are often frustrated and discouraged in their efforts to integrate computer work into their curricula, and art teachers who wish to use the computers may find they have the field virtually to themselves.

Early computer art experiences can overcome students' fear of computers in general, and can become a bridge to skills and experiences that will spur their interest in the "careers of tomorrow," many of which require high-level computer literacy.

If used imaginatively, interactive computer programs for the creation of graphics and page layout can be extremely flexible design tools.

The Computer as a Design Tool

Using the computer as a design tool enables learners to "see" design operations that involve repeating and varying images:

cut	paste	duplicate
shrink	mirror	enlarge
fragment	blur	trace edges
transparency	superimpose	magnification
distort	bilateral symmetry	four-way symmetry

Computers permit students to save progressive stages of a work and to create an infinite number of variations. They foster thinking in terms of scale—students can look at a work normal size and then zoom in for closeup work. Sophisticated visual effects can be achieved by using a range of special tools, for example, and by putting one image one over another using different transparency functions, by making forms grow according to predetermined patterns (fractalizing), or by making forms appear as if they were in a reflecting orb (spherizing). Computers offer sophisticated ways to combine letter forms and words with graphic elements. Thus they can perform a valuable educational role in integrating school art programs with writing programs.

Implementing a Computer Art Program

One problem in implementing a computer art program arises when there is not enough equipment to serve a whole class or a portion thereof. When there are too few computers in the classroom, children can seldom have individual time at the computer.

Fortunately, research indicates that students can learn computer skills as effectively in small groups as individually, and computer art can be taught to small groups of children, one group at a time. However, when this is done, it may be difficult for the teacher to keep the students who are not at computers working on some other task. If the teacher focuses attention on the students engaged in noncomputer activities, the problem becomes one of providing effective instruction in the qualititative production of computer artwork.

One solution may be to have students do computer artwork only after they finish other assignments, or to come in before or after class. Another is to have traditional methods of drawing and painting included as a part of computer-generated projects. For example, a group

Courtesy of Bell South Advertising and Publishing Corporation, 1990.

Top, left: *Children learn computer skills as well in small groups as individually. This painting is made in a technique discussed earlier, tempera resist.* ***Above:*** *An elementary-grade child created a marathon-race effect by multiplying images using the computer's cut and copy or drag functions.* ***Top, right:*** *Geometric forms can be created, overlapped, and filled with hundreds of colors and patterns.*

of students can begin a design on the computer and have a copy printed for each student in the group. Then those students can go to their desks to do the hand coloring, while another group of students, who have been generating design sketches by hand, render them on the computer.

Another way to deal with the problem of a shortage or absence of computers is to approach computer art as an activity in art criticism. Class discussion can focus on the computer art imagery seen by students daily—in special effects in movies, in the animated images that open television programs, in newspaper graphics, and in special lettering effects. Art criticism can be conducted on these mass communication images, and analysis done both of their formal design and on how the design elements complement the idea content. A bulletin board in the room containing found examples of computer art can serve as a center for this collection and analysis.

Another way to develop elementary-school interest in computer art is to have students with computers at home bring in their computer designs, to be mounted in an exhibit. Such an exhibit may serve as a spur to school administrators to support a computer art program in school that will be available to all children. Those who have used computer art programs at home can then use the school computers to teach those who have not had access to computers.

Courtesy of Emily Harris, Athens, Georgia.

Above: *First, the elementary art teacher wrote a grant application to her school system to get a computer in her classroom, and then she and her students learned how to use it. An upper-elementary student made this witch and filled the areas with pattern.* **Above, right:** *Here, in the days before the mouse or joystick was introduced, a middle-school student keyed in the design instructions from the keyboard, and the low-resolution screen has large pixels.*

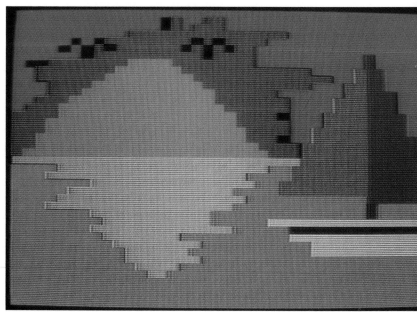

Courtesy of Carole Henry, Athens, Georgia.

The best solution, of course, is for the teacher to convince the school administration that computers should be an integral part of the program, that using computers for art expression is just as essential to students' educational development as using computers for programming, mathematical operations, and word processing.

Photography

The magic of the camera can become real to your students. Using photographic principles, they can capture that most ephemeral of all the art elements, light! Blueprint paper acquired from a local blueprint company or light-sensitive photographic paper obtainable from a photo store can be used by elementary-school children for beginning photographic experiences. Through this medium, they can create designs and learn concepts such as geometric, organic, sinusoidal, pierced, undulating, and lacy.

Before you begin, make sure that there is a totally dark closet somewhere in the school building. Then, with your students, collect an array of opaque, translucent, and transparent objects, of varying color values, that have interesting shapes, patterns, and textures. Suit-

Courtesy of Nancy Elliott, Athens, Georgia.

These photograms are of objects as simple as keys, religious medals, pins, and paper clips. They helped teach middle-school students concepts of overall pattern and positive and negative shape.

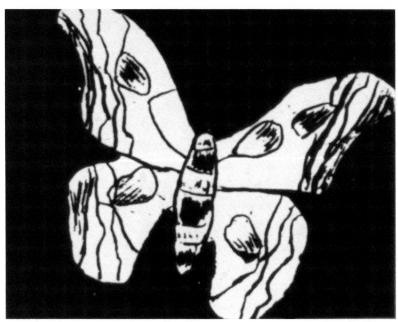

Courtesy of Nancy Elliott, Athens, Georgia.

This butterfly by a middle-school student was created using the cliché verre photographic process. It requires scratching a design through a light-blocking-out painted piece of glass.

able items are fern leaves, grasses, confetti, flowers, ribbon, lace, torn paper shapes, tissue, acetate, window screen, crumpled plastic wrap, shapes of figures and animals cut from paper, checkers, shoelaces, paper doilies, drawings on acetate and on translucent tracing paper, and three-dimensional objects such as coins and keys. Children first plan out their designs. They arrange an assortment of these objects on a stiff sheet of clear acrylic plastic, acetate, or overhead transparency plastic. Properly supervised older students can use a piece of glass with its edges taped. Emphasize consideration of the negative shapes (the empty spaces). Also encourage the students to think about repetition, unity, and variation. To build vocabulary, while the children are waiting for their turn in the darkroom, have them write out a list of the objects they have collected and the design concepts they embody.

For the printmaking stage have a student monitor govern when the darkroom door may be opened. Students take turns carrying their designs into the darkroom. In the dark—by feel or with a red safelight on—they position the design on top of the same size piece of blueprint paper. Then the design of shapes *on* the clear plastic *on* the blueprint paper is taken outside and exposed to sunlight for about 15 minutes, or until the yellow paper turns white.

Then the print is developed. Use a teaspoon of household ammonia on some cotton in the bottom of a large jar with a fitted lid, such as a gallon mayonnaise jar from the school cafeteria. Roll the print enough to fit it into the jar, insert it, and recap the jar. The ammonia fumes will turn the paper blue in a few minutes and the process is complete.

If light-sensitive photo paper is available, the design transfer can be done in a darkroom, using a flashlight to expose the film, and then developed as you would a photograph. With either method, after the print is made, the designs may be left as they are or they may be worked back into with oil pastels and markers to add color. Another variation of this lesson, especially suitable following a contour-line drawing lesson, is to have the students go into the darkroom, using a tiny pocket penlight, and draw the figure as they remember it on the light-sensitive photo paper. Picasso's drawings using this technique may be studied. Another variation is for students to draw on a sheet of translucent paper with a black marker and then make a reverse print in the darkroom. The results will be similar to the cliché verre process used by Corot.

Class discussion afterward should build art vocabulary through listing on the chalkboard names for the shapes, patterns, and textures which the children have created with light. Discuss similarities between their works and those of Fox Talbot and Man Ray. Students

Courtesy of Nancy Elliott, Athens, Georgia.

Middle-school students constructed pinhole cameras. Then they went into the schoolyard to capture light on the forms of sports cars, gravel, walkways, and buildings.

from the fifth grade up can use pin-hole cameras to make their own photographs. Load the camera in a darkroom with slow-emulsion plastic-resin-coated paper. Have the children go out into the schoolyard and point the camera at what interests them—a bicycle wheel, a friend's face, a tree silhouetted against the sky, patterns of bicycle shadows on the ground. Tell them not to worry about composition, or whether the subject moves. An impression is what is sought. Have the children develop the image inside the darkroom. A negative image can be contact-printed back for a positive. This lesson can be correlated with a study of such artists as Corot, Delacroix, Courbet, the impres-

Exhibited at the School Art Symposium, Georgia Museum of Art, Athens, Georgia. Courtesy of Molly Chase and teacher George Mitchell.

Student Molly Chase of Atlanta, Georgia, studying photography at school, captured a special moment of children at the neighborhood store. Probably only a young photographer could elicit the charming expressions of these children caring for children. The photograph is given structure by the geometry, repetition, and perspective in the mammoth shortening display.

sionists, and the futurists, who were fascinated by photography. Discuss what kind of day and light were captured. Was the light direct, or soft, or diffuse? Look at the shadows and describe them.

Another approach is to use Polaroid film or 35-mm print film in a real camera. One roll of 36 pictures will let each child make one picture. Slides are the least expensive. A language-arts-correlated lesson is to have the children make up a story using the slides, then put on a slide show with narration and sound effects, with the children playing the roles. A local photo lab may donate out-of-date film. If the supply of film is limited, have the children work in pairs to plan out the subject of their photo and take the picture. Some other topics to document might include activities on the playground, friends, an architecture field trip, the class garden, and a diorama on almost any subject. The children's photos can then serve as visual complements to art projects using traditional media and methods.

Teach the children the vocabulary of photography. Terms and concepts about light include: light and shadow, direct light and reflected light, contrast, value, low contrast, high contrast, direction of light, high-key delicate lighting containing nothing darker than middle grey, low-key somber lighting containing nothing lighter than middle grey, sharp and diffuse shadows, point of view, low angle, distant shot, foreground, near ground, middle ground, background. Terms about the technical process include: positive, negative, camera, shutter, lens, diaphragm, f stop, focus, film speed (ISO), stop bath, fixer. Historical terms include: daguerreotype, Talbot-type or Calotype, ambrotype, tintype, and cartes de visite (visiting cards with a photograph).

A study of Edward S. Curtis's photos of Native Americans and Matthew Brady's photos of the Civil War can be correlated to social studies units. The lesson can be integrated with a unit on the science of light and art history, replicating the 1830s sun drawings of Henry Fox Talbot. Photos of scientific phenomena, close-up microscopic views, and macrocosmic views of outer space can be studied as works of art, using the above photographic vocabulary. Art criticism can be taught using a collection of photographic masterpieces. For example, cut photographs from an issue of *Life* magazine on the history of photography. With these photos, students can engage in some of the educational gamelike activities discussed in Chapter 15.

Video

Video, the art medium of our time, is transforming the nature of art and of our lives. The famous video artist Nam June Paik said, "Information has to be recognized as an alternative energy source. Informa-

Family of Robot: Aunt, 1986 (video sculpture, 86½ × 21½ inches). Courtesy of Carl Solway Gallery, Cincinnati, Ohio.

Pioneering video artist Nam June Paik (born in Korea in 1932) uses hundreds of television monitors to create video walls of information. He wants them to humanize and demystify television technology, as does the figurative piece shown here which is constructed from TV sets.

An elementary-school child videos a guest speaker discussing his passion, raising horses. Children can also video field trips to sketching sites and peers in the process of making art.

tion changes our life style" (1987). Video's power to capture the affect in human interactions, its accessibility, and its spontaneity, and the ease with which it is disseminated, are awesome. Unfortunately—perhaps because of a fear of technology or an awe of the power of this important medium—too much video equipment stays locked in school closets, gathering dust and becoming obsolete.

Video can provide valuable educational experiences to students. Many homes now have videocassette recorders (VCRs), and families with cameras shoot their own home videos. Teachers of art should put this technology into the hands of our students. Video can be used to document events in the classroom, the school, and community. Art concepts of light, space, movement, and time become real to the students as they make films, and watch and analyze videos and films.

Some instructional objectives for a video program are as follows. In the area of art creation, the students will be able to use the video camera to apply spatial concepts involving the use of closeups and long shots and to manage the art elements of light and space. In the area of art criticism, students will analyze techniques used in art-history videos and videos made by famous artists. Students will learn the vocabulary of motion film. They will identify instances of back lighting, soft focus, and freeze frame, establishing zoom shots, slow disclosure shots, low-angle shots, long shots, and panning shots.

Students will describe how artists have humanized technology, for example, the installations and performances of Nam June Paik and Laurie Anderson. Students can take home the videos they make and view them on the family VCR. With their families they can discuss how they made their shots and how they used light and space and action. Videos of students creating in another art media can be used as a tool to help them critique their performance in achieving their video-related art objectives.

Art displays that the teacher puts up in elementary-school hallways can be videotaped as a way of documenting the quality of work. This video can be shared with the students whose work is depicted as a way to give them feedback. It can also be shared with future classes when they embark upon the same kind of project. Videos documenting the community's older artists, renowned artists, and folk artists can be used as part of an art history curriculum. Videos of seniors telling of their arts and crafts heritage become historical records of knowledge that can be passed on to future generations.

A student can video his or her classmates making art, then take the videotape home and write a critique of the result. The students depicted in the video can take the tape home and watch it, then write a review of their art-making process, telling what they would like to do better or differently. If the museum permits, videos can document your students' museum field trips. This visual documentation can then be used to review the experience and to give the students the opportunity to share their responses. All these videos can provide valuable documentation of a program's effectiveness to be shared with evaluators and at parent-teacher meetings and programs.

Students who have received training in using the camera can document school functions, game days, and seasonal festivities. These can be played in the school hall or in classes to provide feedback to the participants themselves. Art club members can videotape the musical, dramatic, and dance performances of the other arts programs. In many middle schools, where art competes with orchestra, band, and chorus for enrollment, videos of the art program in action can be used as a way of recruiting students and building a program of quality.

Video can be used to bring the art program out into the community. School-produced videos can be shown at the local library as part of a humanities program. Documenting the historical contributions of groups of persons in the community is a way to gain valuable community support for your art education program. Videos can document your students' reactions to social and political events in the community, such as older siblings going off to war and the impact of that event on younger siblings at home. Videos documenting community life can be shown at town festivals; for example, a video of making sorghum syrup might be shown at a local fall festival. For social studies projects, students might make a video in a nearby senior citizens' center, documenting the seniors' memories of fires, riots, wars, and floods. Teachers are amazed at the time and energy that children put into their involvement in video projects. This medium gives students a way to create their own reality.

CHAPTER 24

Three-Dimensional Design: Additive and Subtractive Sculpture

Many challenging sculptural techniques, both additive and subtractive, await those upper-elementary-grade and middle-school students and their teachers who are ready and willing to make a serious, time-consuming commitment to a painstaking yet adventurous task. Too often sculpture in the elementary school has been presented as a therapeutic activity with minor emphasis on its expressive potential. If sufficient time cannot be allotted in the schedule for the students to become thoroughly involved in the sculptural process, postpone it until the middle-school years, when more time is budgeted for art and when the students' perseverance and constructive skills are more developed, for young adolescents definitely enjoy chiseling and carving in substances. However, if the elementary-school teacher of art understands the limitations and possibilities of the various sculptural media, they can be very exciting. If the students can be motivated to carry projects through to culmination, the sculpture experience can be one of the most fulfilling in the art program for upper elementary grades.

The major consideration of these three-dimensional projects is often not so much a matter of motivation as a matter of material resources, preliminary planning, special techniques, cleanup, and storage. A class of 25 or more students working on additive or subtractive sculpture poses several organizational problems. Teachers must decide beforehand whether they want the entire class to use the same medium or to allow the students to work in materials of their choosing. Skilled instructors may be able to control a large class where some students are working on toothpick or balsa-wood construction, some on plaster block carving, and some on wire or metal sculpture. However, the resulting products must show evidence of the students' growth in sculptural design. If, as is often the case, the teacher becomes merely the dispenser of various materials and tools and has little time to evaluate the work in progress with the students, it is much wiser to limit the offering and have the entire class use only one sculptural medium. In such instances the teacher can organize materials, tools, and storage space more effectively. A rich motivational plan and evaluation plan can be developed over the several days necessary for the project.

This chapter will first discuss box sculpture and constructions in space, then masks, and finally subtractive sculpture in plaster.

Box Sculpture and Constructions in Space

Older and more mature children often need a change of pace. New challenges, materials, and techniques can spark them to maintain a growing interest in art. Using cardboard boxes, mailing tubes, and assorted found objects gives upper-elementary-grade and middle school students a rare opportunity to express their individual ideas in a unique three-dimensional form. They can recycle discarded materials using new, environmentally conscious solutions. They can struggle with a problem in complex construction until it is solved. They can come to realize in a creative way the adage that "the whole is greater than the sum of its parts."

An exciting new world of additive sculpture has opened up with the burgeoning exploitation of found materials. These include applicator sticks, drinking straws, thin dowels, assorted toothpicks, reeds, discarded game parts (for example, Tinkertoy pieces), pick-up sticks, scrap lumber, and plastic packing materials. The resulting constructions have many labels: stabiles, mobiles, space modulators, combine art, scrap sculpture, or assemblage. Constructions will definitely add an adventurous dimension to art programs and hold the interest of today's students. A first consideration is to acquire sufficient materials and tools. For this, a letter to the parents listing materials needed will help build a necessary store of discards, scraps, and remnants.

Left: *In box sculpture, allow the shape of the box itself to trigger the student's imagination. Square and rectangular boxes are much easier for young children to assemble.* **Above:** *In view of today's widespread ecological concerns about our earth's vanishing resources, sculptures from recycled materials take on added significance. Some soldering skills were necessary for this metal construction by a middle-school student. It is another example of the adage "The whole is greater than the sum of its parts."*

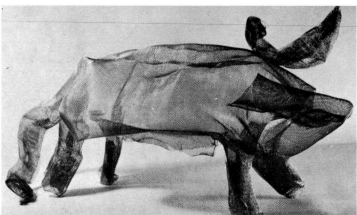

In many instances students will be eager to create nonobjective, abstract, and geometrically oriented constructions, allowing the materials to dictate the form. This is particularly true when straws, applicator sticks, toothpicks, and reeds are the building elements. The design grows, stick by stick, straw by straw, dowel by dowel. Unless the construction itself is stable, an auxiliary support or separate base of wood, plywood, or Masonite is needed. Determine the number and placement of supports required and then drill or hammer holes into the base at these points. Begin the structure by inserting and gluing the initial supports into these holes.

Students and teachers will discover, too, a host of materials to embellish the stick or straw constructions. Experiment, for example, with bottle corks, thread spools, beads, cord, Ping-Pong balls, small rubber balls, pegboard pegs, construction paper, mailing tubes, colored cardboard, cardboard spools from tape dispensers, miniature cardboard boxes, plastic pieces, wood or plastic buttons, and tiny film canisters. Outdoors, the teacher can give the completed constructions a unifying coat of black or white spray paint that will contribute to the striking visual impact.

There are many avenues open to students in upper elementary grades and middle school who want to explore more challenging aspects of additive sculpture. Wire can be combined with found metal pieces. Toothpick and applicator-stick constructions can be dipped into melted crayon, wet plaster, or liquid metal. Corrugated cardboard can be cut into various shapes and then slotted, joined, and glued together into a stabile. Cardboard mailing tubes can be cut into multisized cylinders and rings and then assembled into animals, insects, and figures. X-acto knives, Sloyd knives, or utility knives are necessary to cut cardboard boxes, but they must be used only under the teacher's strict supervision. A coping saw or little vibrating table jigsaw is useful for cutting heavy cardboard, chipboard, Masonite, and heavyweight cardboard tubes.

At least two to four weeks before the project begins, the students should be reminded to start collecting discarded boxes from grocery, stationery, drug, and department stores. This early personal involvement on the part of the students builds interest in the expressive adventure ahead. Store the accumulated boxes and objects until

Wood scraps, rope and yarn remnants, dried corn husks, discarded metal screen, and spools from thread can be recycled in today's school art programs. This lion, elephant, and grasshopper are successful examples. Let the youngsters' imaginations soar.

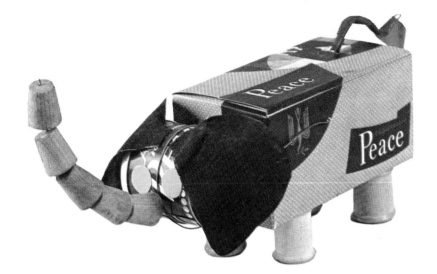

needed in a giant cardboard carton, or students can store their personal collections in their own grocery sack.

Useful fastening materials include straight pins, masking tape, paper clips, string, double-faced tape, rubber bands, gummed tape, white liquid glue, school paste, scissors, paper punch, nails, and wire. Plan ahead for adequate storage facilities for the found objects, for the supply of fastening devices and materials, and for the constructions in progress.

Imaginative box-sculpture themes are almost limitless: astronauts, spaceships, space stations, robots, creatures from another planet, engines, planes, toys, rockets, homes, vehicles and computers of the future, fantastic designs for playground equipment, masks, non-objective space modulators, and imaginative animals, bugs, birds, and fish.

One way to start the project is to invite the students to select three or four different-sized boxes and a set of cardboard mailing tubes (toilet-tissue tubes for small constructions) and juxtapose these in various configurations until an idea is triggered. Another approach is to have a theme in mind and select boxes to form this preconception. After the students decide on a basic shape for their creations, they can make sketches to help them plan the construction. The excitement builds as students see the creation grow. Sometimes an unusual box turns up that is just right for the head of a monster and triggers the design for the rest of the construction. Often a box can be partially opened and hinged to become mouth and jaws of a voracious mythical lion or dragon. What began as a dream car might easily emerge in the final stages as a space station.

The most difficult part is the mechanics involved in fastening the separate boxes together and securing the appendages to the main structure. The recommended method includes first gluing and then tying or taping the boxes together until the glue dries. Fasten the boxes together with masking tape that extends around both boxes. For a strong weld, the glue should be allowed to dry overnight.

Finding an adhesive with ideal properties can be problematic, as many adhesives have some but not all of the desired properties. For example, white glue (e.g., Elmer's glue) is safe, available in most

---

Top: *As is the case with this elephant, it is not always necessary to paint box sculpture. Some boxes already have colorful printed designs.* ***Middle:*** *This cruise ship ingeniously employs box sculptural forms.* ***Bottom:*** *This construction of reeds and construction paper by a sixth-grade student shows a good use of restraint. It employs only triangular shapes, which create a unified design.*

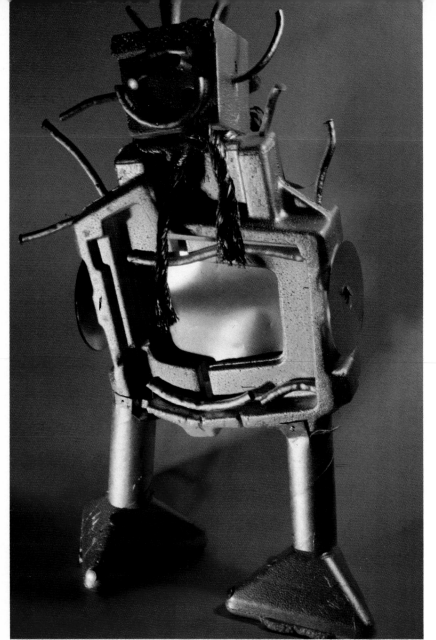

Ann Arbor, Michigan.

Right: *After the boxes have been taped together, the sculpture is allowed to dry and become sturdy. Then the sculpture can be painted.* **Above:** *A sixth-grade student combined plastic discards to produce this imaginatively constructed robot. Then, after working surfaces had been protected with newspapers, the entire sculpture was sprayed with metal paint. Only the teacher, not the students, should use spray paint, and, even then, spray out of doors in good ventilation.*

schools, and reasonably effective, although its tackiness and drying time are not ideal. A new product, Elmer's Tacky Glue, has more tackiness and therefore is superior for box sculptures and wood scrap sculptures. Glues such as airplane glue and Duco Cement should not be used in classrooms because they contain the harmful solvents xylene or toluene. To give added strength to a glued area until the glue achieves maximum strength, use extra bits of tape, paper clips, staples, or pins. Working on a stiff base, such as a 1-foot-square piece of cardboard or Masonite, gives increased stability to the in-progress piece and facilitates rotating the work so that all sides can be seen.

In the construction of standing figures, students must decide how to make the figure stand upright. If necessary, a stabilizing third leg or support can be created. A tail can be added, or the figure can hold gear (for example, a spear or banner standard) that touches the ground.

Unusual combinations of materials can add decoration or texture and heighten interest. For example, consider using egg cartons, corrugated and embossed cardboard, paper drinking straws, plastic packing noodles, clothespins, toothpicks, paste sticks, dowels, corks, pipe cleaners, reeds, beads, Tinkertoy pieces, Ping-Pong balls, and game parts.

Sometimes the containers with their printed designs and logos are so colorful and exciting that painting them would only mask their bold design qualities. If the sculpture is to be painted, the features that give it individuality must be emphasized, especially the eyes,

Top: Milwaukee, Wisconsin. Bottom, *Three-Fold Manifestation II* (steel painted white, 32 feet high), Alice Aycock. Courtesy Storm King Art Center, Mountainville, New York. Gift of the artist. Photo: Jerry L. Thompson.

mouth, nose, ears, and horns. Also, the glossy surfaces of boxes often resist water-based paints and it may be necessary to add soap to the paint to make it adhere. Spray paints are not considered safe for student use, and any spray painting must be done by the teacher and conducted outdoors. Silver, copper, or gold paint may be employed for a robot, knight in armor, or astronaut. Rather than painting the boxes that already contain graphics or lettering, another possibility is to camouflage them with colored paper, comic-book and magazine pages, tissue paper, wallpaper samples, cloth, or gift-wrapping papers. There are endless possibilities in box and found-object sculpture. The teacher and students who are resourceful enough, persistent enough, and patient enough to try this project have a real art adventure awaiting them. Go for it!

Masks

Multicultural education will certainly include the study of masks. An incentive for mask making that is integrated to a social studies cultural unit may be on a firmer academic base than one that comes from overworked Halloween motifs. In Africa, likenesses of departed chiefs are used in memorial services. Native Americans use masks in rain-making and agricultural ceremonies. Judges in New Guinea wear masks to heighten their authority. The masks worn by medieval mummers might signify one of the seven deadly sins, biblical characters, or forces of nature. In China, Burma, and Ceylon masks were worn to prevent illness and to cure diseases. Robbers wear them to conceal their identity. Police officers, firefighters, hospital personnel, and football players wear masks for personal protection.

Mask making in the elementary and middle schools has always been a popular undertaking but, unfortunately, one in which the design considerations have seldom been effectively implemented. Too often basic compositional factors have been minimized and raw colors applied in a random, slap-dash, form-negating manner. Very young children can, on occasion, create colorful, expressively naive masks

---

Top: *A sixth-grade student created this space modulator with construction-paper strips and school paste.* ***Bottom:*** *Perhaps such a project will inspire one of your students to become a sculptor and to create pieces, not 30 inches high, but rather 30 feet high. In any event, because of the school experience you provide, all students will be able to appreciate more intensely the rhythm, repetition, and construction in such works as Alice Aycock's 1987 sculpture.*

Left: *Colored-construction-paper masks. A three-dimensional effect was achieved by cutting short slits into the borders of a square or rectangular sheet of paper and then overlapping the resulting tabs and stapling them together. Masks make highly decorative artifacts to brighten up the classroom.* ***Above:*** *Giant colored-construction-paper masks by Japanese children. (See also page 41.)*

when richly motivated. However, because of the cultural and symbolic connotations of mask making and the often complex techniques required for implementation, mask making is best postponed until students reach the upper elementary grades and middle school.

The most inspired and evocative masks of past centuries and cultures have almost always been based on an abstract, stylized concept rather than on natural appearance. To emphasize certain features, mask makers often abstracted the face, whether human or animal, into combinations of ovals, squares, and circles. A study of masks, such as those by tribal Africans and North Pacific Coast Indians, reveals recurring aspects. Whereas facial features that capture the mood or spirit are usually exaggerated, they are seldom distorted to the extent that they appear as something so alien and trite as star-shaped

Varied approaches to mask making. **Left:** *Boxes, spools, paper cups, and yarn create a face by varying conical forms.* **Center:** *Construction paper is bent into a canoelike shape and raffia added. Feathers could also be incorporated.*

Right: *Papier-mâché over a crumpled newspaper base. Basic mask forms may also be achieved by applying newspaper strips with wheat paste or liquid starch over a balloon or mixing bowl.*

eyes. The most expressive masks are imbued with the essence and vitality of a particular mood or emotion: astonishment, serenity, power, anger, dignity, joy, fury, frenzy, benevolence, or wonder. Another recurring characteristic is continuity of facial forms and features, as exemplified by the linear flow of the nose structure into the eyebrow contour.

Decoration is used to heighten the mask's visual appeal. Taking a cue from mask makers of the past, students should use lines or shapes to reinforce and emphasize the dominant features. They should create pattern and texture on the face and delineate hair and beard and emphasize eyes by using highly contrasting colors and values. However, color must be used judiciously, lest it jeopardize the mask's impact or appeal. Color must be integrated with the features, not super-

ficially applied, and it must complement rather than detract. Subtle, limited color harmonies should be encouraged and primary colors used with discretion, although primary colors may be effectively employed to provide a necessary contrast.

Materials and processes that result in qualitative mask making are in a sense limited. Papier-mâché over a clay foundation is still the most popular and effectively controlled technique, allowing for highly individualized interpretations and detailed facial modeling. Also recommended is papier-mâché or plaster-impregnated gauze applied over a mixing or salad bowl, small dishpan, balloon, or beach ball. As the pasted form develops, it can be embellished with additional pieces of plastic foam, bent cardboard, and found objects to create nose, eyes, mouth, and ear shapes. String, yarn, raffia, and plastic packing

material may be used for hair, beard, and other textures. These details are covered with a final layer of gauze or glue-moistened paper toweling. When dry, the mask can be painted.

A popular mask-making technique is the paper- or cardboard-construction process. This generally requires intricate cutting and scoring of the paper to achieve effective three-dimensional quality. It has many possibilities, however, and can be pursued in the ordinary classroom because of the availability of materials and tools. Unlike papier-mâché projects that involve a lengthy cleanup period and abundant storage space, paper-sculpture masks are simpler to manage and store.

For children in the primary grades, the creation of a paper plate, paper sack, or plastic meat-tray mask is the most practical and successful technique, since it does not involve a complex three-dimensional process.

Totem Poles

A study of early Pacific Coast Indian life provides rich motivation for several art projects, including the group construction of a totem pole. However, the culture of the Northwest Indians must be genuinely examined. Cross-cultural comparisons can be made about the role of art in their culture, and their beliefs about nature, death, and religion and the roles of men, women, and children. For the Native American carvers, art is empty when it omits the spiritual dimension of life. As was the custom of the Native American totem carvers, encourage the students to identify with some other living entity or with an animal or bird school symbol.

Use a sheet of colored construction paper 12 × 18 inches as the background for each totem mask. With the paper placed horizontally on the desk, the 18-inch border at bottom, the students draw with chalk the outline of their mask in the center of the paper. The larger

Observe the highly imaginative and free features which these upper-elementary-grade children invented for their bulletin board full of colored-construction-paper masks. The teacher and students discussed different ways to draw mouths, eyes, and noses. Everyone came up with a unique way to depict each feature; no two are alike. Marker drawings were then enriched with oil pastel and pattern, used in equally unique ways.

At right: Masks created for a totem-pole project. Colored construction paper, 12 × 18 inches, and oil pastels were used. Noses, teeth, ears, and cheeks were made by cutting slits in the mask. These portions were then bent out to create three-dimensional forms. Completed masks were secured to discarded food tins from the school cafeteria. **Above:** *Kindergarten children created their own Halloween costumes by recycling paper garment bags. If such bags are not available, fasten together with glue or masking tape two large-size grocery bags, one with the bottom cut off.*

they draw it, the better, but they should leave some paper plain at each side. However, the top and bottom of their mask should touch the edge of the paper. When the drawing is complete, the mask may be painted with tempera paint or colored with crayon or oil pastels. Students should be encouraged to exploit unusual color combinations in their masks, including the use of black and white; to repeat colors for unity; to create contrast by juxtaposing light and dark colors; and to emphasize important parts of their masks through a selection of vivid, dominant colors.

When the mask is colored, make parts of it three-dimensional by cutting slits with scissors around an ear or nose and folding these pieces outward from the main mask or bending them back. A backing sheet of a contrasting color, 12 × 18 inches, may be added when assembling the several masks into the totem form. Students may also add supplementary shapes of multicolored construction paper for teeth, fangs, horns, ears, earrings, and eyebrows.

There are several ways to construct totem poles out of the separate masks. One method involves the use of gallon food tins from the school cafeteria. Weight them down with sand or clay. Wrap a 24-×36-inch sheet of tagboard around the can and secure it with masking tape, creating a 36-inch-tall cylinder. Build another cylinder above the first, if desired. Secure it again with tape. With the tagboard cylinder as a steady foundation, fasten the masks around it with glue, masking tape, or gum tacker. Another type of foundation pole can be made from a cardboard cylinder from a carpet showroom.

Once the basic totem pole is sturdily constructed, embellish it with supplemental wings, feet, and arms made out of cardboard. Display the completed totem poles at a cultural celebration or in the school foyer as a way of sharing the multicultural learning experience with the school at large.

Courtesy of Alice Ballard Munn, Anchorage, Alaska, and Diane Barret, Athens, Georgia.

Barrow Elementary School, Athens, Georgia.

Subtractive Sculpture in Plaster

Subtractive sculpture (carving) has appealed to artists of all cultures throughout the ages. Wood has probably been the most popular medium for sculptors; but exquisite creations have been carved in a host of materials, including jade, ivory, bone, marble, soapstone, and alabaster. Many of these art materials are, of course, not suitable for the usual art class. They may be banned (such as ivory), too costly (such as jade), or too dangerous (such as soapstone, which may contain asbestos). For school use, ideal materials must be safe, economical, and relatively easy to carve, and allow easy cleanup. Recommended and readily obtainable materials for subtractive sculpture include plaster-of-Paris, leather-hard clay, balsa wood, porous firebrick, and economy-sized bars of soap. A metal casting byproduct, sand core, consisting of sand and binders, may be available free from a local metal foundry.

Plaster is usually the material chosen for subtractive sculpture in school programs because it is cheap and easy to get. Plaster should be mixed with additives such as fine-grain zonolite or white sand to give it a texture and make it easier to carve. Approximately one part additive to one part dry plaster will produce a fairly porous and workable carving block. A half-gallon or quart-size milk or juice carton made of waxed cardboard makes a sturdy, leak-proof container.

Subjects that students can handle successfully include fish, nesting birds, animals (especially those in repose, to prevent thin legs from breaking off), and portrait heads. Organic or nonobjective free forms can be developed from motifs based on rocks, shells, nuts, pods, and other natural or biomorphic forms.

Students begin by making preliminary front-, side-, and optional back-view sketches for their sculptures on paper, cut to the size of their plaster block. While they are sketching, the teacher can help two or three students at a time to make their plaster molds. All necessary materials and tools for making the plaster block should be on a news-

paper-protected table or counter, near the sink if possible. Have ready the molding plaster, vermiculite or sand, scoops or cups, milk cartons opened wide at the top, water, small-size rubber or plastic dishpan, wood stock or paddle, dry tempera colors (if desired), and lots of newspapers to cover the counter and floor around the plaster-mixing area and line the nearby wastebaskets.

Fill a milk carton three-fourths full with water and pour the water into the dishpan. Sift plaster into the water slowly, using hand, cup, or scoop. When islands of plaster appear above the water, add zonolite or sand. Stir the mix gently yet swiftly by hand, squeezing out the lumps until thoroughly mixed. The mixture thickens very quickly, so be ready to pour it immediately into the milk carton. After pouring the plaster into the carton, tap the carton on the table to remove trapped bubbles or stir quickly with a stick or paddle. *Never pour plaster down the sink.* Scrape excess plaster left in the dishpan, on hands, and on tools into the newspaper-lined wastebasket, and then rinse hands and tools in another pail of water. Do not pour the rinsing water down the sink. Allow the plaster mold or block to dry overnight. If color is desired in the plaster block, tempera powder may be used to tint the dry plaster before it is mixed with water. Neutral colors such as umber, ochre, sienna, and earth green are recommended.

Students may transfer preliminary pencil sketches to the block using carbon paper or they may draw directly on the block with pencil or ink marker, using their sketches as a reference. First they cut, file, rasp, or chisel away the excess plaster to delineate the dominant profile or outline view. Next they may refer to their top, front, and rear sketches and carve away to define those contours. They should proceed cautiously as they remove the plaster, turning the block around to define all forms consistently. As they carve, encourage them to think about how each part flows freely and naturally into the next.

The recommended tools for the carving process are a Sloyd or Hyde knife with a 2-inch blade, a utility knife (i.e., a knife with a metal handle encasing a replaceable blade), or a small plaster rasp. Tables and floors in the working areas should be covered with newspapers or plastic dropcloths to expedite cleanup. Cleanup may also be minimized by having the students hold the plaster block inside a large cardboard box as they carve. In fair weather, the class can carve outdoors, away from high-public-visibility areas such as building entrances, and work on dropcloths.

Teachers should help the students evaluate their sculpture in process: to be aware of large masses contrasting with small forms; to capture the characteristic stance or action; to emphasize a feature such as the beak or claws of a bird; and to enrich the surface of their creation through texture and pattern.

---

*Facing page, top left: Totems should be made in conjunction with a study of Native American culture. In a second-grade class, each child selected an animal thought to have special powers and made a northwest Native American totem dedicated to it. **Bottom left:** Northwest Haida women's hats were made and the women's stories told. **Top right:** Cylindrical forms were made by a column of school cafeteria cans being stacked and taped together. **Bottom right:** A tree was used for the vertical column, and masks by upper-elementary-school children attached to the column.*

Subtractive sculptures. **Top, left:** *Sandcore, a by-product from metal casting, and porous firebrick can be carved. Notice how cleverly this child has solved the problem of thin legs breaking off by keeping a central band intact between the legs.* **Top right and bottom left and right:** *Teachers usually add vermicu-* *lite to plaster of Paris so it can be carved more easily. The vermiculite also gives a rough texture. Observe in this bear, mountain goat, and rhinoceros how these sixth-grade artists have solved the problem of delicate parts breaking off by using volumetric compact forms.*

When sculpting animals, heads, or human figures, the students should keep the bottom part of the sculpture undefined during most of the carving process. This way the piece does not become top-heavy and topple over and break. Delicate appendages such as hands, ears, horns, tusks, beaks, tails, and other jutting forms should be kept undefined until the basic shape is well established.

The sculpture should make fullest use of the block. Students should be cautioned against choosing a subject that is too intricate and complex and which might be more easily expressed in wood, wire, metal, or clay. During the final stages, carve textural and decorative details with nails, discarded dental tools, or nut picks. Students should be reminded that no amount of texture, detail, or pattern will redeem the work if the basic form is weak.

The finished sculpture may be stained, glazed, waxed, or metalized. To provide a working surface for the stain or patina, the plaster sculpture should be coated or sealed with slightly water-diluted white

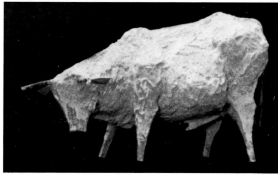

Above: Large-scale cast paper and wood sculpture (55 × 48 × 48 inches). Myth Woman (1991), by artist Ted Ramsay, shows the power of working in large scale, here five times life size. A work such as this can inspire a class and an ambitious teacher to do a project based upon a literary or historical character using large scale. Left: Plaster is often used both additively and subtractively on the same sculpture. Shown here is how a sturdy interior form called an armature can be constructed and covered with plaster. For larger projects, bend and weld reinforcing bars together. Then fill out the form with thinner wire, mesh, string, wood, and paper. Finally, add plaster and carve away the excess. For illustrations of other sculpture projects, see pages 4, 62, 143, 152, and 158.

glue. Allow the glue to dry thoroughly. A paint stain in subtle shades can be applied freely and allowed to penetrate into the incised areas. After letting the stain set briefly, wipe the raised areas to bring out highlights. A complementary sculpture base of driftwood, stained blocks of wood, and sections of tree trunks with the bark left intact can give the carving distinction.

CHAPTER 25

Architecture

Architecture has been called the mother of the arts because it contains all the other art forms. Architectural education conducted in the elementary school can do much to sensitize future citizens not only to the delights of the study of architecture, but also to the importance of wise community design decisions. Yet for too long, architecture has not been a well-established component in elementary school art programs. Nevertheless, architecture is an art form so readily apprehended and so essential to the character of our communities, that architecture education is essential.

One recommended activity is to construct a model of architecturally interesting buildings in the town. Elementary classroom teachers have correlated this activity to the study of social science and careers, and included math and writing skills connected with the various occupations. Some instructional objectives are:

The students will create a model of an existing building incorporating the design qualities of repetition, pattern, and texture.

The students will discuss the reasons why particular buildings have architectural character.

The students will arrange their model buildings to replicate an actual section of a town. (See page 292.)

The design sources can be photographs, slides, or drawings of the actual buildings. Small boxes, such as hand-appliance, cereal, shoe, and drugstore gift boxes, can be used for the basic structure. These can be covered with construction paper or painted. Signs and architectural features can be cut from paper, decorated, and attached. Temporarily arrange the buildings onto a large piece of cardboard, such as that in which a refrigerator is shipped. Then the streets and grounds can be sketched in, the background painted, and models of vehicles, street signs, and street furniture such as benches and stop signs added. The project might be given public display, along with attendant pub-

licity, at a meeting of a community development group such as at the chamber of commerce or downtown development authority.

Models of local architecture can be constructed in other media as well. Designs of individual building facades can be rendered in clay and labeled. These can then be attached with construction adhesive to plywood to make a mural for long-term educational display and appreciation. Three-dimensional clay models of historical buildings may become prize community possessions. Pen-and-ink drawings of buildings can be assembled for a community calendar, or a cloth quilt based on historical community buildings can be made for public display.

Sketching fantasy houses is another architecture lesson. Sketches of one's dream house might include exotic architectural features, such as moats, drawbridges, and crenelated towers. Students of a more practical mind set may want to design something for actual use. They might design the interior for their bedroom or a corner of a garden. Students enjoy expressing their personalities through the choice of artwork, interior design, furniture arrangements, color schemes, plants, and bushes. A scrapbook of examples can be put together from department store newspaper advertising sections, home and garden design magazines, and postcards and photocopies of historical exemplars, and the collection used by students as the basis for a colored overall design plan. A follow-up activity is to have students take before and after photos of places where aspects of their designs were actually implemented.

Young primary-level children can enrich their architectural imaginings about castles and fortresses through use of a sandbox. Using their bodies, they can enact architectural forms, such as arches, tunnels, and tiny spaces, and imagine what it feels like to be a building. With string or rope, several students in a group can make geometric shapes. Students can experience one aspect of architecture by devel-

Above and below: Courtesy of Lawrence Stuek, *The Design of Learning Environments*, Ph.D. dissertation, 1991, University of Georgia, Athens, Georgia.

Courtesy of the National Building Museum, Photo Jack Boucher, HABS.

Top, left: *Children can gain awareness of architectural form by helping to build a playscape.* ***Bottom, left:*** *Fourth-grade children converted their classroom into a model city. They designed and constructed their own buildings: a bank, court, post office, newspaper building, etc. Subjects were taught through an integrated curriculum.* ***Above:*** *The National Building Museum, Washington, D.C., was established by Congress in 1980 to encourage the nation's aesthetic sensitivity to architecture. It is in the National Pension Building, built in 1881 in the Italian Renaissance style. Its Great Hall, shown here, is considered one of America's most architecturally thrilling interior spaces. Outstanding architectural education materials for schoolchildren are available there.*

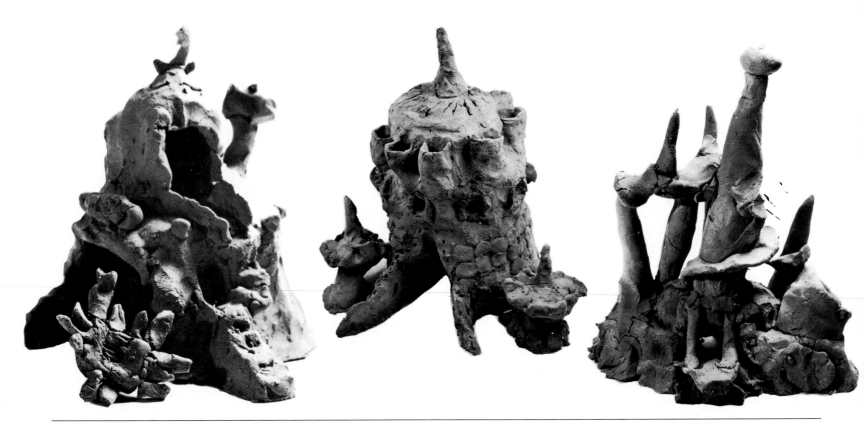

The architecture of Antonio Gaudi and other fantastic architecture can be shown to children to motivate their construction of imaginative structures, such as these sea castles by young Japanese schoolchildren. In most instances constructions like this are assigned as group table projects.

oping design criteria and temporarily rearranging the classroom seats and cabinets.

On a walk around the school, have the students sketch the elements they see: for example, triangular pediments, quoins at corners, columns, arches, fan windows, foyers, and courtyards. In art criticism and art history, teams of students can critique their classroom, school, and community buildings: How do the parts work together? What messages about society are conveyed by the forms? How do you feel about the different spatial arrangements in our school building? How does it show its functions? How would you characterize it, as heavy, serene, lively? If we could redo it, how would we change it?

A local architect can be invited to share building plans with a class, and students can do sketches for the visitor to critique. During a following group discussion, students can share their reasons for preferring modern or traditional styles, classical or romantic designs. Students can go on a sketching tour of their community's most illustrious buildings and list their architectural features.

Informed citizens should be able to interpret architectural plans before buildings are actually constructed. As one way to develop such a skill, students can analyze and critique plans that were used for existing structures or areas, such as their school, a nearby recreation center, park, neighborhood, or subdivision. They can judge whether design strengths and shortcomings found in the built structures were foreshadowed in the plans.

Nelson Goodman wrote, "A building is a work of art only insofar as it signifies, means, refers, or symbolizes in some way." Students can

A drawing of a local historic home by a middle-school student.

discuss the "meanings" of buildings, the messages that buildings send out. Some other aesthetic issues might be addressed by asking such questions as: How does the visual complexity of patterns affect the "interest quotient" of a building? Can a building have too much regularity? Do size and cost determine the quality of a building?

Students can debate what qualities should be considered when ranking buildings (for example, "What is more important, complexity or orderliness?") and then do a class poll to determine whether preference is related to personality. Because architecture is so public an art form and so open to community response, aesthetics and art criticism activities are especially appropriate to the study of architecture.

Top: *Children who are challenged to be aware of their environment and who are encouraged to be "noticers" draw their homes in a personal, individual way. They emphasize those features that make each house unique. Upper-elementary-grade youngsters devoted at least 2 hours to such drawings in felt-nib pens.* **Bottom:** *The world of the future as illustrated in pen and ink by upper-elementary-grade youngsters from Saga, Japan.*

CHAPTER 26

Clay Modeling

All children, in both elementary and middle schools, should have the opportunity to create and express their ideas in clay. Clay is a hands-on wonder—sensuous, malleable, unpredictable, and, on occasion, messy. Some students respond to clay more enthusiastically than others, but all children can benefit from the unique challenges provided by this gift from mother earth.

Clay in the Primary Grades

Young children work in clay in several ways. The majority add clay pieces to the basic form. A few will pat clay into a pancake and draw into it, and a very few will pull out features from a ball or lump of clay. Children may begin a figure with the main body structure, or may start with the appendages and head.

The teacher's main responsibility in the early stage is to provide the children with an adequate supply of workable clay. Check the plasticity of the clay at least a day or two before the project takes place. If the clay is too dry, moisten it; if it is too wet, put it on bats or on newspapers to dry it out. A ball of clay the size of a grapefruit is recommended for each child. Use newspapers or plastic sheeting to protect desk or tabletops. Introduce just enough stimulating subject-matter motivation (for example, animals and their young) to get the class started.

A period of experimentation with the clay should precede every project. Before students can express a particular idea, they need first to acquire the feel of the clay. During these orientation sessions, call the students' attention to the desired plasticity of the clay. Discuss keeping excess clay moist by rolling the crumbs into a single ball. Explain the mechanics of cleanup.

Emphasize how touch experiences help to give shape to objects. One way to introduce students to the exciting tactile potential of clay is to play the clay-in-a-paper-sack game. The students put a ball of clay about the size of a grapefruit or orange into a sturdy paper sack and, without looking, manipulate it until it has an interesting form. Encourage them to think with their hands—to stretch the clay, squeeze it, and poke it. Above all, they must not peek. When completed, the finished pieces are displayed. Ask the students if anyone sees a real form hidden in the clay creations—an animal, a bird, a fish? What did they learn about clay?

The animal kingdom provides a wealth of inspiration for the young clay manipulator. Four-legged mammals such as cows, horses, pigs, hippos, elephants, rhinos, and bears are especially suitable, because the child can model sturdy legs to make them stand up. Other popular animals to construct in clay are cats, dogs, rabbits, turtles, frogs, squirrels, whales, porpoises, and alligators. Group projects such as Noah's ark, a three-ring circus, the zoo, the farm, and the jungle are very popular with young children. Human figures are sometimes difficult for them to master. Children must be guided to provide additional supports or to model thick, sturdy legs to hold the figure erect.

Primary school children especially love clay's plastic changeability as they poke, squeeze, pound, stretch, and roll the moist clay. They may describe a sequence of action with one figure, such as a clown or acrobat, manipulating it to create various postures—standing on its head, bending backward and forward, and falling down. Clay manipulating and modeling may fulfill a therapeutic and storytelling need.

Terra-cotta clay sculpture by a middle-school adolescent, London, England. Notice how the textural quality of the clay has been retained to give the work a spontaneous naturalness. Photo courtesy of London Sunday Mirror.

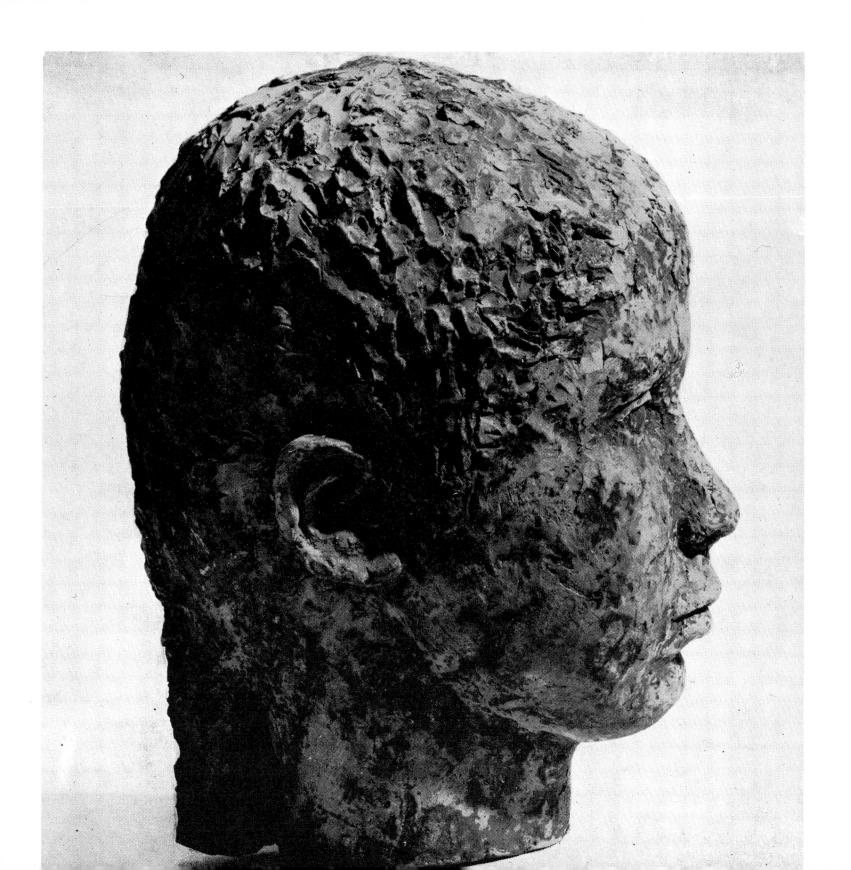

Some students will pat and pound their clay into a flat cookie shape. More advanced students will hold the clay ball in their hands to model their animal's body in three dimensions. They will pull out or add legs, tails, trunks, horns, beaks, and wings. Because figures made in pieces often come apart during drying and firing, many teachers strongly advocate that students be taught to pull out appendages from the body rather than to add them on. Encourage students who insist on adding the appendages to first make holes in the body with a stick or fingers and then insert the appendages into the holes to strengthen the joint. Older students can learn to score and join clay with slip, a pastelike mixture of clay and water. To counteract a sagging form, use temporary clay supports, such as a "fifth leg" under the animal's body, until the clay is leather-hard. Always emphasize the importance of a sturdy basic form.

Although many children in the primary grades are not concerned with detailing, some will enjoy experimenting with textures and pattern on their clay creations. A collection of found objects (which should be washed at the close of the project) such as plastic forks, popsicle sticks, bottle caps, nails, screws, toothbrushes, dowels, and wire mesh will spark their interest.

Clay in the Upper Grades

Older students are more successful in mastering the complexities of advanced clay modeling, but they may ask for help with specific problems. For example, figures and appendages may sag or come apart, and students may need help with balance and proportion, and with intricate delineation of eyes, mouth, nose, and ears.

At this stage effective motivations include: field trips to sketch animals at a farm, zoo, animal shelter, pet shop, or natural history museum; family pets brought to class to model; photographs and art

Left: This elephant's head, neck, ears, and front legs were pulled out from the clay rather than added on. Encourage children to hold the clay in their hands when modeling small sculptural pieces, especially in the beginning stages. This promotes sturdiness. Michelangelo said that a good sculpture should be capable of being rolled down a hill without parts breaking off. Right: The kangaroo's large tail provides support to the burden of the adolescent contentedly sitting in its pouch. The theme of an animal and its young is a surefire hit, one that all children can identify with.

Facing page, top row: Three stages in the construction of a clay hippopotamus are illustrated. First, basic body with legs and tail added. Second, a tongue depressor may be used to create the open mouth. Third, addition of characteristic details: ears, eyes, teeth. Bottom two figures: The directness of clay manipulation holds a universal fascination for children. The delightful clay figure illustrated at right possesses a mobility only the clay medium captures so well. Youngsters can first take a variety of poses themselves and feel the kinesthetic awareness in their own bodies before making a figure in clay perform similar action-packed feats. Children might strut, twist, dance, juggle, bend, and even stand on their heads.

reproductions. As a subject, prehistoric creatures fire students' imaginations. Dinosaurs are uniquely adapted to interpretation in clay. Their ponderous mass, armor-encrusted body, and wrinkled, scaly skin evoke the quality of the ancient earth itself.

Emphasize the structural elements that can give the piece character. Talk about the sway of the body, stance of the legs, swing of the tail, tilt of the head, action of the jaws, flow of the mane, and flare of the wings. An imaginatively expressive creature may also combine the characteristics of several different animals. In the upper elementary grades and middle school a preliminary drawing of figures to be modeled in clay often helps students clarify their ideas.

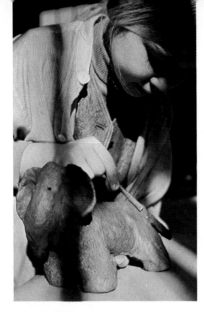

This sturdily constructed clay elephant was made by pulling out forms. Then the elephant was decorated with pattern and texture. Youngsters can employ objects such as tubes, pencil erasers, bottle caps, bark, wire mesh, and pinecones to add imaginative texture and pattern to their clay creations.

pottery on a wheel. Do not frustrate a majority of students by demanding skills that college ceramics majors work long hours to attain. Instead concentrate on hand-building techniques that all can master.

The students must be guided to avoid trite bud vases and ashtrays. Show films and photos of contemporary ceramic techniques and hand-building techniques. Introduce students to the exciting work of contemporary potters such as Peter Voulkos, Andy Nassisse, and Shoji Hamada, and to the beautiful functional clay vessels of the pre-Columbian craftspeople of Mexico, Gautamala, Colombia, and Peru. Encourage students to collect an assortment of stones, shells, seedpods, nuts, and driftwood to trigger ideas.

The basic form must be the first critical concern. No amount of additional embellishment or decoration can redeem a piece weak in formal concept or structure. Critiques of clay work in process should be standard procedure during every studio session, and students should share their discoveries with their classmates.

Variety in the basic sculptural form should be emphasized. Because students are accustomed to symmetrically styled ceramics, the teacher must guide them to see the beauty of asymmetry. Variety can be achieved through contrasting the forms of the appendages, spouts, necks, and feet. It can also be achieved through exploitation of the positive and negative spaces created by openings in the vessel, by the handles and the lids, and by the delineation of incised and relief areas to create dark and light pattern.

Unity is also vital to the total impact of the clay structure. There should be a natural flow from one plane or contour to another. Appendages should grow naturally from the basic body structure and be in scale with it; they should complement, not detract from, the whole. The same is true of decorations: the designs should go with the firm, not compete with it or ignore it.

Clay Slab Construction

Slabs approximately $12 \times 18 \times \frac{1}{2}$ inch should be prepared in advance. Moist clay, a rolling pin, a burlap- or linen-covered board, guiding strips of wood $\frac{1}{2}$ inch thick, and plastic covering to keep slabs moist during storage are needed. Additional slabs can be made as the project progresses. Impress fired clay relief stamps and found objects into the moist slab to enrich the surface before beginning construction of the container. Divide the large slab into the number of slabs needed for the sides and bottom (and sometimes top) of the container. The junctures where two slabs are to be joined should be scored (rough-

Extra clay may be needed, especially for reinforcing junctures. To prevent cracking and exploding when the clay is dried and fired, avoid using armatures, such as sticks, inside the structure. To develop the form three-dimensionally, the sculpture should be viewed from all sides. Use a 12- or 16-inch square Masonite sheet or a turntable as a working base to facilitate rotation.

Whether on a clay pot, a figure, an animal, or a tile, there are almost no limits to clay-relief pattern and textural exploitation. To make scaly, armorlike dinosaur hide, students might roll out balls, coils, and ribbons of clay and apply them to the body of the creature. Slip can be used as an adhesive to secure the pellets and coils of clay to the main surface. Discarded broken saw blades and combs can be used for linear effects. Squeezing moist clay through window screen produces masses of clay strings to employ as manes or tails.

Construction Techniques

Hand Building

In the overcrowded middle-school classes, the beleaguered teacher of art would find it difficult if not impossible to instruct everyone in the sophisticated, highly technical, and time-consuming craft of throwing

Courtesy of David Hodge, Oshkosh, Wisconsin.

The handsome branch pots, made by seventh graders, started as basic coil, slab, and pinch-pot forms. Through the addition of complementary clay and feet and the elegant decoration of surface forms, they emerged as distinctive, one-of-a-kind ceramic containers. Decoration enhances rather than disguises or destroys the fundamental ceramic form. After staining, if stains appear to be too intense, earth can be rubbed into the surface to subdue the effect. Further embellishment can be achieved by inscribing designs through stained surfaces. Liquid wax can provide a subtle sheen as well as a protective surface.

ened) and covered with water or slip before attaching the slabs. When slabs are joined, use a wood paddle to secure them and to form the container's shape. Two or more clay slab constructions in different sizes may be joined to make a larger, more complex structure.

Pinch-Pot Sculpture

For pinch-pot sculpture approximately 5 pounds of moist clay per student is recommended. First, a large portion of the clay is shaped into a large ball and cut in half. Then each half is formed into a pinch-pot shape, keeping the walls fairly thick and each pot similar in size. Then students join together the two pinch pots (scoring and moistening the junctures) and pinch the seams tightly to form a hollow ball. Holding the hollow ball of clay in one hand, the student paddles it until the pinched seams disappear. To create a decorative surface effect, use a piece of wood, approximately $1 \times 2 \times 15$ inches, wrapped at one end generously with cord. Students must rotate the ball as they paddle it so that the entire clay ball will be paddled evenly. This action packs the clay and seals in enough air to support the walls. During paddling, students can change the shape of the ball to resemble a pod, nut, or gourd. Although a cord-wrapped paddle produces an attractive texture, additional decoration may be done by using stamped, incised, and bas-relief motifs.

For unusual effects, students may apply clay pellets, straight and undulating clay ribbons or snakes, and clay coils to the surface. Be sure the surface clay is sufficiently moist for adhesion of such addi-

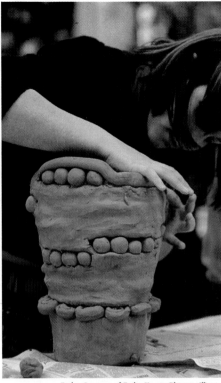

Right: Courtesy of Baiba Kuntz, Glencoe, Illinois.

Students concentrate as they create their clay projects. **Left:** *A boy studying ancient cultures constructs a model of a cliff dweller's home.* **Right:** *This tall pot is being constructed from coils. The coils are then smoothed together for strength. Rows of bold balls and loops give contrast.*

tions. If not, moisten it or use slip. Feet, handles, bases, legs, animal necks, and heads may be added, but to preserve strength the sealed ball should not be opened until the whole container is complete. Once opened, spouts and vase necks may be added. Many exciting forms result when the students combine two or more pinch-pot balls of various sizes and shapes into one unified structure.

Drying, Firing, Glazing, and Staining

If a kiln is available, the clay sculptures should be allowed to dry evenly and slowly in a cabinet or under a sheet of plastic before firing. When firm enough to handle but before becoming too hard, solid

forms over an inch in thickness should have holes or hollows made in their understructures. Another way to allow air to escape during firing is to poke pin holes in the piece while it is leather-hard. Trapped air can cause an explosion, and one exploding piece can destroy a kilnful. Some other precautions are proper wedging of clay to remove air bubbles and adding grog to increase the clay's strength. Another precaution is to keep the kiln lid cracked open for an hour or more when firing begins, then raise the temperature very slowly. Pieces even 2 inches thick can survive firings if the heat is raised *very* slowly over a period of days.

It is relatively easy to fire greenware. Raw clay pieces may be stacked closely inside of or on top of one another, rest against one another in the kiln, and even against the kiln's sides (taking care that they do not touch heating elements). Engobe-decorated pieces, in which the clay slip is applied before firing and scratched through for graffito designs, can be fired in a similar manner. However, do not let the clay get too dry before applying slip decoration, lest peeling and cracking occur in firing.

Glaze firing requires more care. Kiln glazing of bisque-fired clay pieces (those which have already been fired once) is a way for ambitious teachers to bring the ceramic process to a rich culmination. Children create beautiful pieces which frequently become family treasures. (Since old glazes sometimes contained dangerous elements such as lead and arsenic, use only glazes certified as safe, especially for food containers.) The glazed ware must be stacked carefully so that no glazed piece touches another piece or the wall of the firing chamber. Because molten glaze will adhere the piece to the kiln's floor, a protective kiln wash is useful. The bottom and lower ¼ to ½ inch of the piece should be wiped free of glaze, or supports such as stilts or pins used. Weeks of firing may be necessary, especially if the students have created large clay structures.

The large student populations of elementary schools, limited budgets, and limited kiln size frequently make it impractical to glaze large pieces.

An alternate way to beautify fired clay is to rub neutral colors of pigment or moist dirt or soil of another shade into the incised areas. Before the dirt or applied stain dries, the raised surfaces may be partially wiped with a moistened rag to create contrasting effects. In most cases in which staining or coloring (try gluing on torn pieces of colored tissue paper) is applied to bisque-fired clay, it is advisable to add a final coat of liquid wax or clear gloss polymer. Other clay projects are shown on pages 19, 43, 57, 118, 206, and 290.

Ceramics can play a role in a multidisciplinary approach correlating art with science and social studies. **Top left:** *Intermediate-elementary-grade children, studying ocean life, made clay fish. They cut fish shapes out of clay slabs and attached them to the ocean-floor bases. The pieces were then bisque-fired and painted with acrylic paint. The two fish on the left are kissing; the top left fish is dining on another fish.* **Bottom left:** *Second-grade children studied the role of monsters in medieval culture and saw how cathedrals used grotesque gargoyle waterspouts. The children then made these clay monster plaques painted with simulated-stone spatter paint.* **Above:** *Third-grade youngsters studying Anasazi Native American culture created these ceramic pieces decorated with black marker Native American designs.*

Courtesy of Mary Lazzari, Athens, Georgia.

Two attractive plaster reliefs by middle-school youngsters. Notice especially how composition fills the space and how the metal patina brings out the relief highlights. "Animals and their young" is a popular theme chosen by many students for this challenging three-dimensional project. Suggest that students limit the stains to neutral colors at first to achieve unity. Be sure to apply one or two coats of white glue to the plaster relief before staining it. Allow the stain to flow into incised lines.

Clay Plaster Reliefs

Students in the upper elementary grades and middle school are often self-critical concerning their drawing ability and need the satisfaction and challenge of creating in an art medium more dependent on design skills. Creating plaster reliefs, which involves manipulative skills with special tools and materials, and surprise effects, is one such challenging adventure. (Other art projects that belong in this general hands-on, craft-centered category are metal repoussé, ceramics, papier-mâché, stitchery, weaving, and mobiles.)

For a plaster-relief project, you will need moist clay, plaster, a plastic or rubber dishpan, and a container for the clay mold (shoe box, cigar box, or half-gallon or gallon waxed-cardboard milk carton). Also needed are an assortment of found objects (spools, nails, wire, cogwheels, lath, screws, keys, clothespins, buckles, rope, bolts, cord, reed, dowel sticks, bottle caps, jar lids, coins, printer's letters, combs, plastic forks and spoons, and natural objects such as twigs, pinecones, acorns, nuts, seashells, and bark). To finish the piece, you will need a plaster-sealing medium such as white glue or polymer medium, a 1- or 2-inch utility brush, and stains.

The first step is to reinforce the box with masking or strapping tape around the entire box. Use the lid under the box to reinforce the bottom. The inside of the box may be lined with wax paper. Milk cartons requiring no protective lining can be cut in half lengthwise and the open end resealed. If the separate reliefs are to be assembled later into one large group mural design, uniformity of sizes may be desirable. A free-form relief shape can be made by using a sheet of tempered Masonite as the working surface and building a clay wall around the slab of clay.

There are two methods of making the basic slab of clay. The simplest is to roll out the clay into a slab approximately ½ to 1 inch thick, cut the slab to the size of the box, and place the slab in the bottom of the box, ready for the next stage of the process. In the second method, the clay is placed in the box, pellet by pellet, until the bottom is filled with a clay layer ½ to 1 inch thick. If a very flat surface is desired, the clay may be stamped down with the end of a 2- × 4-inch woodblock.

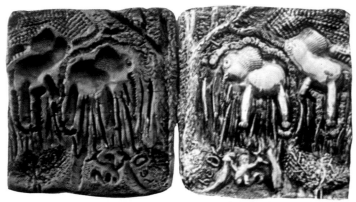

Courtesy of David Hodge, Oshkosh, Wisconsin.

A clay negative mold and the completed plaster relief. Letters and numerals must be impressed backward into the clay mold to read correctly in the final relief. Shapes pressed into the clay bulge out in the plaster version. A seashell was used to make the elephant's ears. Other effective imprinting objects include beads and discarded costume jewelry, plastic forks and spoons, crumpled heavy-duty aluminum foil, heavy cord, reed, and wire.

Before the students begin their relief designs, incisions, and textural impressions in the clay slab, they should practice on a sample slab. Demonstrate that impressions made in the clay will be reversed in the plaster cast. Designs pressed or incised in the clay will bulge out in the plaster version. Show the students examples of relief sculpture throughout art history. For example, the Greek Parthenon frieze, coin designs, and sculptures by the modern artist Marino Marini can be used in discussions of the beauty of low and high relief. Letters and numbers must be imprinted backward in the clay to read correctly in the final product. Once the teacher has made these basic principles clear, the students are free to be expressive and innovative.

There are several ways to model in the slab. A very free and natural approach involves the use of hands and fingers. Commercial ceramic tools may also be employed. Coils, pellets, and ribbons of clay cut out from a thin slab may be applied with water or slip.

With younger children it might be wise to limit the designs to those which can be achieved by pressing into the clay, since it is more difficult to dig lines out of the clay. (In addition, the digging approach often produces sharp and hazardous edges in the final plaster cast.) For straight lines use applicator sticks, popsicle holders, or the edge of

a thick cardboard piece. For curved lines use bent reed, cord, and edges of round containers.

Recommended subject-matter themes for plaster reliefs include birds with plumage, fish, insects (butterflies), animals in their habitat, flowers, theater or clown faces, heraldic devices, personal insignia, monograms, and nonobjective designs. By combining individual efforts into one large "mural" composition, students can achieve a project of significant scope.

When the impressed and incised designs are completed, liquid plaster of Paris is poured over the clay to a ½- to 1-inch thickness. (Plaster-mixing procedures are described in the section on subtractive sculpture.) Before the plaster sets, bent paper clips or wire may be inserted to serve later as a hanger. The hardening capabilities of plaster vary widely. Semihard pieces are easily broken, and the teacher should allow time for the plaster to harden. Hardening takes at least 1 to 2 hours; ideally, plaster should be allowed to set overnight.

If your class does a sand-plaster project at a beach, care must be taken to form the mold far enough up the beach so the plaster will not be affected by dampness at the water's edge; if there is too much moisture in the sand, the plaster will not harden. If you are at a saltwater beach, use fresh water because salt can interfere with the plaster's strength. Since sand will not hold nearly as much detail as clay, the outer edges of sand-plaster reliefs usually form the shape of the object. Sand-plaster reliefs often require coat hangers, wire, or sticks added quickly after the plaster is poured, to give added strength.

When the plaster is quite hard, the student pries open the cardboard container and separates the plaster from the clay. If the separation is done carefully, most of the moist clay in the mold can be salvaged for a future project. (*Note:* If the clay contains bits of plaster, don't re-use it for a clay project that is to be fired; the plaster may cause the clay to explode.)

To prepare the plaster relief for the staining, students should file away or sandpaper the excess edges and any sharp abrasive points. The relief should then be washed with water, using a discarded toothbrush or nail to clean the clay from narrow recesses. Before staining, give it a generous coat of slightly water-diluted white glue and allow to dry thoroughly. Then apply stain and wipe the raised areas to bring out highlights.

Plaster reliefs are a good project for upper-elementary and middle-school teachers and students looking for a different three-dimensional experience. Plaster reliefs are not so dependent on drawing skill, yet they have a sophisticated, finished appearance.

Subject themes for plaster-relief projects are legion. Here animals, both real and imaginary, provided motivation for the designs. **Lower left:** a blue giraffe, a pink elephant, and a hippo behind a tree are surrounded by a decorative border, made by imprinting a circular dowel rod about 1/8 inch deep. **Upper middle:** Jonah appears to contentedly relax inside the whale's stomach; the background is attractively filled with sea urchin and seaweed shapes and painted in subtle colors. **Lower right:** a double-humped Bactrian camel dominates the scene filled in with a tree, a hot desert sun, and textured sand dunes.

Art Materials

To develop the confidence that will help them teach art successfully, teachers must be familiar with the art materials and equipment available for their classes. They should discover the art potential of these materials through actual involvement with them. The following art materials and tools are usually found in the elementary and middle schools today, furnished by either the school or the students. Teachers should learn to use them creatively, know available sources, order them in economy lots and sizes, and store them properly.

Expendable Materials

Pencils	Wax crayons
Fingerpaint	Tempera paint
Watercolors	Colored chalk
Manila paper	White drawing paper
Newsprint	Oaktag (tagboard)
Construction paper	Fingerpaint paper
School paste	School chalk
Clay	

Nonexpendable Supplies and Equipment

Art slides and slide projector	Overhead projector and projection screen
Art reproductions	
Scissors	Rulers, compasses
Easel brushes	Watercolor brushes
Paper cutter	Hammer, saw
	Stapler

Generous Budget Supplies and Equipment

Video player, TV, art videos, and VCR	Computers
Oil pastels	Art gum erasers
Felt-nib or nylon-tip pens	White liquid glue
Printing inks (water, oil-base)	Felt-nib watercolor markers
India ink	Linoleum and tools for block cutting
Brayers (rubber rollers for printmaking)	Clay glazes
Clay kiln	Tissue paper (assorted colors)
Poster board (for mats)	Gloss polymer medium

Toxic Materials and Inhalants

Toxic art materials are particularly harmful to children. Their nervous systems, internal organs, and reproductive systems are more at risk because their cells are still dividing. In 1990, Congress passed a law requiring that all toxic art materials have labels warnings of their toxicity. However, many toxic materials still do not have such labels. Also, old materials purchased before the law went into effect may still be on the shelves, and these materials should be discarded. School shelves may hold pigments containing lead (lead white or flake white), cadmium, mercury, chromates, manganese, and cobalt. All of these are toxic. The main risk is ingestion while working through eating and nail biting.

One in six U.S. children, 3.5 million youths, have harmful levels of lead in their blood. Elevated blood lead is linked to learning disabil-

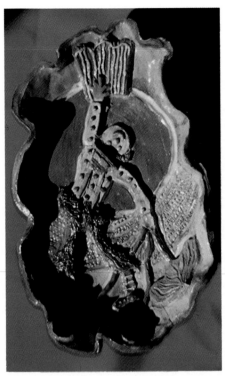

Courtesy of David Hodge, Oshkosh, Wisconsin.

Ceramic glazes add beauty to this ceramic slab dish. A circus clown holding an umbrella balances on one hand. The dish's undulating sides make the piece unique.

ities, lower IQs, and dropout rates. Toxic ceramic glaze chemicals may be especially dangerous if used on ceramics which are then used for food or drink. Wheat paste contains toxic preservatives, yet it is used in over half the schools. All toxic materials should be banned in elementary schools.

Other health hazards are as follows:

Carbon monoxide and often sulphur dioxide and nitrogen oxide from unvented kilns. School kilns should be vented through a canopy hood.

Turpentine and other solvents. Over a 3-hour period, one-fourth to one-half of a small cup of turpentine can evaporate. Inhaling high concentrations of fumes from turpentine or mineral spirits can cause narcosis, dizziness, nausea, fatigue, and respiratory irritation. (Odorless mineral spirits are less hazardous.) Prolonged exposure to all solvents containing aromatic hydrocarbons can cause skin allergies. Ingestion of benzene, toluene, and xylene can be fatal. For this reason, references to varnish and shel-

lac, which require mineral spirits, turpentine, and alcohol as solvents, have been deleted from this edition. Teachers are urged to use gloss polymer medium when a sealant or a high sheen is desired. At this time, alternatives to mineral spirits, akin to baby oil and vegetable oils, are in the developmental stage.

Adhesives. Building supply adhesives and household cements, such as model cement and Duco cement, contain hydrocarbons, which are harmful when inhaled.

Markers. Permanent felt-tip markers contain aromatic hydrocarbons, can be very toxic, and should never be used in elementary classrooms.

Aerosol spray paint contains chemical compounds that can be extremely harmful when inhaled by students who use this "legal drug" for a cheap, brief, and intense high. The student first sprays paint into a plastic bag. Then the student blows the bag up the rest of the way and puts the narrow opening to the mouth and inhales. Some students spray paint into a soda can and then innocently appear to be drinking. Some children paint their nails with typewriter correction fluid repeatedly throughout the day.

Inhalants are particularly prevalent in the eighth, ninth, and tenth grades. Paradoxically, as drug use declines nationally, inhalant use is increasing. Telltale signs are loss of interest in appearance, food, and family activities. Spaced-out behavior, lack of coordination, sores on the nose and mouth, frequent coughing, dried spray paint on clothes, and empty aerosol cans, from hair spray to Scotchguard to Reddi Whip, may be indications. Long-term effects of sniffing are mood swings, depression, hallucinations, memory loss, and impaired judgment. Brain, kidney, and liver damage, damage to the central nervous system, and heart failure may also result.

Practical Suggestions

Keep all tools and materials in order. Store them in cigar boxes, shoe boxes, freezer containers, coffee or vegetable-shortening tins, commercially available tote trays. Label the containers. Paint tool handles with an identifying color.

Keep all tools clean. Do not let metal tools get rusty. Wipe them dry if they get wet, and oil them if they are to be stored. Do not use scissors for clay or plaster projects. Never pour plaster in any form down the sink.

Mount motivational resource photographs on oaktag (tagboard). Store them in labeled accordion folders or flat drawers, or put them in plastic looseleaf protectors and keep them in notebook binders.

Wash brushes clean (use detergent if necessary) and store them with bristle ends up in a jar or tall coffee can. Be sure students rinse and clean watercolor tins. Leave them open and stack them to dry overnight. Order semimoist cakes of watercolor in bulk to refill empty tins.

Courtesy of David Harvell, Athens, Georgia.

Left: *Organized materials not only make teaching go better, but also teach children that order facilitates learning. The wall has adjustable shelves, and matched boxes to fit have been attractively covered in wallpaper and labeled. The display paper dispenser facilitates putting up bulletin board displays.* ***Above:*** *Open bins make collecting, counting, and distributing tools and supplies easy. Bins hold fine and broad markers, crayons, bottles of white glue, and palettes.*

Store scrap construction and tissue paper flat in drawers or discarded blanket cartons to prevent the paper from being crushed.

When placing orders for tempera paint, always order more white paint, because a great deal is used to mix tints of colors. You can also order crayons or oil pastels in colors needed in bulk.

Hardboard in 4- × 8-foot pieces in ¼-inch thickness is excellent for drawing boards and working surfaces on desks or tables. For drawing boards have the lumber dealer cut the hardboard for you into either 18- × 24-inch or 12- × 18-inch rectangles, depending on which size works best in your situation. For longer wear, mask the edges of the boards with tape.

Yarn purchased on skeins should be rewound on balls or spools for ready use. A closed cardboard carton with holes punched in it for the yarn to pass through may be used as a dispenser.

Keep school paste in jars until ready to use; then dispense it on small squares of cardboard. Scrape off the unused paste back into the jar at the close of class; moisten it slightly with a few drops of water and cap tightly.

When crayons break and do not fit easily into the original carton, store them in discarded cigar boxes, coffee or vegetable-shortening tins, or freezer containers.

Powder tempera is much easier to store than the liquid kind, but liquid tempera has definite advantages. It is always ready to use if sealed properly, and it usually has a smoother texture. The most vexing problem in tempera projects is what to do with the liquid tempera remaining in multicompartment muffin tins, plastic egg cartons, or ice-cube trays. It can't be poured back into the original containers. That is why paint should be doled out a little at a time, with refills as needed. To minimize the chance of spills, the teacher should be in charge of paint distribution if possible. Before closing covers on tempera jars, check the plasticity of the paint. If the paint is too dry, add a little water to ensure moistness and then cap the jar tightly. To prevent liquid tempera lids from being difficult to open, wipe the jar rim before closing or put a little petroleum jelly on the rim. To prevent liquid tempera from becoming sour, add a few drops of wintergreen or oil of cloves to each container.

These three works are collages made from wallpaper, patterned paper, and tissue. To prevent crushing of scraps of wallpaper, patterned papers, and tissue, store them flat in drawers or boxes.

Recycling Materials

Recycled materials not only enrich artworks, but their use conveys a valuable lesson about conservation of the earth's limited resources. In America's productive and wasteful society, there are vast resources that teachers of art can tap for nontraditional art materials. Using imagination and skill, discarded items, empty containers, scraps, and remnants ordinarily thought of as worthless can be recycled into artworks. Care must be taken, however, to keep the students from regarding the use of interesting materials as an end in itself. The artwork must transcend the materials to be a whole that is truly more than the sum of its parts.

Interesting sizes of cut-off paper can be secured for free from printing companies, and newsroll ends are often donated by newspapers. Other paper sources are computer printouts from institutions and businesses, cardboard boxes from appliance stores, and unused printed billboard papers from outdoor advertising companies. Virtually every company that produces objects has some discarded materials which may be useful in sculptures, collage, weavings, etc. The company might even underwrite an exhibition crediting their contribution. Most teachers of art are not shy about requesting materials for such a societally worthy cause as children's art expression. Children and their parents can help build a store of materials such as the following:

Recycling materials conveys an important ecological lesson. Wood scraps which would usually be burned can be made into imaginative animal sculptures. Care must be exercised when cutting into plastic. It may be prudent to reserve such construction for upper elementary grades and middle school. Plastic containers, yarn, sticks, and old buttons usually end up in landfills. Instead such materials can gain a reprieve as animal sculptures and can serve a higher purpose, to build the minds and imaginations of tomorrow's creative, adaptive, inventive leaders.

Acorns	Cartons
Baby-food jars	Cellophane
Balls (rubber, polystyrene, Ping-Pong)	Celotex
	Checkers
Bark (tree)	Clock parts
Beads	Clothespins
Blades (saw, broken)	Coat hangers
Blinds (matchstick, plastic)	Confetti
Blotters	Cord
Bolts and nuts	Corks
Bones	Cotton
Bottle caps	Dowels
Bottles	Driftwood
Boxes	Earrings
Bracelets	Fabric remnants
Buckles	Feathers
Burlap remnants	Felt
Buttons	Foam rubber (scraps)
Cardboard	Foil (aluminum)
Carpet samples	Greeting cards

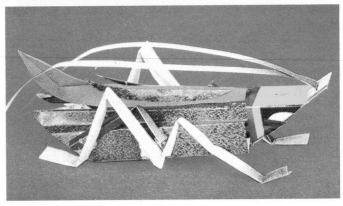

Sculpture can be made from many available and recycled materials.

Gourds
Leather remnants
Linoleum scraps
Magazines
Marbles
Masonite scraps
Meat trays (plastic foam)
Mirrors
Nails
Necklaces
Newspapers
Nuts
Paper bags
Paper cups and plates
Paper tubes (toilet tissue, mailing)

Paper towels
Paper (shelf, gift wrap, crepe, tissue, plain, colored)
Pebbles
Pie plates
Pinecones
Pins
Pipe cleaners
Polish (shoe)
Q-Tips
Reed
Ribbon
Rope
Rubber (innertube)
Rubber bands

Sand
Sandpaper
Sawdust
Screen
Screws
Seashells
Shades (window)
Spools
Sticks (applicator)

Straws
String
Tile (acoustic, vinyl)
Tongue depressors
Toothpicks
TV dinner trays
Wallpaper samples
Wood scraps
Yarn remnants

Special Materials and Tools

Hardboard—For drawing or sketching board, as protective coverage for desks or worktables, and for mural projects.

Brayer (rubber roller)—For inking plate in printmaking. Get the sturdy, soft, black rubber kind for longer wear (not the gelatin type).

Celluclay—Commercially available dry mixture for use in papier-mâché type projects.

Dextrin (powdered)—Add to dry or moist clay (5 to 10 percent) to harden completed work without firing.

Drywall joint cement—For creating relief effects on a two-dimensional surface; can be painted when dry.

Firebrick (porous, insulation type)—For upper-elementary-grade and middle-school three-dimensional and relief-carving projects.

Grog—Aggregate for plaster molds, clay conditioner.

Masonite (tempered)—For clay modeling boards, inking surface in printmaking projects, and rinsing board in tempera or crayon resists; also practical as a portable sketching board.

Pariscraft—Plaster-impregnated gauze in varied widths for additive sculpture projects.

Plaster of Paris (molding plaster)—For plaster sculpture and reliefs.

Polystyrene—For printmaking plates, collage and craft projects, and printmaking stamps.

Posterboard (railroad board)—For multicrayon engraving project; available in several colors.

Sloyd knife (Hyde knife is similar)—All-purpose utility knife with a semisharp blade; excellent for carving in plaster and for delineating details and pattern in crayon engraving projects.

Dressmaker's transfer paper—A white carbon paper useful in crayon engraving projects.

X-acto knife—Craft knife with sharp interchangeable blades for paper and cardboard sculpture. *Caution*: To be used by the teacher only.

Planning Facilities for Art

The elementary classroom or the art room can be the child's first and often most enduring art lesson. It is there, through exciting displays and eye-catching exhibits, that teachers can provide the example for good design through creative, inspiring, and stimulating surroundings. Students should be involved in projects to make the classroom attractive and colorfully stimulating. Bulletin boards and displays should be changed regularly and often to provide evaluative and appreciatory opportunities for completed projects and to whet interest for further art endeavors. Still-life arrangements should be on view for sketching. Students should be encouraged to contribute to the store of found objects and nature's treasures on display.

Most elementary art projects take place in the self-contained classroom. A few schools boast a multipurpose art room. To make rooms function better for art teaching, the changes that need to be made are in the strategic areas of storage, display, and cleanup. If a multipurpose art room is planned, it should be on the first or ground floor, adjacent to the stage of the auditorium or to the cafeteria, and near a service entrance. An outdoor court, easily accessible from the art room, can provide excellent auxiliary space for sketching, mural making, ceramics, and plaster sculpture projects in favorable weather.

Sufficient space should be provided to allow students to work on individual projects with some flexibility of movement. Easy rearrangement of furniture for group projects should be planned. An easy flow of student traffic to the teacher's desk and storage and cleanup areas or stations is desirable. In the elementary art room a space of 55 square feet per student is recommended; there should also be a vented kiln, a separate storage area, and a sink. The self-contained classroom should provide adequate space at the rear of the room and along one or two walls for storage, a cleanup (sink) facility, and counter working space. There should be sufficient room at the rear of

Illustrations on this page show easily constructed plywood storage facilities for both two- and three-dimensional art projects. Notice in the background of the left picture the rack for art magazines and books, and the file cabinets for storage of motivational reproductions. At right, sturdy plastic trays, available commercially, slide in and out on wooden runners tacked to the sides of the cubby holes. Ceramics and reed sculptures with wooden bases are attractively displayed on a background of varied colored papers.

Courtesy of Mary Sayer Hammond, Fairfax, Virginia.

Metal repoussé is an especially suitable material for depicting animal scenes incorporating pattern and texture. **Above:** *two elephants with wrinkled skins jostle with their trunks, surrounded by tall grass and a rich pattern of tree leaves.* **Below:** *a mother horse protectively nuzzles its colt. For details on this tactilely challenging technique, see pages 68 and 69.*

the class for one or two large, sturdy tables suitable for craft activities and group projects.

Tables and desks should be easily movable for special projects. Counter surfaces of nonglare, waterproof, and scratch-resistant materials are recommended. Light-colored laminated plastic working surfaces must be protected during projects involving linoleum or woodblock cutting, carving in semihard substances, or sawing and hammering on wood constructions. In the special art room, stools that can be recessed under tables during cleanup can ease the traffic problem. In the primary grades free-standing easels can effectively augment the limited desk space.

Sufficient storage for art supplies, tools, visual aids, work in progress, and completed art projects held over for future display is helpful. Adjustable shelves and tote trays are helpful for various-size art papers and art materials. Yarn, wood scraps, and found materials can be stored in large cardboard cartons painted in bright colors. Sturdy galvanized or plastic waste containers, water-tight and air-tight, are necessary for clay, and can be used for plaster, zonolite, and sand.

A cabinet or movable cart with shelves and pegboard panels is suggested for storage of small tools. Pegboard secured to a wall and the accompanying hardware can alleviate the most pressing tool-storage problems. Painting an identifying shape or outline of each tool on the pegboard expedites storage and inventory. A hollow box made of Masonite with holes drilled in the top provides an excellent scissors container and inventory device.

Since so much of children's art revolves around painting, there should be adequate horizontal storage spaces for paintings in process. This is especially true in the special art room, where one class quickly follows another. A clothesline and spring clothespins can be used as a drying facility for prints, but not for tempera paintings, which will drip.

To minimize traffic problems, sinks should not be located in a closet or in a corner. They should be large enough to allow two or three persons to use them at once. They should be low enough so children can reach faucets with ease; if not, students should be provided with step-up platforms. Generous amounts of space should be allotted for display purposes and instructional bulletin boards. Display-panel backgrounds should be neutral in color: subtle, nonglare whites, grays, umbers, and blacks are recommended. Surfaces, in most instances, should be matte finish in cork or Celotex; this affords easy pinning, stapling, or tacking of artwork. Acoustic tile can be glued directly to wall surfaces or to Masonite or hardboard panels to provide

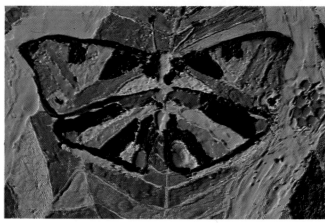

Above: Well-equipped art rooms will accommodate students' efforts in creating drawings in encaustic. **Right:** Drawings of fantasy animals can be stimulated by reproductions of a variety of animals on the room's bulletin boards.

a display facility. Cork-surfaced doors on cupboards, closet doors, and storage cabinets will augment display space.

Floors should be of nonskid materials, hard, yet resilient and easily cleaned. Ceilings should be acoustically treated and provide maximum light reflection. Room-darkening shades or blinds are required for projection of color slides, videos, and films, and a permanent projection screen installed.

Electric outlets should be provided at frequent intervals around the room. For a ceramic kiln, 220-voltage wiring is usually required.

Electric outlets should not be near sink areas. The ventilator fan in the hood also requires wiring.

Special furniture and equipment can promote a qualitative program. The following items are recommended: clay bin or cart, vibrating jigsaw, color slide projector, projection screen, workbench with vises, large-size paper cutter, electric heating plate, utility cart, ceramic kiln, drying rack for flat work in progress, gun tacker, stapler, large scissors, yardstick, and several wastebaskets or large-sized trash containers.

A Brief Chronology
of Art Education
in the United States

1870 — To train artists for industry, Industrial Drawing Act passed by Massachusetts legislature required that drawing be taught to all students over fifteen years of age in communities of over 20,000.

The Oswego Movement emphasized the study of geometric solids in kindergartens.

1871 — The Metropolitan Museum of Art in New York City was established.

1873 — Massachusetts Normal Art School established, the first training school for the preparation of teachers of industrial drawing in the country. Walter Smith was the founder and first principal. As the Boston schools' art instructor, he wrote *Teachers' Manual of Freehand Drawing Designing.* He later organized Massachusetts Art Teachers Association, the first professional art-teachers group, and published a series of graded art lessons to teach geometrical drawing. Copying was encouraged to train the eye and hand.

1875 — Art Students' League, New York City, founded. William Merritt Chase was one of the first instructors.

1876 — Thomas Eakins began teaching at the Pennsylvania Academy of Arts, Philadelphia. He relied little on cast models and instead stressed anatomical studies.

1883 — Department of Art Education established as an integral part of the National Education Association.

1896 — John Dewey started the University of Chicago Laboratory School.

1898 — Arthur Wesley Dow became art instructor at Teachers College, Columbia University, New York City. Dow subsequently wrote the textbook *Composition,* which stressed design and influenced many art teachers.

1901 — First publication of *The Applied Arts Book,* which later became *School Arts,* with H. T. Bailey as editor. The book employed picture-study units that emphasized the storytelling aspects of paintings and the design content.

1904 — John Dewey, author of *Art as Experience,* joined the faculty of Columbia University.

Franz Cizek, called the Father of Child Art, began his influential children's art classes *(Künstgewerbeschule)* in Vienna, emphasizing drawing from memory rather than from life.

1912 — Paintings by children exhibited in Steiglitz Gallery, New York City.

1913 — A. H. Munsell introduced *A Color Notation,* which established a structure by which color theories can be taught. Provided color wheel, color terminology, and color harmonies.

Armory Show opened in New York City, introducing the paintings of the fauvists ("wild beasts"), futurists, cubists, and postimpressionists to the United States art community.

Clive Bell wrote *Art,* a treatise that emphasized formal elements.

1919 — Western Arts Association, the largest of the regional art-education associations, founded. Drawings from nature sources were emphasized.

1920 — Pedro J. Lemos, who served as editor of *School Arts Magazine,* wrote *Applied Art,* emphasizing multicultural contributions.

1923 — Robert Henri wrote *The Art Spirit.*

1924 — Margaret Mathias, art teacher in Cleveland, Ohio, wrote *The Beginning of Art in the Public Schools.*

Belle Boas wrote *Art in the School.*

From 1900 to 1930, the progressive education movement emphasized the child's process of learning, stressed the importance of subjects' correlation, and decried copying.

1928 — Leon L. Winslow wrote *Organization and Teaching of Art.* Sallie Tannahill wrote *Fine Arts for Public School Administrators.*

During the twenties, the picture study movement was responsible for bringing art reproductions, especially those emphasizing patriotic and family values, into the schools.

1933 — With the Carnegie Corporation as sponsor and Edwin Ziegfeld as director, the Owatonna, Minnesota, Community Home Art Project began, emphasizing the role of art in daily life; the project continued through 1938.

1933 (continued) — Joseph Albers, author of *Interaction of Color,* introduced the German Bauhaus design philosophy and techniques at Black Mountain College, North Carolina.

1934 — Works Progress Administration (WPA) provided employment for many artists. Scores of murals in state and federal buildings resulted. John Dewey wrote *Art as Experience.*

1938 — Leon L. Winslow wrote *The Integrated School Art Program.*

1940 — Natalie R. Cole wrote the inspirational book *The Arts in the Classroom.* It describes how painting, drawing, printmaking, and lettering were creatively taught by an elementary classroom teacher.

Art for personal adjustment, emotional release, and leisure-time activity were especially emphasized during this period.

The Progressive Education Association, chaired by Victor D'Amico, published *The Visual Arts in General Education.*

1941 — Kimon Nicolaides wrote *The Natural Way to Draw,* which emphasized contour and gesture drawing.

Ray Faulkner, Edwin Ziegfeld, and Gerald Hill wrote *Art Today,* an art appreciation textbook emphasizing art and design in daily life, for example, furniture design.

1942 — Victor D'Amico, educational director at the Museum of Modern Art, New York City, wrote *Creative Teaching in Art.*

Wilhelm Viola wrote *Child Art,* documenting the teaching methods of Franz Cizek.

During the war years, art for social responsibility and individual freedom received special emphasis.

1943 — Herbert Read wrote *Education through Art.*

The National Committee on Art Education was formed, with Victor D'Amico as chairperson. The committee urged teachers to seek closer ties with practicing artists.

1947 — Viktor Lowenfeld, professor at Pennsylvania State University, wrote *Creative and Mental Growth,* which emphasized art for self expression and creativity.

Rose H. Alschuler and LaBerta Hattwick wrote *Painting and Personality,* a psychological approach to understanding the visual expressions of young children.

1948 — National Art Education Association (NAEA) was established and gradually assumed the administrative functions heretofore held by the four regional art associations.

Henry Schaefer-Simmern wrote *The Unfolding of Artistic Creativity,* which emphasized matching the individual's stage of conceptualization, and documented the role of art in helping people who have disabilities.

1951 — Florence Cane wrote *The Artist in Each of Us.*

Herbert Read helped found the International Society for Education through the Arts (INSEA).

1952 — Charles and Margaret Gaitskell of Ontario, Canada, wrote *Art Education in the Kindergarten.*

Olive L. Riley wrote *Your Art Heritage,* an art-appreciation text for secondary schools.

1955 — Rudolph Arnheim wrote *Art and Visual Perception.*

1957 — National Endowment for the Arts and Humanities established.

1958 — Charles D. Gaitskell wrote *Children and Their Art: Methods for the Elementary School.*

Italo DeFrancesco wrote *Art Education: Its Means and Ends.*

1961 — Louis F. Hoover wrote *Art Activities for the Very Young.*

June King McFee wrote *Preparation for Art,* giving new emphasis to perceptual, sociological, and environmental issues in art education.

1965 — Title V of the Elementary and Secondary Education Act (ESEA) was enacted. Federal funds strengthened state departments of education and made it possible for 36 states to hire a state art director.

The Pennsylvania State University Seminar for Research in Art Education became one of the first federally supported conferences to bring together experts from many fields to discuss content in art education.

Essentialism emphasized the intrinsic value of art study as a discipline itself.

Frank Wachowiak and Theodore Ramsay, both teaching at the University of Iowa, wrote *Emphasis Art: A Qualitative Program for the Elementary School.*

During this period, a movement called "visual literacy" emphasized drawing for perceptual and cognitive development. Newer media such as film and TV began to be studied.

1969 — As a part of an assessment of the quality of education in many subjects in the United States, the U.S. Office of Education funded a National Assessment Program in Art, directed by Brent Wilson.

The National Endowment for the Arts established Artists in the Schools programs.

1970 — Edmund B. Feldman, professor of art, University of Georgia, wrote *Becoming Human through Art, Aesthetic Experience in the School.*

Frank Wachowiak, University of Georgia, and David Hodge, University of Wisconsin, wrote *Art in Depth: A Qualitative Program of Art for the Young Adolescent.*

1972 — Central Midwest Regional Educational Laboratory, directed by Stanley Madeja, developed multiarts aesthetic educational materials.

1975 — Public Law 94-142 mandated that students with disabilities were to receive the full range of educational services.

1976 — Art educators of New Jersey wrote *Insights, Art in Special Education, Educating the Handicapped through Art.*

NAEA begins sponsoring a National Art Honor Society for 12,000 students.

1978 — Francis Anderson wrote *Art for All the Children: A Creative Sourcebook for the Impaired Child.*

Rawley Silver wrote *Developing Cognitive and Creative Skills through Art.*

Reverse stencil spray-painted mural. Courtesy of Jimmy Morris, Athens, Georgia.

Multicultural emphases brought an awareness of sociology, along with popular, folk, and commercial arts into classrooms.

1982 — The Getty Center for Education in the Arts, directed by Lani Lattin Duke, was established. The center supported the establishment of discipline-based art education programs in schools.

Museum education was increasingly seen as a supplement to art classroom instruction.

1984 — Claire and Robert Clements wrote *Art and Mainstreaming: Art Instruction for Exceptional Children in Regular School Classes*.

1988 — The National Endowment for the Arts published *Toward Civilization: A Report on Arts Education* (first draft written by Brent Wilson). Ros Ragans wrote *Art Talk*, a student text incorporating art criticism with studio activities.

1989 — NAEA began sponsoring a National Junior Art Honor Society.

Abrahamson, Roy E. 1980. "The Teaching Approach of Henry Schaefer-Simmern." *Studies in Art Education* **22**(1):42–50.

Anderson, Tom. 1988. "A Structure for Pedagogical Art Criticism." *Studies in Art Education* **30**(1):28–38.

Arnheim, Rudolf. 1966. *Art and Visual Perception: A Psychology of the Creative Eye.* Berkeley: University of California Press.

———. 1983. "Viktor Lowenfeld and Tactility." *Journal of Aesthetic Education* **17**(2):19–30.

Baker, David W. 1990. "Git Real": On Art Education and Community Needs." *Art Education* **43**(6):41–49.

Beardsley, Monroe C. 1966. "The Aesthetic Problem of Justification." *Journal of Aesthetic Education* **1**(2):29–39.

Beittel, Kenneth R., Edward L. Mattil, et al. 1961. "The Effect of a 'Depth' vs a 'Breadth' Method of Art Instruction at the Ninth Grade Level." *Studies in Art Education* **3**(1):75–87.

Berrson, Ron. 1983. "For Cultural Democracy: A Critique of Elitism in Art Education." *Art Education* **39**(4):41–45.

Blandy, Doug, and Kristin Congdon. 1990. *Culture and Democracy.* New York: Teachers College Press.

———. 1988. "A Multicultural Symposium on Appreciating and Understanding Art." *Art Education* **41**:20–24.

Blandy, Doug, E. Pancsofar, and Tom Mockensturm. 1988. "Guidelines for Teaching Art to Children and Youth Experiencing Significant Mental/Physical Challenges." *Art Education* **41**(1):60–67.

Bloom, Benjamin S. 1984. *Taxonomy of Educational Objectives: The Classification of Educational Goals.* New York: Longmans.

Bowers, C. A. 1990. "Implications of Gregory Bateson's Ideas for a Semiotic of Art Education." *Studies in Art Education* **31**(2):66–77.

Broudy, Harry S. 1972. *Enlightened Cherishing: An Essay on Aesthetic Education.* Urbana: University of Illinois Press.

Brown, Eleese V. 1984. "Developmental Characteristics of Clay Figure Modeling by Children: 1970–1981." *Studies in Art Education* **26**(1):56–60.

Burkhart, Robert. 1966. "The Relationship of Creativity to Intelligence." In Elliot Eisner and David Ecker (eds.). *Readings in Art Education.* Waltham, Mass.: Blaisdell.

Chapman, Laura H. 1982. *Instant Art, Instant Culture: The Unspoken Policy for American Schools.* New York: Teachers College Press.

Chijiiwa, Hideaki. 1987. *Color Harmony: A Guide to Creative Color Combinations.* Rockport, Mass.: Rockport.

Churchill, Angiola. 1970. *Art for Preadolescents.* New York: McGraw Hill.

Clahassey, Patricia. 1986. "Modernism, Post Modernism, and Art Education." *Art Education* **39**(2):44–48.

Clark, Gil, Michael Day, and Dwaine Greer. 1987. "Discipline-Based Art Education: Becoming Students of Art." *Journal of Aesthetic Education* **21**(2):130–193.

Clark, Gil, and Enid Zimmerman. 1987. *Educating Artistically Talented Students.* Syracuse, N.Y.: Syracuse University Press.

Clements, Claire, and Robert Clements. 1984. *Art and Mainstreaming: Art Instruction for Exceptional Children in Regular School Classes.* Springfield, Ill.: Charles C Thomas.

Clements, Robert D. 1975. "A Case for Art Education: The Influence of Froebel Training on Frank Lloyd Wright." *Art Education* **28**(3):2–7.

———. 1975. "Instructional Objectives or Objectionable Instructions." *Journal of Aesthetic Education* **10**:107–118.

———. 1978. "Art Teacher Appeals: A Way to Motivate and Discipline." *Art Education* **31**:15–17.

———. 1979. "The Inductive Method of Teaching Visual Art Criticism." *Journal of Aesthetic Education* **13**(3):67–78.

Cohen, Elaine, and Ruth S. Gainer. 1984. *Art: Another Language for Learning.* New York: Schocken.

Colbert, Cynthia, and M. Taunton. 1987. "Problems of Representation: Preschool and Third Grade Children's Observational Drawings of a Three Dimensional Model." *Studies in Art Education* **29**:103–114.

Cole, Natalie R. 1940. *The Arts in the Classroom.* New York: John Day.

Collins, Georgia, and Rene Sandell. *Women, Art, and Education.* Reston, Va.: NAEA.

Congdon, Kristin. 1986. "The Meaning and Use of Folk Art Speech in Art Criticism." *Studies in Art Education* **27**(3):140–148.

———. 1989. "Multicultural Approaches to Art Education." *Studies in Art Education* **30**(3): 176–184.

Cromer, Jim. 1991. *History, Theory, and Practice of Art Criticism.* Reston, Va.: NAEA.

Davis, Don Jack. 1990. *Behavioral Emphasis in Art Education.* Reston, Va.: NAEA.

Degge, Rogena M. 1985. "A Model for Aesthetic Inquiry in Television." *Journal of Aesthetic Education* 19(4):85–102.

Dewey, John. 1934. *Art as Experience.* New York: Minton Balch.

DiBlasio, Margaret. 1987. "Reflections on the Theory of Discipline-Based Art Education." *Studies in Art Education.*

Dissanayake, Ellen. 1988. *What Is Art For?* Seattle: University of Washington Press.

Donougho, Martin. 1987. "The Language of Architecture." *Journal of Aesthetic Education* 22(3).

Douglas, Nancy, and Julia B. Schwartz. 1967. "Increasing Awareness of Art Ideas of Young Children through Guided Experiences with Ceramics." *Studies in Art Education* 8(2):2–9.

Edwards, Betty. 1979. *Drawing from the Right Side of the Brain.* Los Angeles: J. Tarcher.

Efland, Arthur. 1990. *A History of Art Education: Intellectual and Social Currents in Teaching the Visual Arts.* New York: Teachers College Press.

Eisner, Elliot. 1987. *The Role of Discipline Based Education in America's Schools.* Los Angeles: The Getty Center for Education in the Arts.

———. 1968. "Curriculum Making for the Wee Folk: Stanford University's Kettering Project." *Studies in Art Education* 9(3):45–56.

———. 1979. *The Educational Imagination: On the Design and Evaluation of School Programs.* New York: Macmillan.

Erickson, Erik. 1963. *Childhood and Society.* New York: Norton.

———. 1968. *Youth, Identity, and Crisis.* New York: Norton.

Erickson, Mary. 1988. "Teaching Aesthetics K-12." In Steven Dobbs (ed.). *Research Readings for Discipline-Based Art Education.* Reston, Va.: NAEA.

———. 1986. "Which Aesthetics Is the Missing Dimension in Art Education," Part 111, Getty Conference Address.

Ewens, Thomas. 1990. "On Discipline: Its Roots in Wonder." *Art Education* 43(1):6–11.

———. 1990. "Flawed Understandings: On Getty, Eisner, and DBAE." In London. *Beyond DBAE.*

Feldman, David H. 1986. *Nature's Gambit.* New York: Basic Books.

———. 1987. "Developmental Psychology and Art Education: Two Fields at the Crossroads." *Journal of Aesthetic Education* 21(2):243–59.

Feldman, Edmund. 1985. *Varieties of Visual Experience.* New York: Prentice Hall.

Flannery, Merle. 1986. "Art as a Neotenizing Influence on Human Development, *Visual Arts Research* 12(2):34–40.

Freeman, Nancy. 1980. *Strategies of Children's Drawings.* New York: Academic.

———. 1991. "The Theory of Art that Underpins Children's Naive Realism." *Visual Arts Research* **Spring**:70–71.

Freeman, Nancy H., and M. V. Cox. (eds.). 1985. *Visual Order.* Cambridge, England: Cambridge University Press.

Gagné, Robert. 1975. *Essentials of Learning.* New York: Dryden.

Gardner, Howard. 1973. *The Arts and Human Development.* New York: Wiley.

———. 1980. *Artful Scribbles, The Significance of Children's Drawings.* New York: Basic Books.

———. 1982. *Art, Mind, and Brain: A Cognitive Approach to Creating.* New York: Basic Books.

———. 1983. *Frames of Mind.* New York: Basic Books.

———. 1989. "Arts Propel." *Studies in Art Education* 30(2):71–83.

———. 1990. *Art Education and Human Development.* Los Angeles: Getty Center for Education in the Arts.

Gardner, Howard, Ellen Winner, and M. Kirchner. 1975. "Children's Conceptions About the Arts." *Journal of Aesthetic Education* 9:60–77.

Gates, Eugene. 1988. "The Female Voice." *Journal of Aesthetic Education* 22(4):59–68.

Geahigan, George. 1983. "Art Criticism: An Analysis of the Concept." *Visual Arts Research* 9(1):10–22.

——— (ed.). 1980. *Career Education in the Visual Arts: Representative Programs and Projects,* Reston, Va.: NAEA.

Getty Center for Education in the Arts. 1986. *Beyond Creating: The Place for Art in America's Schools.* Los Angeles.

Getzels, Jacob, and Mihalyi Csikszentmihalyi. 1976. *The Creative Vision: A Longitudinal Study of Problem Finding in Art.* New York: Wiley.

Goldsmith, Lynn T., and David H. Feldman. 1988. "Aesthetic Judgment: Changes in People and Changes in Domains," *Journal of Aesthetic Education* 22(4):83–93.

Goldstein, Ernest, Theodore Katz, Jo D. Kowalchuk, and Robert Saunders. 1986. *Understanding and Creating Art.* Dallas: Garrard.

Golomb, Claire. 1974. *Young Children's Sculpture and Drawing: A Study in Representational Development.* Cambridge, Mass.: Harvard University Press.

Golomb, Claire, and D. Farmer. 1983. "Children's Graphic Planning Strategies and Early Principles of Spatial Organization in Drawing." *Studies in Art Education* 24(2):86–100.

Crafts projects in weaving and macramé by elementary-school students. Notice especially the cardboard box loom in the lower left. Teachers are referred to the Sunset Hobby and Craft *book,* Lane Publishing Company, Menlo Park, California.

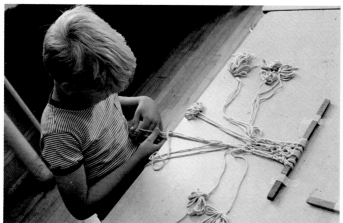

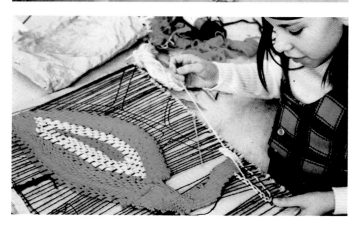

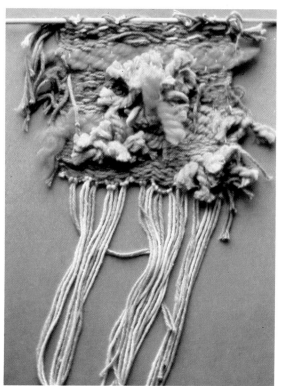

Figures on this page courtesy of David Hodge, Oshkosh, Wisconsin.

Goodlad, John. 1984. *A Place Called School: Promise for the Future.* New York: McGraw-Hill.

Goodman, Nelson. 1976. *Languages of Art: An Approach to a Theory of Symbols.* Indianapolis: Hackett.

Greene, Maxine. 1987. "Creating, Experiencing, Sensemaking: Art Worlds in Schools." *Journal of Aesthetic Education* **21**(4):22.

Hamblen, Karen. 1984. "An Art Criticism Questioning Strategy within the Framework of Bloom's Taxonomy." *Studies in Art Education* **26**(1):41–50.

———. 1984. "'Don't You Think Some Brighter Colors Would Improve Your Painting?' Or Constructing Questions for Art Dialogues." *Art Education* **37**(1):12–14.

———. 1985. "Developing Aesthetic Literacy Through Contested Concepts." *Art Education* **38**(5):19–24.

———. 1986. "Artistic Commonalities and Differences: Educational Occasions for Universal-Relative Dialectics." *Visual Arts Research* **12**:2.

———. 1986. "Exploring Contested Concepts for Aesthetic Literacy." *Journal of Aesthetic Education* **20**(2):67–76.

———. 1987. "Approaches to Aesthetics in Art Education: A Critical Theory Perspective." *Studies in Art Education* **29**(2):81–90.

———. 1989. "An Elaboration on Meanings and Motives, Negative Aspects of DBAE." *Art Education* **42**(4):6–7.

———. 1990. "Beyond the Aesthetics of Cash." *Studies in Art Education* **30**(4):216–225.

———. 1991. "In the Quest for Art Criticism Equity: A Tentative Model." *Studies in Art Education* **17**(1):33.

Hamblen, Karen A. 1983. "Tissue Paper Economics and Other Hidden Dimensions of the Studio Model of Art Education." *Studies in Art Education* **25**(1):32–37.

——— and Camille Galanes. 1991. "Instructional Options for Aesthetics: Exploring the Possibilities." *Art Education* **44**:12–25.

Harris, Dale. 1963. *Children's Drawings as Measurements of Intellectual Maturity.* New York: Harcourt, Brace and World.

Hausman, Jerome. 1990. *"Editorial: Art Education and 'All that Jazz.'"* *Art Education* **43**(5):4–6.

———. 1990. "Unity and Diversity in Art Education." In London, et al. Beyond DBAE.

Heberholz, Donald, and Barbara Heberholz. 1990. Developing Artistic and Perceptual Awareness, Dubuque, Iowa: Wm. C. Brown.

Hewett, G. C., and Jean C. Rush. "Finding Buried Treasures: Aesthetic Scanning with Children." *Art Education* **40**(1):41–43.

Holmes Group Executive Board. 1986. *Tomorrow's Teachers: A Report of the Holmes Group.* East Lansing, Mich.

Holt, D. 1990. "Post Modernism vs. High Modernism: Relationship to D.B.A.E. and Its Critics." *Art Education* **43**(2):42–46.

Hurwitz, Al. 1983. *The Gifted and Talented in Art: A Guide to Program Planning.* Worcester, Mass.: Davis.

Hurwitz, Al, and Stanley Madeja. 1977. *The Joyous Vision: A Source Book for Elementary Art Appreciation.* Englewood Cliffs, N.J.: Prentice-Hall.

Hurwitz, Al, and Michael Day. *Children and Their Art.* New York: Harcourt Brace Jovanovich.

Johnson, Andra. 1989. *Planning Instruction for Performance Assessment: Writing the TPAI Portfolio for the Visual Arts Program.* Athens, Ga.: University of Georgia Art Department.

———. 1992. *Elementary Art Education Anthology.* Reston, Va.: NAEA.

Kaelin, Eugene. 1990. "The Construction of a Syllabus for Aesthetics in Art Education." *Art Education* **43**(2):22–34.

Kellogg, Rhoda. 1970. *Analyzing Children's Art.* Palo Alto, Calif.: National Press.

Kinder, A. 1987. "A Review of Rationales for Integrated Arts Programs." *Studies in Art Education* **29**(1):52–60.

Krathwohl, David, Benjamin Bloom, and Bertram Masia. 1984. *Taxonomy of Educational Objectives, Handbook 2: The Affective Domain.* New York: New Directions.

LaLiberte, Norman, and Shirley McIlhany. 1966. *Banners and Hangings: Design and Construction.* New York: Reinhold.

LaLiberte, Norman, and Alex Mogelon. 1967. *Painting with Crayons: History and Modern Techniques.* New York: Reinhold.

——— and ———. 1966. *Masks, Face Coverings, and Headgear.* New York: Reinhold.

Lark-Horowitz, Betty, Hilda Lewis, and Mark Luca. 1973. *Understanding Children's Art for Better Teaching.* Columbus, Ohio: Merrill.

Linderman, Marlene. 1990. *Art in the Elementary School: Drawing, Painting, and Creativity for the Classroom.* Dubuque, Iowa: Wm. C. Brown.

Lippard, Lucy. 1984. *Get the Message? A Decade of Art for Social Change.* New York: Dutton.

Lommel, Andreas. 1981. *Masks: Their Meanings and Function.* London: Ferndale.

London, Peter, Judith Burton, and Arlene Linderman (eds.). 1990. *Beyond DBAE: The Case for Multiple Visions of Art Education.* North Dartmouth, Mass.: Southeastern Massachusetts University.

Lowenfeld, Viktor. 1947. Creative and Mental Growth. New York: Macmillan.

Mager, Robert F. 1975. *Preparing Instructional Objectives.* Belmont, Calif.: Fearon.

Maitland-Gholson, Jane O. "Judging the Quality of Teachers: Implications of the Holmes Group Report for Art Education." *Visual Arts Research* **14**(1):11–16.

Mattil, Edward, and Betty Marzan. 1981. *Meaning in Children's Art: Projects for Teachers.* New York: Prentice-Hall.

McCann, Michael. 1985. *Health Hazards Manual for Artists.* New York: Nick Lyons Books.

———. 1991. "Oil Painting Hazards in Classrooms." *Art Hazards News* **14**:2.

McFee, June K. 1988. *"Art and Society."* In Getty Foundation for Education in the Arts. *Issues in Discipline-Based Art Education: Strengthening the*

This beautifully detailed ink drawing of an orchard is by Vincent Van Gogh, the late-nineteenth-century Dutch Postimpressionist artist. Notice the bold use of texture in the field, the varied ways of drawing tree forms, and the lower right corner's lines of the road leading into the composition.

Stance, Extending the Horizons. Los Angeles: The Getty Center for Education in the Arts.

McFee, June, and Rogena Degge. *Art, Culture, and Environment: A Catalyst for Teaching.* Belmont, Calif.: Wadsworth.

Michael, John. 1983. *Art and Adolescence, Teaching Art at the Secondary Level.* New York: Teachers College Press.

Morman, Jean. 1989. *One- Two- Three Murals: Simple Murals to Make Using Children's Open Ended Art.* Warren Publishing House.

National Art Education Association. *Position Paper: The Essentials of a Quality School Art Program.* Reston, Va.: NAEA.

National Commission on Excellence in Education. 1983. *A Nation at Risk.* Washington, D.C.: GPO.

National Endowment for the Arts. 1988. "Overview, Toward Civilization." *NAEA News* **30**(3):3–7.

Nicolaides, Kimon. 1941. *The Natural Way to Draw.* Boston: Houghton.

O'Brien, Bernadette C. 1978. *Tapestry: Interrelationship of the Arts in Reading and Language Development.* New York: New York City Board of Education.

O'Keeffe, Georgia. 1988. *Georgia O'Keeffe.* New York: Penguin Books.

Paik, Nam June, cited in Beverly J. Jones. "Toward Democratic Direction of Technology." In Blandy and Congdon. *Art in Democracy,* pp. 64–73.

Parsons, Michael. 1987. *How We Understand Art: A Cognitive Development Account of Aesthetic Experience.* Cambridge, England: Cambridge University Press.

Peterson, Charles R. "Visual Art and the Physically Challenged Person," Videotape, Bloomington, Ind.: Agency for Instructional Technology.

Qualley, Charles A. 1986. *Safety in the Artroom.* Worcester, Mass.: Davis.

Read, Herbert. 1955. *Icon and Idea: The Function of Art in the Development of Human Consciousness.* Cambridge: Harvard University Press.

———. 1966. *Henry Moore: A Study of His Life and Work.* New York.

———. 1973. *Education Through Art,* 3d ed. New York: Pantheon.

Redfern, H. B. 1986. *Questions in Aesthetic Education.* London: Allen and Unwin.

Reiff, J. 1991. *Learning Styles.* Reston, Va.: NAEA.

Rossol, Monona. 1990. *The Artist's Complete Health and Safety Guide.* New York: Allworth.

Rottger, Ernst. 1961. *Surfaces in Creative Design.* London: Batsford.

———. 1963. *Creative Clay Design.* New York: Reinhold.

———. 1969. *Creative Wood Design.* New York: Reinhold.

———. 1970. *Creative Paper Design.* New York: Reinhold.

Rush, Jean C. 1984. "Bridging the Gap Between Developmental Psychology and Art Education: The View from an Artist's Perspective." *Visual Arts Research* **10**(2):9–14.

Russell, R. L. 1991. "Teaching Students to Inquire About Art Philosophically." *Studies in Art Education* **32**(2):94–104.

Sacca, Elizabeth J. 1989. "Invisible Women: Questioning Recognition and Status in Art Education." *Studies in Art Education* **30**(1):122–127.

Sarason, Seymour. 1991. *The Challenge of Art to Psychology.* New Haven, Conn.: Yale University Press.

Saunders, Robert J. 1977. *Relating Art and Humanities to the Classroom.* Dubuque, Iowa: Wm. C. Brown.

———. 1982. "The Lowenfeld Motivation." *Art Education* **11**:30.

Schaefer-Simmern, Henry. 1948. *The Unfolding of Artistic Activity.* Berkeley: University of California Press.

Sharff, Stefan. 1982. *The Elements of Cinema.* New York: Columbia University Press.

Silverman, Ronald (ed.). 1980. *Art Education and the World of Work.* Reston, Va.: NAEA.

Smith, Nancy R. 1982. *Experience and Art: Teaching Children to Paint.* New York: Teachers College Press.

Smith, Nancy, and C. Fucigna. 1988. "Drawing Systems in Children's Pictures: Contour and Form." *Visual Arts Research* **14**(1):66–76.

Smith, Ralph A. (ed.). 1975. *Regaining Educational Leadership: Critical Essays on PBTE/CBTE, Behavioral Objectives, and Accountability.* New York: Wiley.

———. 1986. *Excellence in Art Education.* Reston, Va.: NAEA.

Stokrocki, Mary. 1990. "A Cross Site Analysis: Problems in Teaching Art to Preadolescents." *Studies in Art Education* **31**(2):106–107.

Strommen, Erik. 1988. "A Century of Children Drawing: The Evolution of Theory and Research Concerning the Drawings of Children." *Visual Arts Research* **14**:13–24.

Szekely, George. 1988. *Encouraging Creativity in Art Lessons.* New York: Teachers College Press.

Thorne, J. H. 1990. "Mainstreaming Procedures: Support Services and Training." *NAEA Advisory.*

Torrance, E. Pau. 1966. "Torrance Test of Creative Thinking." Bensenville, Ill.: Scholastic Testing Service.

Vallance, Elizabeth. 1988. "Art Criticism as Subject Matter in Schools and Art Museums." *Journal of Aesthetic Education* **22**(4):69–82.

Wasson, Stuhr, and L. Petrovich-Mwaniki. 1990. "Teaching Art in the Multicultural Classroom: Six Position Statements." *Studies in Art Education* **31**(4):234–246.

Wilson, Brent, and Harlan Hoffa (eds.). 1988. *History of Art Education: Proceedings from the Penn State Conference.* Reston, Va.: NAEA.

Wilson, Brent, Al Hurwitz, and Marjorie Wilson. 1987. *Teaching Drawing from Art.* Worcester, Mass.: Davis Publications.

Wilson, Brent, and Marjorie Wilson. 1981. "The Use and Uselessness of Developmental Stages." *Art Education* **34**(5):4–5.

——— and ———. 1982. *Teaching Children to Draw.* Englewood Cliffs, N.J.: Prentice-Hall.

Winner, Ellie. 1982. Invented Worlds: *The Psychology of the Arts.* Cambridge, Mass.: Harvard University Press.

Young, Bernard. 1991. *Art, Culture, and Ethnicity.* Reston, Va.: NAEA.

Zimmerman, Enid. 1990. "Issues Related to Teaching Art from a Feminist Point of View." *Visual Arts Research* **16**(2):1–9.

———. 1990. "*Questions About My Culture and Art Education or 'I'll Never Forget the Day M'Blawi Stumbled on the Work of the Post Impressionists.'*" *Art Education* **43**(6):8–24.

Zurmuehlen, Marilyn. 1989. "Serious Pursuit of Cultural Trivialization." *Art Education* **42**(6):46–49.

Addresses of Professional Associations and Audiovisual Suppliers

These lists are by no means complete but can serve as starting points to those desiring further information.

Professional Art Education Associations

National Art Education Association, 1916 Association Drive, Reston, VA 22091.

Also, each state has a state art education association.

International Society for Education through Art, c/o Prof. Kit Grauer, University of British Columbia, Dept. of Art Education, Vancouver, B.C. V6T 1Z5 Canada.

United States Society for Education through Art (USSEA), c/o Dr. Ken Marantz, Ohio State University, 340 Hopkins Hall, Columbus, Ohio 43210.

Film Distributors

BFA Educational Media, 11559 Santa Monica Boulevard, Los Angeles, CA 90025

Brandon Films, Inc., 221 West 57th Street, New York, NY 10019

Encyclopaedia Britannica Films, 425 North Michigan Avenue, Chicago, IL 60604

Harmon Foundations, 140 Nassau Street, New York, NY 10038

International Film Bureau, Inc., 332 South Michigan Avenue, Chicago, IL 60604

Santa Fe Film Bureau, 80 East Jackson Boulevard, Chicago, IL 60604

Art Reproduction Sources

Henry N. Abrams, 110 East 59th Street, New York, NY 10022

Art Education, Inc., Blauveldt, NY 10913

American Federation of Arts, 41 East 65th Street, New York, NY 10021

Artext Prints, Westport, CT 06880

Collins and World (SKIRA), 2080 West 117th Street, Cleveland, OH 44111

New York Graphic Society, 140 Greenwich Avenue, Greenwich, CT 06830

Reinhold Publishing Co., 600 Summer Street, Stamford, CT 06901

Shorewood Reproductions, Inc., 475 Tenth Avenue, New York, NY 10018

Shorewood Fine Art Books, 27 Glen Road, Sandy Hook, CT 06482

Van Nostrand Reinhold, 450 West 33rd Street, New York, NY 10001

Color Slides, Filmstrips, and Videocassette Sources

American Library Color Slide Co., 222 West 23rd Street, New York, NY 10011

Art Institute of Chicago, South Michigan Avenue, Chicago, IL 60603

Bailey Film Associates, 11559 Santa Monica Boulevard, Los Angeles, CA 90025

Communacad, The Communications Academy, Box 541, Wilton, CT 06897

Crystal Productions, Box 2159, Glenview, IL 60025

Films Incorporated Video, 5547 Ravenswood Avenue, Chicago, IL 60640-1199

Gould Media, 44 Parkway West, Mt. Vernon, NY 10552

HRW Artworks, 1627 Woodland Avenue, Austin, TX 78741.

International Film Bureau, 332 South Michigan Avenue, Chicago, IL 60604

Life Filmstrips, Time and Life Building, New York, NY 10021

Media for the Arts, P.O. Box 1011, Newport, RI 02840

Middle and bottom: Courtesy of W. Robert Nix, Athens, Georgia.

Left: *Teachers can use their own color slides of nature's phenomena to motivate their students. Build a resource file of photographs and slides of nature.* **Above:** *Ancient ceramic Haniwa horse from the pre-Jomon period, Japan. Hollow clay cylinders form the animal's basic shape. Notice how clay coils were flattened to add characteristic reins and saddle.*

Prothman Associates, 2795 Milburn Avenue, Baldwin, NY 11510
Sandak, Inc., Division of G. K. Hall & Co., 70 Lincoln Street, Boston, MA 02111
Sax Arts and Crafts, P.O. Box 51710, New Berlin, WI 53215
Society for Visual Education, 1345 Diversey Parkway, Chicago, IL 60614
Universal Color Slide, 8450 South Tamiami Trail, Sarasota, FL 34238

Art reproductions and slides can also be acquired inexpensively from many art museums; a few addresses are:

Metropolitan Museum of Art, Fifth Avenue and 82nd Street, New York, NY 10028
Museum of Modern Art, 11 West 53rd Street, New York, NY 10019
National Gallery of Art, Constitution Avenue and 6th Street, N.W., Washington, D.C. 20001

Glossary

Appliqué decorative design made by cutting pieces of one fabric and applying them by gluing or stitching to the surface of another fabric.

Armature framework (of wood, wire, and so on) employed to support constructions of clay, papier-mâché, or plaster.

Balance a principle in art. May be formal or informal, symmetrical or asymmetrical.

Balsa a strong, lightweight wood used for model building and stabiles.

Baren a device made of cardboard and bamboo leaf that is used as a hand press in taking a print (of Japanese derivation).

Bat a plaster block used to hasten drying of moist clay.

Batik a method of designing on fabric by sealing with melted wax those areas not to be dyed.

Bench hook a wood device secured to a desk or table to stabilize the linoleum block during the gouging process.

Bisque clay in its fired or baked state (unglazed).

Brayer a rubber roller used for inking in printmaking processes.

Burnish to make smooth or glossy by a rubbing or polishing action.

Ceramic a word used to describe clay constructions and products thereof.

Charcoal a drawing stick or pencil made from charred wood.

Chipboard sturdy cardboard, usually grey, of varying thicknesses, used for collage, collograph, sketching boards, and in construction projects.

Clay a natural, moist earth substance used in making bricks, tile, pottery, and ceramic sculpture.

Collage a composition or design made by arranging and gluing materials to a background surface.

Collograph a print made from a collage. Relief plate created with an assortment of pasted or glued items such as pieces of paper, cardboard, cord, string, and other found objects.

Color an element of art. Also referred to as *hue*.

Color, analogous closely related color; neighbors on the color wheel: green, blue-green, yellow-green, for example.

Color, monochromatic all of the tints and shades of a single color plus its neutralized possibilities.

Colors, complementary colors found opposite one another on the color wheel: red and green, for example.

Colors, primary red, yellow, blue. Three basic hues.

Colors, secondary green, orange, violet. Achieved by mixing primary colors.

Construction paper a strong, absorbent, semitextured paper available in a wealth of colors and used for drawings, paintings in tempera, crayon, oil pastel, printmaking, collage, and paper sculpture. A staple item in the school art program.

Contour drawing a line drawing delineating the outer and inner contours of a posed model, still life, landscape, or other selected subject matter.

Domination a principle in art. Opposite term is "subordination." They complement each other.

Easel a wood or metal frame to support an artist's canvas during painting. Found in many kindergartens for use in tempera painting but in a simpler version.

Embossing creating a raised or relief design on metal or leather by tooling or indenting the surface.

Emphasis a principle in art. Important elements in a composition are emphasized.

Encaustic a painting process employing hot beeswax mixed with color pigment. Sometimes used to describe melted-crayon creations.

Engobe clay slip, colored or white, used to decorate greenware before firing.

Top and bottom: Courtesy of Jimmy Morris, Athens, Georgia.

Engraving a process of incising or scratching into a hard surface to produce a printed image, as in copper engraving or crayon engraving.

Findings metal clasps, hooks, loops, and so on used in jewelry making.

Firing in ceramics, the baking of clay in a kiln or an outdoor banked fire; also see *Raku*.

Found objects discards, remnants, samples, leftovers, and throwaways that are exploited in collages, junk sculpture, assemblages, and as stamps in printmaking projects.

Frieze a decorated, horizontal band in paint or in relief along the upper part of a building or a room.

Glaze a transparent or semitransparent coating of a color stain over a plain surface or another color used in oil painting, plaster sculpture, or ceramicware.

Gradient a gradual shift from distinct to blended together, as in a textural gradient, or from one color to another, as in a color gradient (or graduated color blending).

Greenware unfired clay in leather-hard stage, firm but not completely dry.

Grout a crevice filler such as the conditioned plaster sealed between clay, glass, or vinyl tesserae in a mosaic.

Gum eraser a soft eraser used in drawing. Available in cube or rectangle form.

Hue another name for *color*.

India ink a waterproof ink made from lampblack. Used for drawing, designing, and in tempera resists.

Kiln an oven used for drying, firing, and glazing clay creations.

Kneaded eraser a gray eraser made of unvulcanized rubber that must be stretched and kneaded to be effective. Used most often in charcoal drawing.

Line an element in art. The basic skeletal foundation of a design or composition.

Loom the supporting framework for the crisscrossing threads and yarn in weaving.

Macramé lacework made by tying, knotting, and weaving cord in a pattern.

Manila paper a general-purpose drawing or coloring paper, usually cream color.

Three-dimensional projects using colored construction paper appeal to children of all ages. They like to fold, fringe, and curl the paper. They like to cut out little doors and windows so they can peek into secret places. The delightful bunnies were part of an Easter-fashion-parade project.

Masonite a pressed board made of wood fibers. Used for clay-modeling boards, inking surfaces in printmaking, and rinsing boards in tempera and crayon resists.

Mat board a heavy poster board, available in many colors and textures, used for mounting or matting artwork.

Mobile a free-moving hanging sculptural construction in space; Alexander Calder's gift to the art world.

Monoprint one-of-a-kind print, usually made by incising or marking on an inked glass plate and taking an impression.

Mosaic a design or composition made by arranging and gluing tesserae or geometric pieces of material next to one another, but not touching, on a background surface.

Mural a monumental artwork on the inside or outside walls of a building. Executed in paint, mosaic, metal repoussé, or a combination of materials.

Newsprint newspaper stock used for sketches, preliminary drawings, and prints.

Oil pastel a popular coloring medium consisting of a combination of chalk and oil; available in a host of exciting colors.

Papier-mâché name given to paper crafts that use newspaper moistened with wallpaper paste or laundry starch. Also called *paper pulp constructions.*

Patina originally the color produced by corrosion on metal—the antique sheen of old age—now artificially obtained through use of patinalike wax pastes.

Pattern design made by repeating a motif or symbol (allover pattern).

Perspective the creation of a three-dimensional space illusion on a two-dimensional surface by means of vanishing points, converging lines, and diminishing sizes of objects.

Plaster a white, powdery substance that when mixed with water forms a quick-setting molding or casting material (sometimes referred to as *plaster of Paris*).

Steps in a fish mobile. **Top:** *Preliminary drawing on sturdy wrapping paper. Discuss the shapes of the dorsal, ventral, and caudal fins. When the drawing is completed, a second matching side is cut out.* **Middle:** *Paint both sides with tempera. Show color reproductions of mobiles to the children, but tell them to use their imaginations freely. Remember that the heads of the fish must be painted facing in opposite directions. When the paint is dry, staple both fish partially, fill with crumpled newspaper, and staple to close.* **Bottom:** *Hang to create an exciting display.*

Postive-negative Positive shapes in a composition are the solid objects—the people, trees, animals, buildings. Negative shapes are the unoccupied empty spaces between positive shapes. Atmosphere, sky, and earth considered negative space are sometimes designated as "foreground" and "background" space.

Radiation lines, shapes, or colors emanating from a central core. Sun rays, fan leaf, ripples around a pebble thrown into a stream.

Raku a ceramic firing process using a primitive kiln and producing smoky and iridescent effects.

Relief a projection from a surface. Low relief as in a coin is called *bas relief.*

Repetition (rhythm) a principle of art. Repetition of lines, shapes, colors, and values in a composition creates unity.

Repoussé a design in metal art in which tooling and hammering are employed to achieve relief effects.

Scoring (clay) to make rough indentations in clay with a nail or similar tool as a step in cementing two pieces of clay together. Also used to describe the guiding indentation in paper-sculpture curved-line folding

Selvedge the edge of a fabric where the weft returns to weave its way to the opposite edge.

Shade refers to the darker values of a color or hue. Maroon is a shade of red; navy blue is a shade of blue.

Sketch usually a preliminary drawing made with pencil, pen, crayon, charcoal, brush, pastel, or similar tool.

Slip clay diluted with water to a creamy consistency. Used as a binder to join two pieces of clay in ceramic construction.

Stabile a sculptural construction in space resting on the ground, akin to a mobile which hangs.

Still life an arrangement of objects, usually on a table, as a subject for drawing, painting, collage, and so on.

Subordination a principle of art in which parts of the composition are subordinated so that others may dominate and be emphasized.

Tagboard sometimes referred to as *oaktag.* A glossy-surfaced, pliable cardboard used in collage, collographs, glue-line prints, and paper constructions.

Tempera paint an opaque, water-soluble paint available in liquid or powder form. Also referred to as *showcard* or *poster paint.*

Tessera a small segment of paper, cardboard, vinyl, ceramic, and so on (usually in geometric shape: square, rectangle) that is fitted and glued to a background surface to produce a mosaic (plural: *tesserae*).

Texture the actual or visual feel of a surface—bark on a tree, fur on an animal, sand on a beach.

Underwater themes are most effective for crayon-resist paintings. This illustration is from a Rangoon, Burma, children's art class taught by the author.

Tint the lighter values of a color or hue. Pink is a tint of red.

Unity a principle of art. When everything in a composition falls into place through use of fundamental principles of art, unity is achieved.

Value in color terminology, the lightness or darkness of a hue.

Warp the thread or yarn that supports the weft in weaving.

Watercolors water-soluble colors, generally transparent or semitransparent. Can be employed thickly to become opaque. Available in semimoist cakes or tubes.

Wedging a method of preparing moist clay by kneading and squeezing to expel the air pockets and make it more plastic.

Weft the thread that goes across the warp from side to side in weaving; also refers to the yarn used as weft.

Photo Credits

Art Education Magazine, 118
Barrett, Diane, 5, 115, 252
Bell South Publications, 235
Binney and Smith, Educational Materials Division, 72
Brassie, Fay, 15, 61, 259
Chase, Molly, 238
Clements, Robert, 60, 118
Davis Publications, 207
Elliott, Nancy, 237, 238
Exelrod Press, 26
Fein, Sylvia, 26
Georgia Museum of Art, 61
Hammond, Mary, 10, 19, 21, 22, 68, 92, 94, 100, 102, 160, 163, 166, 187, 189, 192, 193, 195, 202, 203, 206, 215, 219, 221, 226, 227, 228, 259, 278
Harris, Emily, 236
Harvell, David, 84, 105, 115, 273
Henry, Carole, 167, 236
Hirshhoren Museum, Smithsonian Institution, 145
Hodge, David, 8, 16, 19, 47, 63, 69, 74, 80, 87, 91, 95, 97, 110, 160, 162, 165, 168, 169, 176, 178, 189, 202, 212, 213, 214, 220, 222, 233, 265, 268, 269, 272, 285
International Child Art Collection, 1, 12, 36, 44, 53, 65, 75, 87, 130, 134, 170
Kuntz, Baiba, 20, 48, 52, 54, 81, 92, 97, 103, 133, 167, 179, 266
Lazzarri, Mary, 267
London *Sunday Mirror,* 261
Lucas, Shirley, 17, 180, 114

Mallett, Marla, 90
McCuthen, Mary, 190
Mitchell, George, 238
Moore, Mary Ruth, 9
Morris, Jimmy, 19, 22, 25, 28, 49, 76, 83, 129, 163, 182, 183, 192, 198, 200, 221
Museum of Fine Arts, Boston, 135, 210
Munn, Alice Ballard, 5, 115, 252
National Building Museum, 257
National Gallery of Art, 128, 141, 149
Nix, W. Robert, 74, 109, 152, 174, 290, 109
Oldenburg, Claes, 4
Oliver, Teddy, 60
Ramsay, Ted, 23
Robinson, Virginia S., 206
Sapp, William, 82
School Arts Magazine, 60, 7
Solomon, Holly, Gallery, 67
Solvay, Carl, Gallery, 239
Steuck, Lawrence, 118, 252
Storm King Art Center, 247
Swanson, Mary, 150
Thomas, Charles C Publishing Co., 120
University of Georgia Art Department, 113, 197
Van Bruggen, Coosje, 4
Varon, Malcolm, 147
Wilkinson, Knox, 235

Index

In this index, topics and related illustrations usually appear on the same page or within a range of pages. For this type of situation, page numbers are given in regular type. When an illustration on a particular topic appears elsewhere in the text, and not on the same page with its related text topic, the page number is given in italic type: 478.